AF731986

Yearbook of Cultural Property Law

## YEARBOOK OF CULTURAL PROPERTY LAW

***Series Editor:*** Sherry Hutt

*Sponsored by the Lawyers' Committee for Cultural Heritage Preservation*

The *Yearbook* provides those in the heritage-management world with summaries of notable court cases, settlements and other dispositions, legislation, government regulations, policies, and agency decisions that affect their work. Interviews with key figures, refereed research articles, think pieces, and a substantial resources section round out each volume. Thoughtful analyses and useful information from leading practitioners in the diverse field of cultural property law will assist government land managers; state, tribal, and museum officials; attorneys; anthropologists; archaeologists; public historians; and others to better preserve, protect, and manage cultural property in domestic and international venues. All royalties go directly to the Lawyers' Committee for Cultural Heritage Preservation.


| | |
|---|---|
| *Editor, 2010* | Sherry Hutt |
| *Assistant Editor* | David Tarler |
| *Section Editors* | James Van Ness<br>Eve Errickson<br>Rob Roy Smith<br>Nathaniel R. Orpen<br>Lucille A. Roussin<br>Thomas R. Kline<br>L. Eden Burgess<br>Patty Gerstenblith<br>David Tarler<br>Gary Nurkin |
| *Contributing Editors* | Caroline Blanco<br>Anita Canovas<br>Elise Foster |

*Lawyers' Committee for Cultural Heritage Preservation*

| | |
|---|---|
| *President* | Patty Gerstenblith |
| *Secretary/Treasurer* | Anita Canovas |
| *Executive Director* | Terressa Davis |

# Yearbook of Cultural Property Law

# 2010

**Sherry Hutt**
*Editor*

**David Tarler**
*Assistant Editor*

Routledge
Taylor & Francis Group
LONDON AND NEW YORK

First published 2010 by Left Coast Press, Inc.

Published 2016 by Routledge
2 Park Square, Milton Park, Abingdon, Oxon OX14 4RN
605 Third Avenue, New York, NY 10017

*Routledge is an imprint of the Taylor & Francis Group, an informa business*

Copyright © 2010 Taylor & Francis

All rights reserved. No part of this book may be reprinted or reproduced or utilised in any form or by any electronic, mechanical, or other means, now known or hereafter invented, including photocopying and recording, or in any information storage or retrieval system, without permission in writing from the publishers.

Notice:
Product or corporate names may be trademarks or registered trademarks, and are used only for identification and explanation without intent to infringe.

ISSN 1931-5627
ISBN 978-1-59874-442-2 (hbk)
LCCN 2006213755

# Contents

# Preface

Welcome to a review of the year 2009 for the genre of law that is cultural property law. It has once again proven to be a substantive year as measured by the number of news articles, court actions, and journal articles that were generated and are noted in this volume. The *Yearbook* series seeks to bring together thoughtful pieces that explain these issues, inform and educate, and assemble source materials useful to those who will seek to represent clients and use the law as a means to protect cultural property.

As well as inform the reader and support cultural property practitioners, the *Yearbook* seeks to give identity to cultural property law, or cultural heritage law as some refer to it, as an identifiable area of legal practice. The *Yearbook of Cultural Property Law* series joins together federal, state, local, tribal, museum, historic preservation, marine resources, art market, international, and criminal law in one volume, where the common thread of cultural property law is identified, discussed and analyzed. In this manner, the components of cultural property law can be seen and precedent can be addressed in a meaningful context. The reader will note that cases or discussions may appear in more than one section or article in the volume, allowing them to be viewed from different perspectives within cultural property law. It is hoped that genre identification will allow meaningful precedent to be developed in court cases. Cultural property law, although unique, is of the same standing as other well-recognized legal areas, which interrelate, such as: environmental law, Indian law, contracts, torts, administrative, international and criminal law.

At the core of the *Yearbook* are the Practice Area sections, each with a section editor who is a practitioner and scholar in that particular area of cultural property law. If you the reader feel that something should be covered in the coming year, the editors would be pleased to receive your comments. In some instances, cases that saw litigation during the year are not reported, as the sentencing or culminating event had not occurred by year's end.

The articles in the *Yearbook* are peer reviewed and the topics are chosen to add further depth to the Practice Areas, to give the reader insight into major events, and to provide source data that are not published elsewhere. The *Yearbook* is intended as an ongoing aid to legal practice, ranging from scholarly analysis of emerging issues to practical aids for practitioners and educators. The *Yearbook* is similar to a law journal in the scholarly treatment of cutting edge topics, but it strives to blend cross-disciplinary styles of writing and combine legal and scientific forms. Contributors to the *Yearbook* are creative and forward thinking, seeking to identify the course of the law, but they are also mindful of their responsibility to fully inform the reader of the parameters of issues. The series strives for credibility upon which practitioners can rely. Thus, items accepted for the *Yearbook* are not advocacy pieces, except to the extent they generally promote cultural resource protection through use of the law.

Once again this year, the *Yearbook* has been produced as a project of the LCCHP, the nonprofit organization of lawyers, which is dedicated to scholarship, education, and cultural heritage preservation, and which receives the proceeds from the sale of this volume. The regular contributors to the *Yearbook* are members of LCCHP. For more information on the benefits of membership please visit www.culturalheritagelaw.org. The editors, editorial board, the LCCHP and authors who contributed to this volume also offer their appreciation to Mitch Allen and the staff at Left Coast Press, our publisher, for their continued efforts to seek out and promote scholarship to benefit cultural resource preservation, protection, and education.

The *Yearbook* editors continue to seek information for the next edition, particularly actions that may not have been published or may have been resolved without a final judgment. Expression of interest to publish articles that meet the mission of the *Yearbook* are also welcome. Articles are desired that address topics of current interest in a scholarly and complete manner, that will be of assistance to practitioners, but that leave advocacy to those practitioners. Please send information or inquiries to: Hutt_Sherry@yahoo.com. Thank you.

*The information in the Yearbook is drawn from public records. The views expressed in the Yearbook are those of the LCCHP members and the authors, and do not necessarily reflect the views or policies of the federal agencies or the public or private firms whose employees contributed to this volume.*

# Introduction

• • •

## Introduction to Yearbook 2010

The *Yearbook* strives to provide substantive information on current topics of interest, in papers, interviews, articles and Practice Area sections, authored by those who have sufficient expertise in the field to offer meaningful analysis and insight. Each volume presents cultural property law topics that have featured in press articles and conferences, and which will inform court cases. Sometimes, different perspectives on the same topic might appear in more than one Practice Area section in order to illuminate various facets or issues.

Appearing for the first time in this edition is State and Local Practice Area Section Editor, Eve Errickson, who is on the staff at the National Trust for Historic Preservation and thus provides a national look at preservation actions. Returning this year to edit Practice Area sections for the Yearbook are, in Federal Land Management, James Van Ness, the acting Deputy General Counsel (Environment & Installations), Department of Defense, responsible for advising senior DoD officials on legal matters related to natural and cultural resources management, environmental planning, and consultation; in Tribes, Tribal Lands, and Indian Arts, Rob Roy Smith, who is of counsel with the Indian Law Group of the law firm Ater Wynne, LLP in Seattle, Washington; in Marine Environment, Nathaniel R. Orpen, a private practice attorney at Galena Law Firm, in White Bear Lake, Minnesota; in Museum, Lucille Roussin, a private practitioner, art museum advisor, faculty member at the Benjamin Cardozo School of Law in New York City, and expert on Holocaust Restitution

Claims; in Art Market, Thomas R. Kline and L. Eden Burgess, practicing in the Washington, D.C., office of Andrews Kurth LLP, where they represent governments, museums, churches, foundations, and families, including Holocaust survivors and heirs, in recovering stolen art appearing in the United States; in International Cultural Property, Patty Gerstenblith, a frequent speaker and author on cultural property law, particularly international cultural heritage, and the Director of DePaul University College of Law Center for Art, Museum and Cultural Heritage Law; and in Enforcement, David Tarler, who is the enforcement and training coordinator in the Washington, D. C., office of the National Park Service, in the National NAGPRA Program.

The Yearbook is also assisted by the following contributing editors: Caroline Blanco, the Assistant General Counsel for the Environment at the National Science Foundation, where she provides advice on the environmental and cultural resources laws implicated by the Foundation's mission in promoting cutting edge science; and Elise Foster, who is an attorney with the U.S. Department of Agriculture, Office of the General Counsel in Ogden, Utah, where, since 1997, she has been active in the development of ARPA civil penalty practice.

The *Yearbook* is aware that ethics and the responsibilities of practitioners should always be a consideration in any legal anthology. Last year we began a new feature: an introductory comment focusing on the ethics of collecting. This year's comment is by Gillian Bearns, formerly a professor of historic preservation at Mary Washington College in Virginia, and now a historic preservation cultural property lawyer in Washington, D.C. She answers the question that we so often hear from new cultural property practitioners: What do we do with the things from grandmother that my client just discovered in the attic? Her treatise on cultural property laws is basic and intended to assist the new practitioner to well represent their clients.

The *Yearbook* is also pleased to publish winning submissions of the 2009 Lawyers' Committee for Cultural Heritage Preservation (LCCHP) Law School Writing Competition, generously sponsored each year by the law firm of Andrews Kurth LLP. The entries this year presented in-depth analyses of several areas of interest to cultural property practitioners, making it beneficial to publish three of the top papers. Author of the 1st place article Amelia Borrego Sargent is a law student at Stanford University and a Ph.D. candidate at the University of California at Berkeley. In *New Jurisdictional Tools for Displaced Cultural Property in Russia: From "Twice Saved" to "Twice Taken,"* she draws upon her considerable experience in Russia and her research into international cultural property dilemmas. In the 2nd place article, *Deaccessioning: A Necessary Evil?,* Melanie Greer provides a deep understanding of problems in museum administration. Finalist Lydia Grunstra is a student at American University, Washington College of Law. In *The Duty Under NAGPRA to Inform Repatriation Recipients of Potentially Hazardous Substances: A Best-Practice Guide* she offers a best-practices manual and analysis of liability in failing to notify recipients of repatriated items of the possible presence of toxins in preservatives. Although written by a law student, each article, after screening in the competition process, was subjected to peer review by the *Yearbook* editorial board. These articles are presented not as mere student work but as well-researched and vetted scholarship on the topics presented.

The *Yearbook* editors are pleased to recognize those cultural property practitioners who inspire us and who have made a positive impact on the field. This year we focus on David Griffel, retiring as a law enforcement agent with the USDA Forest Service. David has not only been an inspiration and driving force in successful cultural resource criminal prosecutions, but he has given of his time to train the next generation of cultural resource investigators. In addition, the *Yearbook* sadly notes the passing this year of Blackfeet religious leader and noted advocate of Native American cultural property rights, Clarence "Curly Bear" Wagner. Curly Bear lived to see repatriations from some of the major museums in the United States, brought about in part by his tireless efforts to see the enactment of NAGPRA. Nominations for recognition are welcome.

In a continuing effort to meet the needs of practitioners and law professors, the *Yearbook* includes a section on published resources, websites, and blogs. Gary Nurkin has once again compiled a comprehensive list of items and electronic resources published and created in the last year. It is notable that each year the list of newly published items is long, reflecting the attention by scholars to the importance of cultural property law as an identified area of practice.

It is our hope that you, the reader, will find the information in the *Yearbook* to inspire your practice.

*Sherry Hutt*
*David Tarler*

*2010*

# The Fate of Private Collections

*by Gillian K. Bearns*

Cultural resource law is a newly recognized and evolving area of law. Few general practitioners ever have occasion or cause to delve into it, and therefore may be unaware that these laws exist and may have impact on their client and their client's property rights.

This article seeks to provide basic information about the most commonly used federal cultural resource laws that affect domestic cultural resources and the issues raised when cultural resources are part of private collections or in the possession of private individuals.[1] Using a select case study, the article explores how federal cultural resource laws might affect property rights where the property at issue is a cultural resource. It also attempts to offer some guidance for legal practitioners confronted by the question of what to do with the cultural resources owned by private clients, particularly the stuff discovered in grandmother's attic.

## Cultural Resources As Property

The term "cultural resource" includes a vast realm of objects, documents, and materials. Typically, cultural resources are thought of as objects on display in a museum, or items acquired by universities and public and private institutions for their historical, scientific, artistic, or cultural value. However, many such objects are acquired by private individuals and private institutions. Their reasons for collecting may, in many circumstances, mirror those of public museums and institutions, or may be based on an object's value and desirability as a commodity. Yet, in either circumstance, an object's value, whether cultural, historical, or monetary, is almost always intrinsically connected to its history, the culture that produced it, who used it and how it was used.

Unlike other types of movable property, the physical characteristics of cultural objects, such as the material from which it was made, does not necessarily determine its value. It is the relationship of the present to ephemeral cultural traditions and history through the object that distinguishes many cultural resources. Yet, because at their most general level, cultural resources are still property, traditional principles of property law provide a legal framework and body of legal precedent that may tie into an array of cultural resource laws. This relationship should provide some reassurance of familiarity to practitioners when faced with the question of what to do with the artifacts and objects in grandmother's attic.

## The Provenance Problem

In determining what laws apply, the answers to the questions "what is the object?" and "where did it come from?" are important factors. The term "provenance" refers to where an object came from originally, which may mean different things, including where it was made, used, stored, or discarded. An object's original or intended provenance provides context, that is, meaning beyond what can be gleaned from the object itself. Context relates to the nexus between the object and the culture from which it came, or with which it properly belongs. An object's context may reveal where and by whom it was created, its intended purpose, how it was used, where and when it was used, and by whom. For example, the shape and glaze pattern on a vase may indicate that it was manufactured in the shop of a particular artisan during the eighth century B.C. in Greece. However, its discovery in an Etruscan tomb in the hills of Tuscany reveals that it was traded and transported by a fairly sophisticated network of merchants, was eventually acquired by a wealthy Etruscan patriarch, and retained its value as a luxury good sufficient to be included in his tomb at his death. When objects are removed from their true context with little or no documentation, it becomes incredibly difficult to determine their true provenance, which in turn means that little information can be gleaned from the object and its meaning, and potential significance as anything more than an aesthetically pleasing object may be lost forever.

The "where" relates not only to provenance but also to the chain of custody leading to the current owner. The legal term of art "chain of custody" immediately conjures up the ominous realm of criminal law. In fact, criminal laws governing personal property may apply, and there are specific cultural resource laws establishing criminal liability for the theft, misappropriation, or fraudulent sale or transfer of cultural resources under certain circumstances. Fortunately or unfortunately, depending on your or your client's position in the chain, chain of custody is often extremely difficult if not impossible to establish for the vast majority of cultural resources in private hands. Quite often such objects were removed from their context many years ago, and no records exist documenting the removal and subsequent transfer of the object. Archaeologists also refer to the location of the find and the precise place of the archaeological retrieval as provenience, to distinguish this information from the place where the object was created and its travels in use and from the time it was retrieved in history. As described below, some relevant information may be obtainable through diligent historical research and from scientific analysis of the object itself by trained professionals. The information obtained should help ensure that an appropriate plan in accordance with applicable laws is developed for the conservation and disposition of the object. Knowing the provenance of an item and the circumstances surrounding its provenience may assist in having all of the relevant data to determine accurate context, not only for historical and scientific purposes but to establish legal chains of title.

## Questions of Law

Under American law, property is divided into three categories: real property (meaning land), tangible personal property (movable objects), and intangible personal property (intellectual property when in the marketplace). Different laws apply depending on which category of property is at issue. Property ownership, whether of real or personal property, has traditionally been described as a bundle of rights including the right to buy, sell, lease, transfer, donate, alter and destroy.[2] Property laws, including cultural resource laws, at the federal, state, and local levels impact or restrict certain of those private property rights while still respecting the Fifth Amendment prohibition against the taking of property without due process of law and just compensation applicable under the United States Constitution.

The legal hierarchy places those laws set forth in the U.S. Constitution, which reflects America's highest values as a culture, as supreme. Federal laws enacted by Congress apply broadly to the federal government, particularly to federal agencies, to federal property (real and personal), and to use of federal funds, but are limited by the Tenth Amendment in their application to matters traditionally controlled by state and local governments and by the Bill of Rights, the first ten amendments, specifically the First and Fifth Amendments, with respect to private individuals' personal freedoms and personal property. The U.S. Constitution provided an overlay of freedoms on the traditional use and control of property, often called the "common laws." These laws were not written, but were a real community ethic. As specific property rights statutes are enacted, to the extent they codify or modify the common law, the statute controls.

State governments, often through their subsidiary local governments, have traditionally been responsible for regulating real and personal property held by their residents and for regulating the use of land within their jurisdictional boundaries. Thus, most transfers of real and personal property, whether by sale, gift, or inheritance, will be governed by state and local laws. But if a federal law applies, it will trump the state and local law. And finally, as a general rule, if a more specific law applies to the facts or circumstances at issue, that law will govern over a more general law. This means that applicable cultural resource laws will supersede any more general property laws.

The delicate balance between property rights and cultural resource protection is somewhat fluid and continues to change as society's understanding of the role of history has shifted and recognition of the importance of preserving the cultural heritage of the United States and other influential cultures has increased.

## Real Property v. Personal Property

The ownership of land under American jurisprudence is a sacred right protected by the Fifth Amendment of the U.S. Constitution, by similar state constitutional provisions and by over 200 years of court decisions restricting the circumstances under which the government may use the power of eminent domain, that is, government control, to take private property for a public purpose. Traditionally, under the Tenth Amendment, states retained the power to regulate the land within their borders, and the extent of such regulations is also limited by the Fifth Amendment and state constitutional provisions.

The federal government has engaged in the regulation of private land within state borders in limited areas, such as protection of the environment, endangered species, and religious rights, under the Enforcement, Commerce, and Spending Clauses of the U.S. Constitution. As a general rule, because the federal government has limited jurisdiction over private land, federal cultural resource laws do not apply to private lands or to the objects attached to that land under traditional principles of property law, but may apply when objects are placed in the market place for interstate commerce.

Similarly, the ownership of personal property is protected by the Fifth Amendment and by corresponding state constitutional provisions. And states have traditionally been responsible for the regulation of personal property held by residents within their borders. Thus the federal government has very little authority to regulate private personal property. Practitioners must look to state law to determine whether any specific laws or regulations apply to cultural resources. In fact, few states have adopted cultural resource laws pertaining to privately owned personal property. This reflects the weight of private property rights versus the public interest under American law. Thus, regardless of the potentially national historical or cultural significance of an object, if it, or the land to which it is attached, is privately owned and was acquired by legitimate and legal means, neither the state nor the federal government has any right to the object and any government controls must be consistent with comparable laws governing ordinary personal property within the limits imposed by the Fifth Amendment and the applicable state constitution.

Because of this legal hierarchy, and the potential overlap of federal and state laws affecting cultural property, the question of what to do with cultural resources held in private collections can be complex. The following discussion attempts to outline the applicable laws and a means of determining whether any federal laws apply or might be triggered for situations that a general practitioner, or even a trust and estate practitioner, might encounter.

## Determining Applicable Law

### Is It a Cultural Resource or Just a Rock?

Some objects are easily identified as having historical or cultural value—a sword from the Civil War, a collection of Native American projectile points, or a needlepoint sampler from the early 1800s are seemingly self-evident. Other objects, by contrast, may not be recognized as historically significant, or even as a cultural resource. The shape of a black rock may not clearly reveal that it is a broken Native American projectile point, while a piece of the Berlin Wall may be mistaken for a mere hunk of cement. In trying to determine what an object is, where it came from, how old it is, and how the owner acquired it, multiple avenues of inquiry should be pursued including obtaining information from the owner, or his or her family, through historical research and from analysis of the object itself.

Quite often those who collect such objects know the historical or cultural significance, history, and provenance of the objects in their possession. If the collector is no longer available, friends and family members may be able to provide some information. Rarely is there any documentation for such objects; however, keen collectors often document their acquisitions in journals, perform their own historical research, and communicate with others who share their interest about their acquisitions. These sources can provide invaluable information as to what it is, when and from whom the object was actually acquired.

Historical research can be performed in varying degrees by interested laypersons, by amateur historians, archaeologists, and collectors. Local libraries, historical societies, and local colleges and universities often have good reference materials concerning cultural resources from the local region. For objects obtained from outside the immediate geographic area, or for foreign cultural resources, the expertise of a specialist may be necessary.

The object or resource itself should be analyzed, preferably using nondestructive techniques, by a knowledgeable professional. The types of analysis that can be performed will depend on whether the item is moveable or attached to land, its material composition, its integrity, and practical considerations, such as the availability of technology and experienced professionals, and the costs associated with the use of more advanced analytical tools.[3] A specialist in the appropriate field can generally determine what the object is, its material composition, and possibly its approximate age by visual inspection, taking measurements, comparison to objects of a similar typology, and examination using a microscope. The need for more invasive analyses will depend on how much information can be derived using noninvasive techniques: the object's significance; its scientific, monetary, sentimental or personal value; the existence or need for an appropriate disposition plan; the expense of such additional testing and the amount of time available for such analyses. Additional factors such as the material composition and physical integrity of the object will also determine whether invasive analyses can and should be conducted.

A surprising amount of information can usually be obtained from even a preliminary examination, and technological advances have increased the amount of information that can be obtained through noninvasive means while decreasing the impact of more invasive processes. Analysis and investigation of the object should reveal what the object is, its type, category, or defining characteristics; its material composition; the culture with which it is or was most closely associated; when it was made and used; and its provenance. The information obtained will help determine whether any federal or state cultural resource laws apply and will also help the owner or successors in interest to develop an appropriate disposition plan.

## Federal Jurisdiction: Hook, Line, or Sinker?

Federal cultural resource laws apply in only three circumstances: where the federal government owns the property; where federal officials or agencies undertake an action or project, including permits; and where federal funds are expended. Determining whether any of the three jurisdictional "hooks" apply may be quite simplistic if the critical information has been obtained from the analyses in step one. Unfortunately the information that may be most determinative of federal jurisdiction may also be the most difficult to glean: the object's provenance and the chain of title or chain of custody leading to the current owner. Is the private possession lawful?

Federal laws control where the federal government retains ownership of property, whether personal or real. Although federal lands are located within the jurisdictional boundaries of state and local governments, only federal cultural resource laws apply to federally owned lands. Federal ownership of real property is usually open and obvious. Encroachment on federal lands must be removed. Federal ownership of personal property is self-evident if the agencies have the object in their possession, the object is located on federal property, or the federal government produced or commissioned the object to be produced and never relinquished ownership, such as sunken aircraft and ships. But the federal government retains title despite the fact that it no longer has control or possession of the object, such as archaeological items taken from federal land, either with permission for study under a permit, or without permission. This can create confusion as the person in possession of the object may have reason to know that the object truly belongs to the federal government, based upon what is known about how the object was collected.

Federal laws apply to so-called "major federal actions"—where a federal agency undertakes, directs, or authorizes an infrastructure development project. This is the broadest category of activities to which federal cultural resource laws apply. State and local laws may also apply to a "major federal action" if the project occurs on state or local lands, involves state or local agencies, or state or local funds are expended for the project or activity. Potentially overlapping federal, state, and local cultural resource laws can create some confusion as each layer of government may apply different standards for determining significance, may protect different types of cultural resources or different aspects of the same cultural resource, and may impose very different review and mitigation procedures. Actions on tribal land can be confusing as the United States Supreme Court ruled that tribes do not have an interest in federal projects on tribal land, but certainly the tribal status as landowner otherwise is controlling.

The final area of federal influence occurs when federal funds are involved. An entity, institution, or organization that receives federal funds, whether it is public or private, may be subject to federal cultural resources laws. When federal funds are used for a specific project, such as building a road or building, federal laws will apply to the projects. However, this may give rise to application of federal control to general operations. For instance, a university may receive federal funds for a building and then find that as a result its museum collections are subject to federal curation and repatriation laws. It is not the amount of federal funds expended that determines whether federal laws apply. In addition, there are regulations implementing these laws, with specific guidance, and regulations that apply to particular federal lands.

Combined, the three circumstances in which federal laws apply affect a surprisingly wide range of entities and activities, both public and private at the federal, state, and local levels. Federal cultural resource laws should not be ignored; rather, asking and answering a few questions to determine whether the resource at issue involves or triggers any of the three federal jurisdictional "hooks" (federal property, federal action, federal money) will help private clients avoid criminal or civil liability.

**Practitioner's Tip**

Federal legislation aimed at protecting cultural resources has largely been enacted over time and often in reaction to federal programs, projects, and activities that have had a detrimental impact on cultural resources. More than one law may apply to a situation. Legal practitioners should follow the lead of those involved in the field of cultural resource management and review each and every situation or issue carefully to ensure that no federal laws apply or could possibly be triggered.

A two-step review process addresses both the subject-matter jurisdiction of federal laws, over specific types of cultural resources—such as eagle feather protection wherever they may be held—and the general jurisdictional reach, the federal hook of land, permits, and funds, of federal law. The information obtained will determine whether any state laws might apply, in addition to federal law or in absence of federal law, which will help the practitioner develop a plan.

In the first step, the inquiry focuses on the object itself, where it came from, and how it was acquired by its current owner. This analysis should seek to establish what the object is based on its material characteristics, to which category of cultural resource the object belongs, with which cultural group it was previously associated, where geographically it came from, and the probable age of the object. Certain types or categories of cultural resources are more likely to trigger a federal or state cultural resource law than others. For example, the discovery of human remains should wave a red flag that federal and state cultural resource, civil rights, and potentially criminal laws, may apply. The analysis should also attempt to establish how the object was acquired by its current owner, when it was acquired, and, if possible, the chain of title or chain of custody leading to the current owner. The type or category of cultural resource to which the object belongs may help determine whether a particular federal law applies or if any state law applies. Nonhuman burial objects will likely trigger federal and/or state laws. One good rule to use would be, if you do not know how it was obtained and have a sense that the acquisition was lawful in the first instance, given all of the circumstances, then legal review is prudent.

The second step requires a review of the general federal jurisdictional "hooks" (federal property, federal action, or federal money) to determine whether there is any legal basis or grounds for the application of federal law. Typically, the ownership of raw undeveloped land will not implicate any federal laws, while ownership of land improved with a historic building may require a more thorough analysis.

For those unfamiliar with the fields of historic preservation and cultural resource management, there are numerous ways to find specialists capable of identifying and analyzing objects of historic and cultural significance. Practitioners can locate such specialists through history, anthropology, archaeology, and sociology departments at local colleges and universities; through cultural resource management firms, state agencies such as departments of culture, history, historic preservation, or archaeology; the State Historic Preservation Officer; or relevant nonprofit organizations. Additional information and assistance concerning the parameters of federal jurisdiction over cultural resources can be obtained from practitioners specializing in cultural resource law. Although the number of lawyers who specialize in cultural resource law is extremely small, various other specialists and consultants are familiar with federal and state laws concerning cultural resources, including cultural resource management consultants; State Historic Preservation Officers; state agencies for history, culture, historic preservation and archaeology; the National Park Service; and national, state, and local nonprofit organizations.

## Federal Cultural Resources Laws: An Overview

Cultural resources have, historically, been valued as aesthetically pleasing remnants of the past to be discovered, claimed, and displayed, or as objects containing valuable information about the past to be studied, tested, and analyzed. From the beginning, federal cultural resource legislation placed tremendous value on scientific inquiry, academic study, and increasing our knowledge about the past. To that end, federal cultural resource laws were written to provide access to cultural resources, not only to scientists and academics, but to the American public through national parks and museums, and to allow for the acquisition of cultural resources by qualified individuals and institutions for research, study, and display. As interest in cultural resources grew and conflicts over access and possession arose, the focus of federal legislation shifted towards developing processes to identify cultural resources, determine their historical significance, assess the potential impact on those resources, and find an appropriate balance between the protection of those cultural resources and the pursuit of other goals and activities. More recent laws also require an analysis of priority of ownership and control. There is a recognition that cultural resources actively embody the history and maintain the continuity of the cultures from which they derive. More recent laws have emphasized preservation planning and the proactive development of resource management plans to identify goals and establish appropriate parameters for the preservation of our resources, involving all stakeholders.

The first federal law to express control of cultural resources by the United States was the Antiquities Act, enacted in 1906.[4] This Act made it a federal offense to "appropriate, injure or destroy any historic or prehistoric ruin or monument, or any object of antiquity, situated on lands owned or controlled by the Government of the United States. . . ."[5] and imposed permitting requirements on qualified individuals for the "examination of ruins, excavation of archaeological sites, and the gathering of objects of antiquity. . . ."[6] The liability and permitting provisions were largely replaced by more specific permitting requirements and a more comprehensive liability and penalty scheme contained in the Archaeological Resources Protection Act (ARPA) enacted in 1979. The Act also gave the President the authority to declare "by public proclamation historic landmarks, historic and prehistoric structures, and other objects of historic or scientific interest that are situated upon the lands owned or controlled by the Government of the United States to be national monuments. . . ."[7] This provision was used, for example, by President Clinton to create new national monuments, including Canyon of the Ancients in Colorado and Aqua Fria in Arizona, and to expand existing monuments and parks such as Giant Sequoia National Monument in California and Craters of the Moon in Idaho.[8] Almost thirty years later, in 1935, with the Historic Sites Act, enacted during Roosevelt's New Deal, Congress declared that it was "a national policy to preserve for public use historic sites, buildings, and objects of national significance for the inspiration and benefit of the people of the United States," thereby launching the federal government into the field of historic preservation.[9] The Act required the federal government, through the National Park Service under the authority of the Secretary of the Interior, to identify and document historic buildings and sites and to preserve historic buildings and sites owned or acquired by the federal government for the benefit of the public.[10]

Following the deaccession and distribution of surpluses and property after World War II, Congress enacted the Federal Property and Administrative Services Act, which required the federal government to consider the historic and/or cultural significance of real and personal property before disposing of it.[11] In the same year, Congress chartered the National Trust for Historic Preservation and designated the private institution as a recognized partner of the federal government in the field of historic preservation.[12]

The field of historic preservation and the relationship of the built and natural environment began to take root in the public conscience in the1960s and early 1970s, prompting Congress to enact a series of new laws that transformed American policies at all levels of government towards cultural resources. The Archaeological and Historic Preservation Act (AHPA) was enacted in 1960, followed by the National Historic Preservation Act (NHPA) in 1966 and the National Environmental Policy Act (NEPA) in 1970.[13] The AHPA was enacted in response to federal projects to construct reservoirs and dams resulting in the flooding of vast areas of land and the submersion and destruction of historic and archaeological resources, most of which were never identified, documented, or salvaged. The NHPA and NEPA are considered process-oriented legislation as they both require that the federal government identify and document historic and natural resources, respectively; accumulate and make public information indicating the impacts that a proposed federal action or federally funded project will have on those historic or natural resources; and make a decision whether to proceed with the proposed federal action or federally funded project.

The success of those acts in transforming government policies towards cultural resources prompted review of older legislation like the Antiquities Act and, in 1979, Congress passed the Archaeological Resources Protection Act which provided greater protection to archaeological resources from looting and from a rapidly growing black market for cultural resources.[14] Growing interest in the monetary and market value of shipwrecks and the contents of those vessels located in American waters prompted passage of the Abandoned Shipwreck Act in 1988.[15] And, in 1990, with the passage of the Native American Graves Protection and Repatriation Act, Congress attempted to redress decades of desecration of Native American graves and assign presumption of control of cultural items located on federal lands.[16] The American Battlefield Protection Act was passed in 1996, in an effort to stem private development of lands on which historic battles were fought, primarily those associated with the Civil War.[17] The most recent piece of legislation, the Sunken Military Craft Act, was adopted in 2004 to protect sunken federal military vessels and aircraft located anywhere in the world and foreign craft sunken in American waters.[18]

## Federal Property

The largest category of property in private collections to which federal cultural resource laws will apply is federal property. The federal government owns and manages millions of acres of land and hundreds of thousands of historic and archaeological buildings, sites, and objects that are or were attached to that land.[19] Over time, objects have been removed, with and without the permission of the federal government. Some of those objects have been acquired by private individuals who may not know that the object was previously located on, or attached to, federal lands or that the federal government retains title to all personal property, such as ships and aircraft, absent an explicit action to transfer or terminate title. Furthermore, the object itself may not reveal that it is the property of the federal government. If, however, the provenance is known and federal law applies, a thorough analysis of the applicable laws should help determine who owns the object and what should be done with it. A recent story about federal property in private hands provides an excellent case study to test the proposed two-step analysis for determining whether federal cultural resource laws apply.

In October 2009, items that were once part of a formal silver tea set aboard the *USS Arizona*, a battleship sunk in Pearl Harbor during the attack on December 7, 1941, were listed for auction by a private individual who claimed to have inherited the pieces from her father. Her father was aboard the *USS Oklahoma* during the attack and served as a diver during recovery efforts conducted immediately afterward. He may have obtained the silver tea settings during salvage operations, perhaps believing that they were destined to be deemed refuse and dumped out at sea by the Navy. Upon his death, his daughter inherited the silver settings as part of his estate. She retained the items for nearly seventy years and reportedly chose to put them up for auction to help pay medical expenses for a family member.[20]

News of the items to be auctioned off spread quickly among veterans' groups and historians and, within days, the National Park Service and the U.S. Navy got involved. The U.S. Navy, through its Judge Advocate General, contacted the auction house and the items were removed from the auction list pending a formal determination of the legal status of the silver items.[21] Although the seaman's daughter inherited the items, she might not be the true legal owner. Despite the fact that some sixty-eight years have passed since the attack and the items were inherited by an innocent third party, the items may be deemed as initially stolen property and therefore still the property of the Navy. And because the objects were once the property of the United States military, they remain so until formally deaccessioned. The family will likely lose any rights they believed they had to the silver objects that they inherited, including rights to possess, transfer, or sell the silver objects, but they are not likely to face criminal charges. Being an innocent owner may relieve criminal liability, but does not confer property ownership.

**Object Analysis**

The objects at issue were clearly movable, personal property. An examination of the objects, even by a trained specialist, would not necessarily have revealed that they belonged to the U.S. Navy or that they came from the *USS Arizona*. Reportedly, the only visible stamps revealed the names of two common silver manufacturers, Reed & Barton and Gorham Manufacturing Company. It is possible that the objects did have a Navy stamp or seal that, although not visible to the naked eye due to a crust of lime that had formed, may have been discernible using more advanced analysis techniques or by the careful removal of the lime crust by a trained conservator. Nothing about the objects themselves revealed their unusual provenance. It was only through information provided by the purported owner that the provenance of the objects was known. Luckily, the object was only one generation removed from the salvor and the story behind the objects was passed down. Authenticity can be verified through additional analyses.

Based on the information provided by the family, the U.S. Navy pressured the auction house to remove the items from sale and began an investigation to determine if the items were authentic and, if so, which federal laws and claims would apply. That inquiry is still pending; however, this analysis reveals that it is highly likely that the U.S. Navy is the true owner and that title never vested in the seaman who allegedly took the items, even though it was his purpose to protect them.

**Legal Analysis**

Various specific cultural resource laws affect movable objects the vast majority of which were, at some point, in, on, or attached to land. If historical or archaeological objects are removed from federal land without permission—whether outright stolen or removed in violation of an issued permit—the civil and criminal liability provisions of the Antiquities Act or the Archaeological Resources Protection Act (ARPA) will apply. General federal criminal laws pertaining to theft and destruction of federal property may apply as well, but this analysis will review the specific cultural property laws. The Antiquities Act applies to objects of antiquity illegally removed from lands owned or controlled by the United States after 1906, the date of its enactment. In 1979, some of its enforcement provisions were enhanced by the ARPA.[22] The Antiquities Act will still apply to submerged resources controlled by the United States, even if not on U.S. land, given the specific language of these two laws. ARPA imposes criminal liability on any person who excavates, removes, damages, or otherwise defaces "any archaeological resource located on public lands or Indian lands" without a validly issued permit;[23] and on any person who sells, purchases, exchanges, or transports such a resource.[24] ARPA also establishes that the federal government, through the Secretary of the Interior, retains ownership and ultimate control over archaeological resources removed from public lands under the Antiquities Act, ARPA, and the Reservoir Salvage Act of 1960, as amended by the Archaeological and Historic Preservation Act of 1974.[25] ARPA also establishes that the exchange or ultimate disposition of archaeological resources removed from Indian lands is subject to the consent of the Indian tribe that owns or has jurisdiction over such lands.[26] Thus, any person involved in the removal, transport, purchase, sale, exchange, or potential purchase, sale, or exchange of archaeological resources obtained in violation of federal law is potentially subject to criminal and possibly civil liability, in addition to forfeiting the items to the government or tribal owner.

ARPA creates two categories of cultural resources obtained from federal public lands or Indian lands: those removed under a validly issued permit, i.e., the permission of the landowner, and those removed illegally. The former can remain in the possession of the individual or institution to whom the permit was issued, for access to enable scientific study for the time allowed, but title does not transfer to the possessor as the federal government retains title.

Additional federal cultural resource laws apply to objects that are in, on, or attached to lands that are submerged underwater. The Abandoned Shipwreck Act (ASA) of 1987, which became effective in 1988, and the Sunken Military Craft Act (SMCA) enacted in 2004 apply to privately owned vessels that have been abandoned in the navigable waters of the United States and to sunken military aircraft and water vessels, respectively.[27]

Prior to the enactment of the ASA in 1987, the fate of shipwrecks was determined by the laws of salvage and finds. Those laws were focused on determining who had legal title to vessels that appeared abandoned, i.e., shipwrecks. Legal status depended on whether the person or entity that owned the vessel when it sank still retained title, whether some successor in interest to that person or entity had asserted and maintained legal ownership, whether it had been abandoned, or whether a subsequent valid claim had been made by another party. Even following the enactment of the ASA, salvage operations continued as claims established prior to 1988 remained valid. Some states that obtained title to numerous shipwrecks under the ASA allow select salvors to obtain permits to salvage materials from shipwrecks and shipwrecks sites deemed to have little historical significance, limited environmental benefit, or low value as a recreational diving site. In addition, some vessels have been removed or salvaged because they inhibited the use of waterways for transportation and recreation or their eventual disintegration posed an environmental threat.

The ASA provides that any vessel "embedded in submerged lands of a State" or "embedded in coralline formations protected by a State on submerged lands of a State" or "on submerged lands of a State and . . . included in or determined eligible for inclusion in the National Register" that has been abandoned by its owner becomes the property of the federal government.[28] The Act then provides that title, once vested in the federal government, shifts to the state in which the shipwreck is located.[29] Following more traditional jurisdictional principles, title to any abandoned shipwreck located in or on public lands vests in the federal government while any abandoned shipwrecks on Indian lands become the property of the tribe that owns that land.[30] The unusual transfer of title, by operation of the statute, from the federal government to the state where the abandoned shipwreck is located was intended to encourage the states to take control of abandoned shipwrecks within their boundaries and, for the benefit of the public, protect them from private salvage activities.

The stated goals of the ASA include encouraging the exploration of abandoned vessels for tourism, recreation, scientific and historical research, and their preservation as natural resource and habitat areas and as cultural resources and, in limited circumstances, to allow for the recovery of shipwrecks "consistent with the protection of historical values and environmental integrity of the shipwrecks and the sites."[31] The ASA provides protection for certain abandoned shipwrecks and the objects associated with such vessels by excluding the application of the law of finds, which the common law uses to establish title to abandoned personal property in the finders of such property. The common law of finds, when included in maritime/admiralty law, had encouraged shipwreck hunters to actively assert claims over abandoned shipwrecks, and to excavate these vessels and remove any materials and objects associated with them. This activity resulted in the destruction of abandoned shipwrecks located off the coast of the United States and in major navigable waters, such as the Mississippi River, and the loss of vast amounts of historical information pertaining to a broad range of subjects, from Spanish exploration of the New World, to colonial mercantile activities, to military campaigns during the Civil War.[32] The ASA limits the destruction of shipwrecks and the resulting loss of information by establishing federal, state, or Indian control over such shipwrecks and encouraging their protection as historical, archaeological, and environmental resources.

It is not known exactly how many shipwrecks have been claimed and salvaged since Spanish explorers first sailed to the New World. It is rather unlikely that practitioners will encounter clients who claim title to a shipwreck located in or on state, federal, or Indian lands.[33] It would not, however, be unusual for private individuals to own objects and materials that were removed from a shipwreck. A review of public auction houses and private dealers reveals that thousands of objects salvaged from shipwrecks in the United States are in commercial circulation.[34] The primary consideration is whether the object or material was obtained legally, either under a valid claim of title or a valid permit issued by the federal government or a state. If the object was removed prior to 1988, the laws of salvage and finds controlled and the salvor must have established a valid claim of title to the vessel prior to conducting any salvage activities. After 1988, objects could be legally removed under a claim of title established prior to the enactment of the ASA, a valid transfer of title from the relevant governmental entity (state, federal or Indian tribe) to the salvor, or under a valid permit to salvage issued by the relevant governmental entity.[35] A permit issued under ARPA may be required for the removal of any objects or materials from a shipwreck located in or on federal or Indian lands.[36] Typically, salvage permits are issued to allow access for historical, scientific, or archaeological research of the shipwreck, its contents, and the site. These permits often provide that the acquired materials remain the property of the issuing authority and prohibit any transfer, sale, or exchange.

This quickly leads the analysis back to questions of provenance, age of the object, and chain of title or chain of custody. In some instances, the objects and materials can be easily traced back to a particular vessel based on characteristics that can be gleaned from the object itself, such as the type of material used, a unique design, style, or motif, or the purpose or function of the object. If the provenance can be determined, additional historical research may reveal whether the object was legally removed pursuant to a title or a permit allowing for the transfer, sale, or exchange into private hands. No special action is required if the object was removed under legal title or pursuant to a permit allowing for private acquisition as such objects are considered the personal property of the owner and can be bought, sold, exchanged, transferred, or destroyed. If so, the possessor should have a copy of the authorizing document, or some record to substantiate ownership that began with legal authority. Credible dealers keep track of such documentation, and it may increase the value of the object. If the objects were stolen (meaning the salvor did not have legal title) or objects were taken in the absence or in violation of a permit, the person who acquires those objects will not have legal title. Under traditional property law, true and legal title vests if the object is purchased for value by a bona fide purchaser, i.e., one who had authority of ownership in the first instance. Lack of criminal knowledge may protect a client from criminal charges, but does not also ensure ownership title.

**Practitioner's Tips**

If a private client is in possession of objects that appear to have been or purportedly were removed from a shipwreck, every effort should be made to determine the provenance of such objects and discern whether the objects were legally salvaged, stolen, or inherited without indicia of ownership.[37]

If provenance can be determined, the next step would be to find out who owns the vessel or who owned it when it or its contents were salvaged. Under the ASA, many states have created inventories of the abandoned shipwrecks in or on their lands.[38] The federal government also maintains records of shipwrecks located on federal and Indian lands and records pertaining to those shipwrecks transferred to their respective states under the ASA.[39] If the vessel was privately owned and salvage operations were conducted prior to 1988, or thereafter pursuant to a claim established prior to 1988, few records may exist. Under the laws of salvage and finds, legal controversies often erupt over whether a shipwreck was in fact abandoned and whether a valid legal claim had been established. Thus state courts in the relevant jurisdiction may have records pertaining to such claims. Federal courts control admiralty law claims concerning ships involved in interstate commerce and international trade and therefore may in some instances have records. If salvage operations were undertaken on federal or Indian lands, some records should exist indicating that the salvor had permission, or after 1988 had a valid permit. If the shipwreck was located on the submerged lands of any state, a permit may not have been required prior to 1988; after 1988, the state should have records identifying shipwrecks within its borders over which it has control pursuant to the ASA and records indicating whether a salvage permit was ever issued.

In the absence of any information as to provenance, the owner must make a potentially difficult decision as to what to do with the objects. He or she may choose to retain ownership having been fully advised of the potential risks and liabilities, both civil and criminal, associated with the possession of objects to which there may not be legal title. If choosing to dispose of the objects, he or she should be made aware that the lack of information about the provenance may limit or complicate any transfer, sale, or exchange. Such clients should be advised that the transport, transfer, sale, or exchange of such objects may give rise to additional liabilities and may make the recipient or purchaser also liable. Donation of the object to an educational, scientific, research, or public institution may be a viable option as such institutions comport with the goals of federal cultural resource laws such as the ARPA and ASA and may provide a safe haven from liability; and they are better equipped to provide for the proper conservation, interpretation, and public display of the object. However, both private and public institutions may be unwilling to accept an object of unknown provenance that may have been acquired illegally. In such circumstances, it may be possible to donate the object to the relevant state, federal agency, or Indian tribe. Many states, through their State Historic Preservation Officer, historic preservation office, state archaeologist, or state parks agency, willingly take cultural resources that came from private or public lands within their borders and hold them in trust until they can be returned to their appropriate owner.

## Sunken Military Craft Act

The Sunken Military Craft Act (SMCA) provides that the federal government retains title to any sunken federal military craft, whether a water vessel or an aircraft, "regardless of when the sunken military craft sank" and such rights cannot be extinguished "except by express divestiture of title by the United States."[40] It specifically prohibits anyone subject to federal jurisdiction from possessing, disturbing, removing, or injuring any sunken military craft unless authorized by a permit or regulations issued under the Act.[41] It protects sunken military craft by suspending the laws of salvage and finds with respect to any sunken federal military craft, wherever located, and any foreign sunken military craft located in United States waters.[42] The final section imposes civil liability on anyone who violates the terms of the Act and clearly provides that the Act in no way affects or prevents the pursuit of criminal sanctions for violations of applicable criminal laws.[43]

**Practitioner's Tips**

Consistent with the prior analysis under the ASA, knowledge of provenance is highly determinative of whether the SMCA applies. In addition, because such laws cannot be applied retroactively, actions taken prior to 2004 that if taken after 2004 would violate the SMCA are exempt and subject only to the laws of salvage and finds and possibly criminal statutes in force at the time.

As noted throughout, if provenance cannot be determined, additional effort should be made to determine the age of the object in question and potentially how old it was when it was transferred to a private collector. Age and the likely date of transfer or conversion from federal property to private property may help to determine which federal cultural resource laws apply.

Thus, although the SMCA seems applicable to the removal of the silver tea set from the *USS Arizona*, the objects were taken sixty plus years prior to the enactment of the SMCA. Instead, as lawyers for the Navy have mentioned, other laws concerning federal property, particularly federal military property, may apply. It is highly likely, given all of the policy and precedent considerations against allowing private individuals to convert federal property, that title will have been retained by the federal government.

## Conclusion

It should be stated that because this is a relatively nuanced area of law, the circumstances surrounding the transfer, acquisition, or disposition of any specific object or item as well as the nature of the object itself can dictate which laws apply and the outcome of their application. Therefore, decisions should be made based on as complete information as can be obtained and only after consideration of the potential consequences not only for the current and prospective owner but also for the resource itself. Efforts should be made to obtain the critical information and to cross-reference what can be gleaned from the object itself against what can be learned about the object from its purported owner. Any legal analysis should be careful and deliberate to ensure that all potentially applicable state and federal cultural resources are considered. Finally, because of the potential liability under various federal statutes, general practitioners and those involved in asset management and trust and estate practices should give special consideration to involving specialists to assist with the analysis of the object itself and with the legal analysis. As practitioners, our goal is to protect our clients and their resources. In some instances, that may mean giving up cultural resources in their possession.

## Notes

1. This article addresses only "domestic" cultural resources, the physical remnants of the cultures and peoples that are part of the prehistory and history of what is now known as the United States.
2. The Latin term "fasces" meaning a bundle of sticks is used to describe property rights. *Black's Law Dictionary*, 2 ed., ed. Bryan Garner, West Group (St. Paul, Minn., 2001).
3. Typical analysis methods include visual examination, detailed measurements, digital photography, thermography, x-ray, CAT scans, chemical analyses; *see also* National Park Service, Index of Conserve-O-Grams, available at http://www.nps.gov/history/museum/publications/conserveogram/cons_toc.html#collectionpreservation (accessed Jan. 1, 2010); National Center for Preservation Technology and Training, available at http://www.ncptt.nps.gov/ (accessed Jan. 1, 2010).
4. 16 U.S.C. §§ 431-433 (2009).
5. 16 U.S.C. § 433.
6. 16 U.S.C. § 432. *See also*, "'Cultural Property' Begins: The Centennial of the Antiquities Act," in the YEARBOOK OF CULTURAL PROPERTY LAW, 2006.
7. 16 U.S.C. § 431.
8. National Park Service, National Park Service History, "National Monument Proclamations under the Antiquities Act," available at http://www.nps.gov/history/history/hisnps/NPSHistory/monuments.htm (last accessed Jan. 1, 2010).
9. 16 U.S.C. §§ 461-467 (2009).
10. 16 U.S.C. §§ 462, 462 (a)-(j).
11. 40 U.S.C. §§ 484-550 (2009).
12. 16 U.S.C. § 468 (2009).
13. AHPA: 16 U.S.C. §§ 469-469c-2 (2009); NHPA: 16 U.S.C. §§ 470-470x-6 (2009); NEPA: 42 U.S.C. §§ 4321, 4331-4335 (2009).
14. 16 U.S.C. §§ 470aa-mm (2009). *See* generally, PRESENTING ARCHAEOLOGY IN COURT, Hutt, Forsyth and Tarler eds. Alta Mira Press, 2006.
15. 43 U.S.C. §§ 2101-2106 (2009).
16. 25 U.S.C. §§ 3001-3013 (2009).
17. 16 U.S.C. § 469k (2009).
18. 10 U.S.C. §§ 113 Note -118 (2009).
19. U.S. Geological Survey, "Federal Lands and Indian Reservations," National Atlas project, available at http://nationalatlas.gov/printable/images/pdf/fedlands/fedlands3.pdf (last accessed Jan. 1, 2009).
20. Chris Ayers, "Plans to sell tea set from sunken Pearl Harbor ship USS Arizona spark anger," THE LONDON TIMES (Nov. 12, 2009), available at http://www.timesonline.co.uk/tol/new/world/us_and_americas/article6913431.ece (last accessed Jan. 1, 2010).
21. Burl Burlingame, "USS Arizona items pulled from auction," HONOLULU STAR ADVERTISER (Nov. 12, 2009), available at http://www.starbulletin.com/

news/20091112_uss_arizona_items_pulled_from_auction.html (last accessed Jan. 1, 2010).
22. *See* 16 U.S.C. §§ 470cc(g) & (h) (clarifying jurisdiction of Antiquities Act).
23. 16 U.S.C. § 470ee(a).
24. 16 U.S.C. § 470ee(b).
25. 16 U.S.C. §§ 470cc(b)(3) and 470dd(2).
26. 16 U.S.C. § 470dd. And see, 25 U.S.C. 3001, NAGPRA for disposition to tribes.
27. ASA: 43 U.S.C. §§ 2101-2106 (2009); SMCA: 10 U.S.C. §§ 113 Note–118 (2009).
28. 43 U.S.C. § 2105(a).
29. 43 U.S.C. § 2105(c).
30. 43 U.S.C. § 2105(c) & (d).
31. 43 U.S.C. § 2103.
32. *See, e.g.*, Harold Heckle, Associated Press, "Spain files suit for $500 million shipwreck treasure," National Geographic online (May 9, 2008), available at http://news.nationalgeographic.com/news/2008/05/080509-AP-spain-shipw.html (last accessed Jan. 1, 2010).
33. Such a claim may require the assistance of a specialist in admiralty law, preferably one with experience in the jurisdiction where the shipwreck is located.
34. *See, e.g.*, auctions held by Daniel Frank Sedwick, LLC, available at http://www.sedwickcoins.com/ (last accessed Jan. 1, 2010).
35. North Carolina Gen. Stat. Ann. § 121-22: Salvage of Abandoned Shipwrecks and Other Underwater Archaeological Sites (2009), available at http://www.ncga.state.nc.us/EnactedLegislation/Statutes/PDF/ByArticle/Chapter_121/Article_3.pdf (last accessed Jan. 1, 2010).
36. 16 U.S.C. §§ 470cc(a)-(j); 470ee.
37. When it comes to shipwrecks, the golden nugget of information is the registered name of the vessel. That alone can lead to vast amounts of information including shipping records, historical accounts, purchase and sale agreements, and state and local records concerning import taxes, property and business taxes, and harbor and port entry fees.
38. *See, e.g.*, Wisconsin Historical Society, "About the State Underwater Archaeology Program," available at http://www.wisconsinhistory.org/shipwrecks/about.asp (last accessed Jan. 1, 2010).
39. *See, e.g.*, Barbara Voulgaris, "The Navy's Computerized Shipwreck Database Inventory," Dept. of the Navy, Navy Historical Branch, Underwater Archaeology Branch, available at http://www.history.navy.mil/branches/org12-7c.htm (last accessed Jan. 1, 2010).
40. 10 U.S.C. § 113.
41. 10 U.S.C. § 1402.
42. 10 U.S.C. § 1406.
43. 10 U.S.C. § 1406.

# Federal Land Management

• • •

## *Section Editor: James Van Ness*

### Introduction

This year's cases address recurring themes. In each case, the decision reached by the court will likely come as no surprise to experienced cultural property law practitioners. On the other hand, the fact that each of these cases was litigated to a decision suggests that maybe the outcome was not so predictable, at least to the litigants involved. With that in mind, perhaps we all may add to our knowledge base by reexamining these themes through the prism presented by the facts in these cases.

### NHPA Section 110 Obligations

Section 110 of the National Historic Preservation Act requires federal agencies to establish a preservation program to ensure "historic properties under the jurisdiction or control of the agency are identified, evaluated, and nominated to the National Register [of Historic Places]."[1] In *Oglala Sioux Tribe of the Pine Ridge Reservation v. United States Army Corps of Engineers*,[2] the United States Court of Appeals for the District of Columbia was asked to determine whether these duties must be satisfied within any certain time frame.

The case concerns several federal government properties located along the Missouri River and under the jurisdiction of the Army Corps of Engineers. These properties were once part of the Great Sioux Reservation, which encompassed the western half of present-day South Dakota until the Reservation was dissolved by an Act of Congress in 1889. The Water Resources Development Act of 1999 directed the Secretary of the Army to transfer title to—or grant perpetual leases for—many of these federal properties to the State of South Dakota, the Cheyenne River Sioux Tribe, and the Lower Brule Sioux Tribe. Seeking to enjoin the transfers of these federal properties, the Oglala Sioux Tribe filed a complaint in 2001 alleging the Army Corps of Engineers owed the Tribe a duty under the National Historic Preservation Act to "locate, inventory and nominate for inclusion in the National Register of Historic Places all Native American cultural items and other historic properties" within the federal lands encompassed by the former Great Sioux Reservation. The United States District Court for the District of Columbia determined that mandamus relief[3] was inappropriate because the Army Corps had no plainly prescribed duty to evaluate federal properties in the manner requested by the Tribe; the Tribe appealed.

In a single brief and admirably to-the-point paragraph, the Court of Appeals held that "the National Historic Preservation Act establishes no clear duty for agencies to evaluate potential historic sites within a certain time frame or in a certain manner."[4] Echoing the United States District Court for the District of Columbia's oft-cited (if somewhat murkier) 1996 opinion in *National Trust for Historic Preservation v. Blanck*,[5] the Court observed that the National Historic Preservation Act establishes for federal agencies two principal statutory duties: the Section 106 duty to "take into account the effect of the undertaking on any district, site, building, structure, or object that is included in or eligible for inclusion in the National Register";[6] and the Section 110 duty to "establish . . . a preservation program for the identification, evaluation, and nomination to the National Register of Historic Places, and [for the] protection of historic properties."[7] Because the Tribe did not allege that the Army Corps had failed to meet either of these affirmative responsibilities, arguing only that the Army Corps had failed to act quickly enough in meeting its Section 110 obligations, the Court determined it had no choice but to dismiss the Tribe's mandamus claim.

## The NHPA and the "Small Federal Handle" Question

In *Harrison v. United States Department of the Army*,[8] the United States District Court for the Western District of Kentucky addressed what is commonly referred to as the "small federal handle" question: at what point does federal participation in a project proposed by a nonfederal entity "federalize" the action and render the entire project subject to the requirements of the National Historic Preservation Act?

Although the administrative record considered by the Court spanned more than 1,200 pages, the facts are not complicated. In 2005, the Louisville Gas & Electric Company and Kentucky Utilities Company proposed to construct a 41.9 mile–long transmission line to connect a generating station in Jefferson County to a substation in Hardin County. The utilities' preferred route intersected the Army's Fort Knox Military Reservation, so the utilities requested an easement across the military reserve. For the purpose of analyzing the potential effects on historic properties of granting the easement, the Army defined the "undertaking" as the 10.9 mile stretch of Fort Knox that the transmission line would cross. The Army then determined the "area of potential effects" to include, in addition, the distance from which the transmission line could be seen from Fort Knox property, or 3,000 feet from the military reserve. Using this APE, the Army found that only one National Register–eligible property, Fort Duffield, would be affected, and recommended certain changes to the transmission line, including lowering the height of the poles, to eliminate any potentially adverse effects. After assuring the State Historic Preservation Office that other than its approval of the requested easement, the project involved no federal control, funding, or permits, the SHPO issued a finding of "no adverse effect" on historic properties and, in January 2008, the Army Corps of Engineers, which manages the land at Fort Knox for the Army, issued the utilities the requested easement on the Army's behalf.

The plaintiffs, Dennis and Cathy Cunningham, are members of the CDH Preserve, a 150-acre nature preserve. The Cunninghams live on the CDH property, which is in the "immediate vicinity" of Bethlehem Academy, a historic property listed on the National Register of Historic Places. Although the plaintiffs' property and nearby Bethlehem Academy are not within the area of potential effects of the undertaking as the Army defined it, a different portion of the 41.9 mile transmission line crosses the plaintiffs' property and is within the "viewshed" of the Bethlehem Academy. Seeking to block the construction of the transmission line across the CDH Preserve, the plaintiffs sued the Army, alleging that the Army wrongly limited its Section 106 review by defining the "undertaking" under the National Historic Preservation Act as just the 10.9 mile portion of the transmission line crossing Fort Knox, rather than the utilities' entire 41.9 mile transmission line.

The Court initially addressed the plaintiffs' standing to bring the suit. To establish standing, the plaintiffs must show they have "suffered a concrete injury to aesthetic, recreational, or scientific interests."[9] In this case, however, the plaintiffs appeared to allege no injury to their own land, but only injury to a neighboring property, Bethlehem Academy, which was not a party to the suit. While acknowledging that the plaintiffs were rather vague when describing the relationship between the Bethlehem Academy property, their own property, and the proposed location of the transmission line, the Court concluded that the plaintiffs had alleged injury insufficient to establish standing. Nonetheless, because the vagueness of the plaintiffs' pleadings left the Court unable to determine accurately whether the plaintiffs had standing to bring the claim, the Court proceeded to determine whether the Army improperly defined the "undertaking" or "APE."

The Court first considered the Advisory Council's definition of an "undertaking" as a "project, activity, or program . . . requiring a Federal . . . approval."[10] Applying this definition, the Court concluded that the entire 41.9 mile transmission line did not fit within the definition, as only the much shorter 10.9 mile portion crossing Fort Knox land required federal approval. In the Court's view, the Army's limited approval authority did not serve to define the "undertaking" as the entire project.

Next the Court considered whether the Army's definition of the "area of potential effects" squared with the Advisory Council's definition of an APE as "the area or areas within which an undertaking may directly or indirectly cause alterations in the character of historic properties."[11] The Court concluded that it was not arbitrary, capricious, or an abuse of discretion for the Army to define the APE and the undertaking's indirect effects based on the farthest distance from Army property that the transmission line could be seen—3,000 feet.

Lastly, the Court acknowledged that several circuits have treated an "undertaking" under the NHPA and a "major federal action" under the National Environmental Policy Act (NEPA) similarly.[12] As a consequence, the Court applied the test set forth in *Southwest Williamson County Community Ass'n, Inc. v. Slater*[13] for determining when a nonfederal action becomes a "major federal action" under NEPA to the facts in this NHPA case. In pertinent part, the *Slater* test asks whether federal decision makers have authority to exercise sufficient control or responsibility over the nonfederal project so as to influence the outcome of the project. The Court concluded that the Army's control over the transmission line was limited to its ability to grant or deny an easement over its property;

the Army did not otherwise approve the line, fund the line, or determine the route of the line over plaintiffs' property. Under these circumstances, the Court reasoned that "[t]o find that the grant of an easement over federal land serves to federalize an otherwise private project, is both contrary to the weight of the case law and to the Court's reasoned judgment."[14] In short, the Court found the "federal handle" in this case to be simply too small to force the Army to have to examine the potential effects of the transmission line on historic properties neither on Army property nor visible from it.

## NHPA and NEPA—Separate Requirements

Although the Advisory Council's regulations encourage federal agencies to coordinate compliance with Section 106 with any steps taken to meet the requirements of the National Environmental Policy Act (NEPA),[15] the requirements of the two statutes remain separate. Just how separate is well-illustrated by the United States District Court for the District of Columbia's decision in *Lemon v. McHugh*.[16]

The salient facts of the case are these. In 1998, the Army issued a Final Environmental Impact Statement evaluating the planned reuse of Fort Ritchie, a military post in Washington County, Maryland, selected for closure pursuant to the Defense Base Realignment and Closure Act. The FEIS was based on Washington County's April 1997 Comprehensive Redevelopment Plan. This Plan assumed that Fort Ritchie's historic parade ground—part of the Camp Ritchie Historic District—would remain untouched and would be integrated into any new development scenario as open space. As a consequence, none of the reuse alternatives analyzed by the Army in the FEIS addressed building on the parade ground.

In 2004, six years after the Army's FEIS was issued, Corporate Office Properties Trust (COPT), a development company selected by the Local Redevelopment Authority (LRA) for the Fort Ritchie site, developed a new Master Plan for the Redevelopment of Fort Ritchie (COPT plan). Upon issuance of the COPT plan, the Army prepared a Record of Environmental Consideration (REC), which it issued in January 2006. Although the COPT plan contemplated the construction of buildings and sports facilities on the historic parade ground, the REC concluded that the COPT plan presented "no significant new circumstances or information relevant to environmental concerns" and that no additional analysis under NEPA was required. The Army thereafter transferred the Fort Ritchie property to the LRA, which immediately transferred it to COPT.

The plaintiffs filed suit alleging the COPT plan imposes significant new impacts on Fort Ritchie's historic district that the Army failed to evaluate in either its initial FEIS or its subsequent REC. The plaintiffs asked the Court to find that the Army had violated NEPA and must therefore prepare a Supplemental EIS (SEIS). In response, the Army argued that it had taken adequate steps to mitigate any adverse effects that the COPT plan may have on Fort Ritchie's historic district by entering into a Programmatic Agreement with the Maryland State Historic Preservation Office to reduce impacts on historic resources.

In finding for the plaintiffs, the Court rejected the Army's assertion that its satisfaction of the NHPA's requirements was sufficient for the purposes of NEPA and therefore obviated the need for an SEIS. Instead, the Court emphasized that compliance with the NHPA does not relieve a federal agency of the independent duty to comply with NEPA. The Court determined that the COPT plan proposed substantial and obvious changes to Fort Ritchie's historic district—changes that were not addressed in the REC (beyond a mere reference to the existence of a Programmatic Agreement related to the original comprehensive Redevelopment Plan). As a consequence, the Court held that—irrespective of the fact that the Army had concluded a Programmatic Agreement with the SHPO—the Army was required to prepare either an SEIS analyzing the changes to the parade ground contemplated by the COPT plan or a REC convincingly demonstrating how the mitigation measures required by the terms of the Programmatic Agreement would render effects on the historic parade ground less than significant, making an SEIS unnecessary. In short, although the Court chose to rest its decision principally on the Council on Environmental Quality's NEPA regulations,[17] the Army would have been well advised to have heeded the Advisory Council's advice in 36 CFR §800.8(c)(5):

> If the undertaking is modified after approval of the FONSI or the ROD in a manner that changes the undertaking or alters its effects on historic properties, . . the agency official shall notify the Council and all consulting parties that supplemental environmental documents will be prepared in compliance with NEPA. . . .

## Notes

1. 16 U.S.C. § 470h-2(a)(2)(A).
2. 570 F.3d 327 (D.C. Cir. 2009).
3. *See* Mandamus Act, 28 U.S.C. § 1361. *See also In re Cheney*, 406 F.3d 723, 729 (D.C. Cir. 2005) (A plaintiff seeking mandamus relief has the burden of showing that the defendant owes it a "clear and compelling" duty).
4. *Oglala Sioux Tribe*, *supra* note 2, at 334.
5. 938 F. Supp. 908 (D.D.C. 1996).
6. 16 U.S.C. § 470f.
7. 16 U.S.C. § 470h-2(a)(2)(A).
8. Civil Action No. 3:08CV-105-H, 2009 WL 3347109 (W.D. Ky.).
9. *Id.* at 6, citing *Center for Biological Diversity v. Lueckel*, 417 F.3d 532, 537 (6th Cir. 2005).
10. 36 C.F.R. § 800.16(y).
11. 36 C.F.R. § 800.16(d).
12. *Harrison, supra* note 8, at 7 (and case cited).
13. 243 F.3d 270, 281 (6th Cir. 2001).
14. *Harrison, supra* note 8, at 8.
15. 36 C.F.R. §800.8.
16. Civil No. 05-949 (RCL), 2009 WL 3747218 (D.D.C. Nov. 10, 2009).
17. *Id.* at 9-10.

# State and Local

• • •

## *Section Editor: Eve Errickson*

### Introduction

This year, the most notable development on the state and local practice front was the remand of *Hanna and Mwroka* to the trial court level for hearing on the issue of the constitutionality of Chicago's historic preservation ordinance. In this highly publicized case, Albert Hanna and Carol Mwroka challenged the designation of their neighborhoods as historic districts because they believed the language of the local ordinance was unconstitutionally vague. Although this case is as yet pending, its larger effects are still being felt. Sympathetic challenges to local preservation activities, such as permitting and district designations, were decided this year in a number of jurisdictions, including *Covel v. Town of Vienna*, in which a group of property owners requested permits for repair and for removal and then challenged the district ordinance in trial court in order to rezone for commercial development. Likewise, a redrafted local New Jersey ordinance was upheld, allowing projects to bypass historic preservation review if they met objective criteria for height, setbacks, and square footage, on the grounds that the existing context-based criteria for the district were too subjective. In May 2009, the National Trust for Historic Preservation filed an *amicus curiae* brief in support of the City of Seattle's decision to deny an application to build on the grounds of the Satterlee House based on the traditional use contextual standards used by many districts. Property owners are appealing the decision of the trial court to the Washington State Court of Appeals.

## Compliance with Federal Law

### Historic Preservation

**New York** The plan to relocate the home of Alexander Hamilton, a National Memorial and National Historic Monument, to St. Nicholas Park in Manhattan was challenged in federal district court.[1] In 1990, the Hamilton Heights Homeowners Association (HHHA) and the National Park Service (NPS) entered into a Memorandum of Agreement. The HHHA agreed to raise funds and contribute historic materials, and the NPS agreed to "administer and develop the Hamilton Grange National Memorial according to plans developed through a documented process of public participation, commensurate with available funds."

In the early 1990s, a draft General Management Plan (GMP) and Environmental Impact Statement (EIS) were issued after consultation and public participation. Plaintiffs allege that in 1994, the NPS convened the Friends of the Hamilton Grange, and that they provided mediation and outreach to support the plan to move the Grange to St. Nicholas Park.[2] One of the four alternatives in the draft GMP entailed moving the Grange to St. Nicholas Park and orienting the house front to face northeast, although it had faced southeast in its historic location. The northeast orientation was questioned during the official comment period by the New York City Landmarks Preservation Commission, reflecting that the siting and orientation should be considered so that the mansion could be read "as a free-standing country retreat in the middle of a landscape." The NPS agreed to consider a southerly orientation during the design process, "in consultation with the Friends of Hamilton Grange group, the State Historic Preservation Office [SHPO], the Landmarks Commission, and other state and local organizations."

The following year, a final GMP was issued by the NPS with the same four proposals. In alternative 4, however, the Grange would be oriented to the southwest to retain historic authenticity. The NPS also stated in the final GMP that the Convent Avenue site would be developed simultaneously with restoration of the Grange. The final GMP was conceptual in nature, and lacked architectural and engineering plans, but allowed that "The Friends of the Hamilton Grange would be actively involved in all aspects of planning the new structure."

From 1995 to 2001, the NPS worked to acquire an easement so that the Grange could be situated on the St. Nicholas Park site. During review under the New York City Uniform Land Use Review Procedure, the orientation of the Grange was changed to face northeast. Documents prepared during this review reflected the new orientation, in which the rear of the Grange faced Steinman Hall of the City College of New York. The windows of the dining room and study, which had previously been sunlit, would now face a solid wall. The review was completed, and the application was approved in 2002.

In March 2006, the NPS executed a Programmatic Agreement with the New York State Office of Historic Preservation, the New York City Department of Parks and Recreation, and the New York City Landmarks Preservation Committee, as required by the National Historic Preservation Act (NHPA). This agreement included continued comment by the New York SHPO, Landmarks Preservation Commission, and New York City Parks. In addition, according to the Programmatic Agreement, "a public-private partnership" would continue to inform plans for a multiuse facility on the Convent Avenue site as a separate 106 action. Plaintiffs, however, claimed this decision had been made as early as 2001 without the benefit of public involvement.

In public meetings, community residents expressed concern that the Grange, if oriented to the northeast, would face onto a street, rather than the park, and the interior experience of the house would be compromised. In response, officials promised to revisit the issue and prepared scale drawings and models for three redesign options allowing a southwest orientation. By memorandum dated April 10, 2007, the New York City Landmarks Commission approved proposed plans for the Grange, which now included a northeast orientation, which it found satisfied conditions issued in 1993 and "relates to its original siting as a mansion on a promontory." Further, the Commission endorsed location of a wheelchair lift on the Grange's front porch, integrated into a portico so as to be out of sight when not in use.

During a site visit conducted two days after the issuance of the memorandum with community representatives, including some members of the Friends, the issue of the northeast orientation was revisited, as well as the cost of Americans with Disabilities Act (ADA) compliance on the project. NPS officials again promised to look at the issue of orientation. On April 16, 2007 the Art Commission of the City of New York approved the plan as presented. Likewise, a final decision was issued by the NPS on the $16^{th}$, finding the northeast orientation was the best option for the Grange. Substantive considerations included the appearance of the Grange in its northeastern and southwestern orientations, ease of compliance with the ADA, and aesthetic impact. Visitors to the Grange would understand it in the most historically accurate manner if approaching it from below as Hamilton's guests had, with its unique front door and tripartite window design. The northeastern orientation allowed the Grange to be sited as a free-standing country retreat, without retaining walls or railings, satisfying an explicit condition of the New York Landmarks Committee. By contrast, the southeastern orientation would obscure the front façade, would require visitors to approach the rear and walk around the building to the front, and would require removal of three of the front steps. Additionally, the hill behind the Grange would have to be extensively reshaped to accommodate its foundation. In several design schematics developed to consider the southwest orientation, retaining walls and fences would have been constructed approximately five feet from the front door; another would have required a railing across a portion of the front façade.

Officials acknowledged that the northeast orientation would expose the dining room mirrors to the façade of Steinman Hall. To compensate for this effect on the interior experience, the NPS planned to plant thirteen sweet gum trees to provide a more sylvan setting. The trees would be reflected in the dining room mirrored doors, and would replicate the original view to some degree.

Some of the community members who attended the site visit on April 17 and 19, 2007 were notified of the final decision. The letters reflected the importance of the view of the Grange from its public access point on West 141st Street and the extensive site modifications required for ADA compliance in the conceptual plans proposed for the southwestern orientation. The New York State Preservation Office approved the plans on June 21, 2007, in accordance with NHPA Section 106.

In the last week of May 2008, Hamilton Grange was lifted from its foundations, conveyed to the St. Nicholas Park site and on June 7, placed on a bed of dirt in preparation for setting on its permanent foundation.

The Friends of the Hamilton Grange commenced suit on June 6, 2008, seeking a temporary restraining order and preliminary injunction enjoining the defendants from situating the Grange on its new foundation in any orientation than the northeastern orientation.[3] After a hearing on June 17, plaintiffs withdrew the motion for injunctive relief. An amended complaint was filed August 8, 2008, alleging violations of the NHPA Sections 106 and 110 and the APA. The claim made reflects that 1) the defendants' design decisions will harm the Grange; 2) defendants' abandonment of the Convent Avenue site will harm the Grange and/or harm the Hamilton Heights neighborhood; and

3) the defendants failed to follow required procedures in developing plans for the Grange and the Convent Avenue site.

Primarily, the plaintiffs contended that the defendants failed to "take into account the effects of the undertaking on any district, site, building, structure, or object that is included in or eligible for inclusion on the National Register,"[4] and "to the maximum extent possible, to undertake such planning and actions may be necessary to minimize harm to (National Historical Landmarks)."[5] The plaintiffs sought relief under the APA which permits a court to set aside agency action undertaken without "observance of procedure required by law."[6]

They sought declaratory and injunctive relief—1) a declaration voiding the Programmatic Agreement; 2) an injunction directing the defendants to comply with the NHPA by consulting the Friends group prior to any further undertakings related to the Grange; and 3) ordering the construction of the community center as directed in the Final GMP.[7]

Defendant filed a motion to dismiss under Rule 12(b)(1) for lack of constitutional standing to challenge the design of the Grange, the Convent Avenue site, or the proceedings. Further, the defendants claimed that NHPA provides no private right of action, and invoked mootness and laches to bar the claims based on orientation of the Grange and the requirement to initiate development of the Convent Avenue site.[8] The defendants claim that the APA claims regarding the Convent Avenue site should be barred on the basis of ripeness as no final agency decision had occurred.

The court granted the motion to dismiss, finding that claims premised on harms to the Grange and on allegations of procedural harms were not supported by a showing of a specific concrete injury. Claims relating to the Convent Avenue site were premised on the NPS commitment to develop the site concurrently with the Grange. As the government controls future development of the site, the court found that the plaintiffs had standing to bring claims relating to Convent Avenue development.[9] Under a review of the relevant statutes, the court held that the Congress directed the language of the NHPA to government agencies; accordingly it could not be interpreted to support a private right of action and plaintiffs' claims arising directly from the NHPA were dismissed. Finally, the court addressed similar claims under the APA alleging defendants failed to "initiate and actively support a public/private partnership to plan and develop a new multi-use facility" on the Convent Avenue site "as a separate Section 106 action" under the Programmatic Agreement.

## Department of Transportation Act

**Idaho** North Idaho Community Action Network (NICAN) sued the United States Department of Transportation, the Federal Highway Administration, and the Idaho Transportation Department in district court to challenge a proposed construction project on a portion of US Highway 95 located in northern Idaho, but lost when the court granted summary judgment to the defendants. On appeal, the ninth circuit considered NICAN's claims under NEPA and Section 4(f) of the Department of Transportation Act.[10]

NICAN's claims derive primarily from the third phase of a project to improve a section of I-95 that runs through Sandpoint, Idaho. In 1999, defendant agencies issued a final environmental impact report for the project, but in 2005 and 2006 proposed substantive changes to the project. As part of the review process for the project, the impact reports issued for the 2005 and 2006 modifications concluded that the changes would pose no significant effects beyond those in the 1999 statement. NICAN challenged the approvals issued in 2005 and 2006, alleging that the agencies violated NEPA by failing to consider alternatives to the proposed modification and failing to disclose and assess plans to dredge and excavate approximately 17,035 cubic yards of material from Sand Creek. In addition, NICAN claimed that defendants' "phased approach" to reviewing the project's impact to historic properties violated NEPA. The court, reviewing *de novo,* found the agencies had conducted adequate review of the modifications and affirmed the district court's decision with regard to claims brought under NEPA. NICAN brought similar claims under Section 4(f) of the Department of Transportation Act and Section 106 of the National Historic Preservation Act for failure to survey, identify, and evaluate historic properties for all phases of the project and for determining that one historic structure, a depot, could be excluded from review required under Section 4(f).[11] The court cited 23 CFR s771.135(b), which provides that "any use of lands from a section 4(f) property shall be evaluated early in the development of the action when alternatives to the proposed action are under study." By necessity, the section 106 review required for section 4(f) must be completed by the time the record of decision is issued. Phased projects, then, are required to complete section 4(f) for all phases before issuing the record of decision.[12] Defendants conceded that only one of the four phases of the project had received a detailed review under Section 106, and had therefore violated section 4(f). The court concluded that the scope of injunctive relief granted on this claim be limited to precluding the defendant agencies from commencing construction under the remaining phases until they had completed review under section 4(f).

**New York** The Concerned Citizens of Chappaqua sued for a temporary restraining order and preliminary injunction to prevent the US Department of Transportation from proceeding with planned demolition and reconstruction of a historic Route 120 bridge in the Hamlet of Chappaqua, New York.[13] The plaintiffs alleged that the defendants failed to comply with NEPA, Section 106 of the NHPA, and Section 4(f) of the Department of Transportation Act.

The Route 120 bridge was constructed in 1930 and designated to the National Register of Historic Places in 2005. In 2004, the New York State Department of Transportation (NYSDOT) began a major repair effort on the bridge, which was found to be structurally deficient and in need of urgent attention. By agreement with the Federal Department of Transportation, NYSDOT evaluated general proposals for repair or replacement of the bridge. Either option required the addition of a third lane to accommodate traffic during construction and after completion, which entailed replacement and expansion of the bridge's existing retaining wall. Subsequent design modification expanded the replacement retaining wall from an initial 25 feet in 2005 to 298 in 2007.

NYSDOT issued a finding documentation identifying three properties that would potentially be impacted by the project—the bridge itself, which would be removed and replaced, and a nearby Chappaqua train station and depot plaza. NYSDOT concluded the project would not adversely affect the train station and depot plaza. Federal Highway Administration officials concurred in the report, which included specific mitigation measures to minimize harm to the historic properties. As required by the NHPA, the FWHA notified the Advisory Council on Historic Preservation in 2006. The ACHP, with the New York State Historic Preservation Officer, NYSDOT and FHWA entered into a Memorandum of Agreement, which concluded that retaining the bridge was not a reasonable alternative and outlined appropriate measures to preserve the historic property. The ACHP reviewed and approved the MOA under Section 106 requirements. The NYSDOT had concluded no environmental or ecological impact was likely. When the Town of New Castle requested the expansion of the bridge project to encompass a nearby intersection, the NYSDOT redesigned the project, and concluded the proposed changes to the project would not impact earlier agency findings.

The Concerned Citizens of Chappaqua and neighbors filed for injunctive relief, citing that the felling of several trees near the bridge during preparation and execution of the proposed project would constitute irreparable harm. The court reviewed plaintiffs' claims under the APA, under a " likelihood of success" standard on any of the plaintiffs' five claims premised on NEPA, NHPA, and 4(f).

Under NEPA, the project was designated as a categorical exclusion as a highway modernization and bridge replacement project under subsection 117(a) CFR 771.117(d)(1)(3). The plaintiffs claimed this designation was improper on the basis of the bridge's historic designation. In review, the court reflected that "a mere finding of 'adverse effect' was insufficient to overcome the categorical exclusion, especially where the agency's final design report provided for mitigation of such effects and assessed the project's impact on surface waters and wetlands, water sources, general ecology, and wildlife, historical and cultural resources, visual resources, parks, farmland, air, noise, energy and contaminated materials."

Under Section 106 of the NHPA, the plaintiffs claim that after the expansion of the retaining wall from 25 feet to 298 feet, the SHPO was not provided with revised plans. The court considered whether the defendants were required by law to conduct the second evaluation, and found that the expansion posed a visual impact on the bridge, the train station, and the depot and that the agencies had allowed no opportunity for the SHPO to avoid, mitigate, or minimize the adverse effects. However, under 36 CFR 800.5 the "visual element" must "diminish the integrity of the property's significant historic features," to be considered. The plaintiffs had failed to show that the features of the train station and depot then would be "affected." "The SHPO has reviewed project plans for this project . . . including . . . the 298 foot retaining wall . . . the retaining wall is separate and distinct from the Route 120 Bridge historic resource and it is not material to SHPO's evaluation of the effects on the resource."[14] Thus the Court found the plaintiffs did not meet their burden of proof to show a likelihood of success on its NHPA-based claims.

Section 4(f) of the Department of Transportation Act permits the FWHA to use land of a historic site only if "there is no prudent and feasible alternative" and the project "includes all possible planning to minimize harm" to the historic site resulting from the use. Under Section 4(f)(1), "feasible" means capable of development through sound engineering and "prudent" means "a common sense balancing of practical concerns." An agency may reject feasible alternatives based on a variety of factors, including cost, traffic considerations, safety, traveler convenience, and failure to meet project objectives.

The court determined that, while not clearly articulated in the Final Design Report, it is reasonable to conclude that rehabilitation fails to meet the following objectives: provide a safe, non-deficient structural condition for more than 30 years and minimize maintenance and repair. Therefore, the court found the plaintiffs did not meet their burden of proof to show a likelihood of success on 4(f)-based claims.

## Compliance with State Law

### Environmental Law

**New York** Union Square Community Coalition, individuals and others filed suit seeking an order that the renewal of a permit for Luna Park, a restaurant operating at the Union Square Park Pavilion, to renovate its existing structure and construct a nearby comfort station would constitute a "blanket rule" that all restaurants are consistent with park purposes, and that "the Parks Commissioner has carte blanche to establish a private commercial restaurant wherever he so chooses."[15] Additional claims include the plaintiff's allegation that the Restaurant Initiative will lead to an alienation of New York park land; that the Luna Park renewal application was not supported by an Environmental Impact Statement required under the State Environmental Quality Review Act (SEQRA); and that the renewal application also required a zoning amendment and compliance with the Uniform Land Use Review Procedure.

The court reserved review of the claim that the Restaurant Initiative will alienate park land as unripe. As to claims relating to SEQRA, the court found that Luna Park's plans fell under a Type II designation and were exempt from further SEQRA requirements as the expansion would entail less than 4,000 square feet. No zoning amendment was required, as no relinquishment of control of the facility had taken place.

## Compliance with Local Code and Zoning Permits

### Local Codes

**California** The City and County of San Francisco initiated the process to designate St. John's United Methodist Church as a landmark pursuant to Article 10 of the City's Planning Code in 2007.[16] In 2005, the Church was vacated in order to allow seismic retrofitting due to its construction of unreinforced masonry. The owner, the California-Nevada Annual Conference of the United Methodist Church, concluded in 2004 that the property had no use in its mission except for sale and revenue therefrom.

Pacific Polk Properties, LLC contracted with the church to purchase the property in 2004, and filed applications with the City for permission to raze the structure and proceed with new construction. In 2007, a Draft Environmental Impact Report was filed for the proposed project, and the local Landmarks Preservation Advisory Board conducted a public information hearing on the report. Less than a week after the hearing, the board's Land Use and Economic Development Committee recommended a resolution to initiate proceedings to determine whether the property should be designated as a Landmark over the church's objections. The grounds for the proposed designation reflected that the property was "the only extant California example by nationally renowned architect George Washington Kramer and is a valuable example of early twentieth century church architecture that combines elements of the Mission Revival and English Gothic Tudor styles." The Landmarks Advisory Board accepted the resolution and the recommended approval of the Landmark designation. After the approval of the resolution, Pacific Polk and the church filed a writ of mandate seeking to halt the process. The court, after review of the administrative record, conducted a hearing and granted the writ, finding the Board had exceeded its authority. The City appealed.

The appeals court considered interpretation of the applicable government code provisions, which hold that county and city boards of supervisors may, "by ordinance, provide special conditions or regulations for the protection, enhancement, perpetuation, or use of places, sites, buildings, structures, works of art and other objects having a special character or aesthetic interest or value." By amendment in 1994, the code provision was amended to exclude:

> non-commercial property owned by any association or corporation that is religiously affiliated and not organized for private profit, whether the corporation is organized as a religious corporation, or as a public benefits corporation, provided that both of the following occur: (1) The association or corporation objects to the application of the (provision) to its property. (2) The association or corporation determines in a public forum that it will suffer substantial hardship, which is likely to deprive the association or corporation of economic return on its property, the reasonable use of its property, or the appropriate use of its property in the furtherance of its mission, if the application is approved.

The crux of the City's appeal was its contention that the church was not "noncommercial property" because of plans to sell the property to Pacific Polk for the purpose of a condominium development. However, the appeals court noted the extremely high cost of the seismic retrofitting required for continued viable use and the legislative intention of the 1994 amendment, which expressly addressed this issue. Issuance of the writ was affirmed.

**Delaware** The Supreme Court of Delaware reviewed the Superior Court's final ruling reversing a decision of the City of Wilmington's Board of Zoning Appeals (ZBA) to grant a variance to CCS Investors, LLC (CCS) allowing CCS to develop the Gibraltar Estate into commercial office space. The Gibraltar Estate, owned by Preservation Delaware, Inc. (PDI), is a historic estate at the edge of the Highlands neighborhood.[17] The area is zoned as residential, but commercial and residential uses exist in the surrounding neighborhood.

At the variance hearing, PDI presented evidence on the advanced state of Gibraltar's deterioration, its solicitation process for developers, and the cost of rehabilitation of the historic structure. Experts for PDI opined that residential development could not adequately generate returns to salvage the mansion and gardens. The ZBA granted the variance on the basis of "circumstances and practical difficulty" supported by a finding of ten separate factors.[18] The Superior Court reversed the BZA and denied the use variance on the grounds that it was granted on the basis of hardship self-imposed by the owner. On appeal, the Supreme Court of Delaware noted that failure to join all material parties under the relation back doctrine was fatal to the property owners' challenge to the ordinance, as PDI, the actual property owner, was indispensible to the initial claim. Thus, the Superior Court erred in its conclusion that applicants self-imposed the hardship from which relief was required, by attributing the easements on the property owned by PDI to CCS. Delaware has no *per-se* rule against self-imposed hardship.

**New Jersey** ***Bowie-McCready v. Morristown Zoning Board of Adjustment*** The New Jersey Superior Court considered development plans for Willow Hall, a late 19th century mansion and grounds of the Vail Family, former owners of Speedwell Iron Works.[19] Eventually the Vail property was divided into four parts; two publicly owned and two owned by Frederick Steadman. K & K Developers contracted to purchase the properties owned by Steadman with the purpose of developing the land as condominiums and to preserve Willow Hall. In order to bring the project into compliance with local zoning designations, K & K submitted applications for a variance to construct townhouses in an area zoned for single-family residences, a dimensional variance, a variance from restrictions against developments on steep slopes, and for final site plan approval. The condominiums were styled to minimize interference with Willow Hall through the use of tiered roofing.[20] Although K & K did not conduct a feasibility study for construction of single family homes, its position at the public hearings was that single family homes would compete visually with Willow Hall. The Board concluded that the K & K proposal was the best to ensure the preservation of Willow Hall, which was in need of $200,000 in structural repairs, and adopted a resolution granting the use variance, provided K & K obtained site approval and preserved Willow Hall.

Neighbors and Friends of Historic Speedwell filed suit. After reviewing the Board's resolution, the trial court entered judgment in favor of the Board. On appeal, plaintiffs asserted 1) the Board engaged in *ultra vires* conduct by effectively re-zoning of the property *ad hoc*; 2) the use variance was *ultra vires* because the Board may not trade a use variance for a good deed; 3) there is no presumption of correctness to the Board's actions; and 4) K & K failed to satisfy the remaining grounds for issuance of a use variance.

The appeals court reversed the trial court decision. The court noted that less deference is accorded use variances. Use variances may be issued where "special reasons" exist and where the public good is served and will not substantially impair the intent and the purposes of the zone plan and the zoning ordinance. "Special reason" variances include both inherently beneficial uses and uses shown to be "particularly suitable for the proposed use."[21]

On review, the court found no substantial credible evidence in the record to support the Board's conclusion that the property was particularly suitable for the construction of twenty townhomes, or that the factual record demonstrated that the property was "particularly suited" for condominiums. Rather, the Board was primarily concerned with the preservation of Willow Hall, and accepted K & K's assertion that condominiums were suitable without the benefit of comparative information on single family homes. The court also noted K & K's plans to build into the steep slopes of the property which required an additional variance, and which did not support a finding of particular suitability. The relative profitability of townhouse development was not relevant, given that no comparative analysis had been proffered on the development of single family homes. The Board's decision was reversed on the grounds that K & K failed to satisfy the required criteria for a use variance.

### *Philogene v. CPR Holdings, Inc.*

The Plainfield Board of Zoning Appeals granted a variance to a nursing home facility, subject to conditions, allowing the expansion of the facility onto an adjacent vacant lot and adding parking. Plaintiffs, neighbors and members of the Plainfield Historic Preservation Commission, challenged the Board's decision. The Superior Court of New Jersey vacated the decision. On appeal, the Board of Zoning Approval's decision was reinstated.[22]

In 2000, CPR Lapid Holdings, owner of a 35-bed nursing home facility, Abbott Manor Convalescent Center, applied for a use variance and bulk variance for expansion plans at the facility due to technical obsolescence. The facility, in operation since the 1950s, would expand from a 35-bed nursing home to a 65-bed assisted care facility, with a skilled nursing unit and additional parking. The Board denied the application in 2002. In lieu of an appeal, CPR sued the Board and the city under the Federal Fair Housing Act of 1968, as amended by the Fair Housing Amendments Act of 1988, and equal protection and due process violations. The case was reported by the parties to have been settled, and the court entered a dismissal order. CPR's application was reopened by the Board as a condition of the settlement.

Later in 2002, the Abbott Manor property was rezoned. The new zoning scheme rendered the property undersized and without conditions allowing a nursing home. In addition to the problems of technical obsolescence, fire code waivers kept the facility operating despite deficiencies in stairwells, exits, and elevator shafts. Mandatory construction standards for long-term care facilities required that any renovations bring the entire facility up to code, necessitating expansion of the facility.

Abbott Manor is an 8,000-square-foot historic brick mansion, with an attached, two-story framed addition at the rear, forming a "T." The proposed expansion would extend onto an adjacent vacant lot, forming an "L" with the mansion. CPR's architectural expert testified that the expansion's bulk and orientation was "essentially mandated" by standards for supervision for long-term care residents. The mansion-front elevation would be unaffected by the height or roofing of the proposed addition.

To evaluate CPR's proposal, the Board appointed legal, architectural, accounting, and health care consultants. After a review of CPR's financial information, the accounting consultant concluded that CPR's operating figures reflected that the current state of Abbott Manor was not financially viable; the 35-bed facility was "generally unprofitable."

The planning and historic preservation consultants requested multiple changes and multiple rounds of review. CPR's architect incorporated some comments and developed architectural and landscaping changes, including window style, lowering the extension's roofline and raising the first floor. However, CPR refused to reduce the extension to two stories or hide the third floor under a gambrel roof. Ultimately CPR's designs were submitted to the Board without the consultants' endorsement, who cited the bulk and appearance of the expansion as problematic to the district.

After touring the site, the Board received testimony on the required standards recommended by its special counsel, and voted unanimously to approve the application, subject to conditions. As CPR's residents required fulltime skilled nursing care, the Board determined as a matter of law that CPR's use of the building was beneficial. The Board attached multiple conditions to its approval of the project, including modifications to the roofline to mitigate the bulk of the rear "L," increasing a setback along a rear street front without concomitant footprint reduction and reducing the size of a multistory rotunda. Further, the Board mandated deed restrictions for tree screening, shade trees along the property lines, as well as delivery and waste removal restrictions and related maintenance obligations.

The Van Wyck Historic District and neighbors filed suit to invalidate the Board's approval asserting claims of res judicata, collateral estoppel, lack of jurisdiction, and fraud on the basis of the settlement order entered on the 2002 suit filed by CPR. These claims were considered by the trial court and denied. In a later decision addressing the merits, the trial court concluded instead that the Board "took a tortured path" to approve the variance in order to avoid a fair housing lawsuit and set the approval aside.

CPR argued that the trial court substituted its decision for the Board's. The appeals court found the Board's decision satisfied positive criteria that CPR's use of the property as a nursing home promoted the general welfare.[23] Acknowledged detrimental effects of the bulk, density, and use of the expansion on surrounding properties' value and preservation of the district would "reasonably be mitigated" by CPR's redesign.

On appeal, the court held Abbott Manor's beneficial use was supported by the Board's review and administrative record. Interestingly, the court cited substantial evidence in the record to show that CPR's expanded use would cause substantial detriment to the historic district, the neighborhood, the zoning ordinance, and the master plan. However, the public interests that were not considered by the trial court included CPR's improvements to the mansion, demolition of the present, nonconforming addition, and construction of a fire and health compliant structure.[24]

### *Chambers v. Neiffer*

Defendants contracted to purchase a 40-room hotel in the Historic District Oceanfront Zone of Ocean Grove, New Jersey.[25] The zone "recognizes the character and historic land-use pattern of the oceanfront blocks in the Ocean Grove portion of the Township," and does not allow multi-family homes, with the exception that "unique circumstances may exist along . . . prominent avenues where the preservation and adaptive reuse of a large historic structure is dependent on a mix of uses not envisioned in this plan."[26]

Neiffer and co-defendant Rudolph embarked on a plan to develop the property as eleven condominium units, and applied for variances under NJSA 40:55D-70(d), design waivers and site plan approval, in addition to certificate of appropriateness for partial demolition of existing structures and permits for partial demolition. Citing the hotel's historic importance and contribution to the Ocean Grove neighborhood streetscape, the Historic Preservation Committee approved defendant's applications. At variance hearings in June 2006, defendants described their plans to convert the hotel to condominiums with a height of four stories and to restore its appearance to its turn of the twentieth century appearance. Concerns about the density of the area were expressed during the hearing and the Board agreed. Defendants revised their proposal and reduced the number of condo units to 9.[27]

Plaintiff filed suit challenging the grant of use variances, bulk variances, design waivers, and final site plan approval. A bench trial resulted in an order affirming the Board's action. On appeal, plaintiff argued that the Board usurped authority of the Township Committee by granting the variances. The appeals court found that the variances would not substantially alter the character of the district as described in the zoning ordinance, and will "promote the general welfare because the site is particularly suitable for the proposed use."[28] The appellate court, citing expert testimony on the architectural style and density of the new development, agreed that the neighboring properties would not be impacted, and would likely benefit from the decrease in density and the concomitant reduction of "noise, trash, vehicular traffic and pedestrian traffic."

## Zoning and Use Permits

**Montana** The Supreme Court of Montana reviewed a state district court decision enjoining construction of a house for violating development and site zoning permits in *Virginia City v. The Estate.*[29] The City challenged the construction of a home because it allegedly violated the city's setback requirements.

In his initial application for new construction, Mason submitted to the City's Historic Preservation Officer drawings reflecting a plot plan of his property, showing a new house on co-defendant Olsen's property. The dimensions reflected on the drawings were in compliance with the City's requirements. On that basis and after review by the Historic Preservation Advisory Committee, the City approved the applications and granted permits allowing construction of the new house to proceed. Almost immediately after beginning construction, Mason received complaints that the house did not meet setback requirements. An investigation ensued, and he was found to be in violation of the requirements. The City issued a letter requesting that construction stop, and requested Mason meet with the Historic Preservation Officer to resolve the matter. Mason continued construction, and a month later the City confirmed the setback violation via survey, revoked the permits, and filed a complaint and application for preliminary injunction in the District Court alleging violation of City ordinances regarding setback distances, height, window size, window placement and general structure. A show cause hearing took place and the District Court entered an order granting the City's application for preliminary injunction.

Mason and Olsen's answer to the City's complaint raised affirmative defenses and counterclaims, among them that Ordinance 503 was unconstitutionally vague, and the City's enforcement of the ordinance was arbitrarily and discriminatorily enforced, thereby violating their right to due process and equal protection. After discovery, the City alleged the evidence showed Mason's construction violated the granted permits, and both parties moved for summary judgment. The District Court again granted summary judgment in favor of the City and permanently enjoined Mason from resuming construction. On appeal from this order, Mason made three arguments—(1) that Ordinance 503 was unconstitutionally vague; (2) that the District Court erred in granting permanent injunctive relief in ordering the removal of the house and re-contour of the property; and (3) that the District Court erred in granting summary judgment on Mason's counterclaims.

Mason's appeal as to constitutional vagueness centered on a section of City code incorporated by reference into Ordinance 503, regulating the setback for the affected property as "50 feet from the center of the abutting street or road," arguing that the ordinance fails to specify whether the setback is to be measured from the street as indicated on the City plat or the actual traveled way currently in use by the public. The Supreme Court relied on the setbacks stated in the permits and supporting documents—25 feet from the lot-line along Warren Street and 35 feet from the lot-line along Fairweather Street, and found the District Court did not err in granting summary judgment in favor of the City.

Next, the Supreme Court reviewed the injunctive relief, which consisted not only of the cessation of construction, but also an order to return the property to its former appearance by removing the violating structure and recontouring the lots. Mason alleged that a variance should have been considered allowing the house to be constructed in a manner that was historically appropriate. As Mason offered no evidence that the City was required to consider such a variance nor of the District Court's manifest abuse of discretion in granting the injunction, the District Court's ruling was affirmed.

The third argument was premised on the Plaintiff's request for a jury trial. However, having made requests for summary judgment motions, the Montana Supreme Court affirmed the lower court's order granting summary judgment to the city as well as its orders for permanent injunctive relief.

**North Carolina** Carl Meares began plans for a development project in the Beaufort Historic District in 2001. As part of his preparation, he met with the chair of the Beaufort Historic District Commission, Linda Dark, in November 2001 and obtained a copy of the design guidelines for the district.[30]

In October 2003, Meares submitted plans for a three story building developed in consultation with a preservation specialist and architect recommended by Dark. In December 2003, the HPC proposed a technical correction to its guidelines without publishing notices to the public, approved as Historic District Design Guideline 8, which provides in part that:

> Therefore, under no circumstances shall any proposed building visually encroach in height or scale upon the remaining public landscapes of Beaufort's Historic District . . . these include . . . views of the historic district, particularly Front Street . . . unless it can be demonstrated that an historically significant building previously existed on the site of the proposed building.

The following year, the HPC denied Meares' application, in partial reliance on Design Guideline 8. Meares appealed to the Beaufort Board of Adjustment, where the HPC's decision was vacated and a new hearing was ordered. Meares filed suit before a new HPC hearing could take place, seeking declaratory judgment decreeing that the technical correction to the design guidelines was void and unlawful, or that Meares had acquired a vested right to construct and occupy the structure he had designed for submission to the HPC. The trial court granted Meares' motion, holding the correction was void and unlawful, and that even if Historic District Design Guideline 8 was upheld, Meares had acquired common law vested rights, as a matter of law, to develop the project on his property. Further, the trial court ordered Guideline 8 stricken from the Beaufort Historic District Guidelines in its entirety.

On appeal, the town argued the trial court committed reversible error by holding that (1) Guideline 8 was unlawful and void as a matter of law; (2) Meares acquired common law vested rights to develop the proposed structure; and (3) Meares' action is justiciable.

The Court of Appeals of North Carolina affirmed the trial court. In particular, the appeals court held that the North Carolina General Assembly is limited to a contextual analysis of the total physical environment of the Historic District:[31]

> The commission . . . shall take no action under this section except to prevent the construction . . . which would be incongruous with the special character of the landmark or the district.[32]

As Guideline 8 imposed a standard that new structures not be incongruent with a historically significant structure which had previously existed on the site of the proposed structure, the HPC exceeded its authority. The trial court's decision was affirmed.

### District Designation

**Illinois** In 2006, Plaintiffs Hanna and Mrowka filed a 20 count complaint against the City of Chicago,[33] the Commission on Chicago Landmarks, and several city officials, alleging that the Chicago Landmarks Ordinance was invalid on its face as applied to Plaintiff's properties. The City moved to dismiss all but one of the claims on the grounds that the plaintiffs failed to state a cause of action, which the trial court granted. On appeal in 2008, the judgment of the trial court was reversed and remanded.

The cause of action stems from the City's designations of two neighborhoods as Landmark Districts. Albert Hanna's property, in the Arlington-Deming neighborhood of Lincoln Park, and Carol Mrowka's property, in the Elk Grove Village neighborhood, were recommended for designation as Landmark Districts by the Commission on Chicago Landmarks in 2006.

Plaintiffs sought a declaration that the Chicago Ordinance was unconstitutionally vague and ambiguous on its face and violative of state due process rights under article I, section 2 of the Illinois Constitution. The criteria, of which two must be satisfied for Landmark status, are as follows:

1. Its value as an example of the architectural, cultural, historic, social, or other aspect of the heritage of the City of Chicago, the state of Illinois, or the United States;
2. Its location as a site of a significant historic event which may or may not have taken place within or involved the use of any existing improvements;
3. Its identification with a person or persons who significantly contributed to architectural, cultural, historic, social, or other aspect of the development of the city of Chicago, state of Illinois, or the United States;
4. Its exemplification of an architectural type or style distinguished by innovation, rarity, uniqueness, or overall quality of design, detail, materials, or craftsmanship;
    1. Its identification as the work of an architect, designer, engineer, or builder whose individual work is significant in the history or development of the city of Chicago, state of Illinois, or the United States;
    2. Its representation of an architectural, cultural, economic, historic, social or other theme expressed through distinctive areas, districts, places, buildings, structures, works of art, or other objects that may or may not be contiguous;
    3. Its unique location or distinctive physical appearance or presence representing an established and familiar feature of a neighborhood, community or the city of Chicago.[34]

The City responded that these provisions are not ambiguous when viewed as a part of the Ordinance as a whole and that the terms "important," "critical," and "significant" provide sufficient guidance to the Commission, which is made up of professionals in the disciplines of history, architecture, historic architecture, planning, archaeology, real estate, historic preservation, or those with a special interest in such fields. The Illinois Appeals Court was not persuaded by this argument, finding that the Commission members' qualifications were as vague as the language of the Ordinance. Accordingly, Plaintiffs' complaint was sufficient to establish a cause of action.

Count II of Plaintiffs' complaint challenged the delegation of authority as an impermissible grant by a legislative body, the city council, to an administrative body, the Commission. The City argued that the Ordinance does not amount to a delegation because decisions of the Commission are subject to approval by the City Council. In response, the Plaintiffs argued that the Commission's recommendations can become final within 365 days, without Council approval.[35] Further, any declaratory authority granted by a legislative body must be accompanied by a provision of intelligible standards to guide the administrative body. Dismissal of Count II was reversed and remanded by the appellate court. On this basis, Count III was also reversed and remanded.

Counts V through XX of Plaintiff's complaint alleged that the designation of Arlington Deming District and the East Village District, and the inclusion of Plaintiffs' properties therein, constituted a violation of Plaintiffs rights to substantive due process and equal protection. The appellate court declined to address these matters, pending decisions on Counts I, II, and III.

**New Jersey** In 2003 and 2004, the Rocky Hill Planning Board considered the rezoning of certain areas of the Borough consistent with its master plan.[36] A property owner in the affected area, David Schafer, objected to the rezoning and secured a settlement with the Board, to remove his property from the proposed zoning and place it in a newly created zone for age-restricted traditional neighborhood development. The ordinance and master plan, including Schafer's settlement, were adopted after extensive public hearings and discussions on December 31, 2004.

A development application was filed by Pulte Homes for preliminary and final approval and for historic preservation plan approval on May 19, 2005. Six public hearings and extensive expert testimony was elicited to address various parts of the development. Ultimately, the plan was approved under the approved ordinance, despite lingering questions as to whether the application was compliant with the historic preservation ordinance (Section 713). The planning board referred to Section 704(F)(8) which provides:

> Within the development variations in architectural style are encouraged. Buildings and fences shall be designed to be compatible with the architecture and land-

> scape of the [district]. A development meeting the following standards and the standards set forth in Section 704(F)(6) and (7) shall be deemed to comply with [district] requirements set forth in Section 713.

Following this section, sixteen subparts set out various design standards. Provided that the application met requirements at Section 704(F)(6-8), the board claimed the authority to deem the application in compliance with the historic preservation ordinance without further review under 713. After further review of the adoption of Section 704 and the Schafer settlement, the board found that the units submitted in the application were consistent in "bulk and design" to the settlement agreement and were consistent with Section 704. However, the board declined to apply Section 704(F)(8)(i), which required that "all massing, building and roof forms respect the general scale and proportions of the historic homes of the Borough. . . ." Rejecting this standard as "subjective" and "without defined standards," the board found that actual height and bulk standards specified in Section 704(E)(3) were appropriate if larger than existing buildings in the Borough and could not "*per se* be deemed a lack of respect for the Borough's historic character."

In response, property owners stated concern over the size of the new homes. The board cited the units' open porches, setbacks, and changes in elevation. They determined a mix of scale and mass among existing structures would prove compatible with the district's architecture and landscape. Finally, the board concluded that the development met all requirements.

Rocky Hill Citizens for Responsible Growth and individuals filed suit challenging the board's grant of the application and preliminary and final subdivision approval, and challenging the validity of Section 704. The trial court granted defendants' motion for summary judgment, finding the plaintiffs' suit untimely. On appeal, plaintiffs argued that they were entitled to an enlargement of time on the grounds of public interest. As the district ordinance was premised on compatibility with existing structures and landscape, units allowed in Pulte's application would change the measure of compatibility in future applications. Defendants responded that the plaintiffs' claims were based in their subjective displeasure with the size, scale, and footprints of the units allowed in the ordinance. The trial court decision was affirmed, and the appeals court held that the plaintiffs were not entitled to an enlargement of time on public interest grounds: "Plaintiffs' primary argument is that the ordinance will undermine the 'efficacy' of the district. . . . this is not the public interest envisioned by the Court in permitting limited expansion of the rule."[37]

Further, the appeals court relied on the public record in the consideration and adoption of the ordinance:

> Concerns about the interaction of Section 713 and 704 were known and articulated. . . . plaintiffs adopted a wait and see attitude that . . . should not form the basis of seeking extraordinary relief . . . to attack the *bona fides* of the ordinance.[38]

Plaintiffs' claim that exemption of the Schafer property was impermissible spot-zoning likewise failed at the trial court and appeals level.[39] The appeals court affirmed the trial court's ruling in its entirety, rejecting plaintiffs' arguments that the Board's action was capricious and arbitrary and finding that the decision of the board was grounded in appropriate findings of fact.

**New York** Developer Stahl initiated proceedings to annul the designation of two buildings by respondent city as New York City, N.Y., landmarks known for their significance as "light court tenements" in Manhattan.[40] Previously, the developer had attempted to carve out several buildings in a block designated as a New York City Landmark, but failed.

In 2008, the developer made extensive renovations to the designated structures, eliminating many of the structures' significant features. Before the Landmarks Preservation Commission, Stahl claimed that previously the buildings were wrongly designated because they were not architecturally "special" and no longer shared architectural features with other designated buildings. The trial court denied the developer's petition, citing the historic significance of the buildings, as well as their unchanged size, footprint, shape, and height.

**Virginia** *Covel v. Vienna* is a group of consolidated cases brought in Fairfax County Circuit Court in Virginia, related to properties in Windover Heights Historic District.[41] Multiple petitioners claimed that the district in which their properties were located was established in a manner inconsistent with statutory and constitutional law, and that decisions made by the Town of Vienna were arbitrary and capricious. Each of the six properties involved in the suit have been part of the Windover Heights Historic District since its adoption in 1979. Five of the six properties were the subject of requests to be removed from the district in 2003. One of the properties, owned by PMY Associates, was the subject of a request made in 2005 to be removed from the district. All requests were denied by unanimous votes of the Town Council.

Michael Covel filed for Declatory Judgment in 2003 after the denial of his request for removal.[42] The complaint sought declaratory relief that (1) by the denial of a COA to build on his property, the Vienna Town Code was unconstitutionally vague; and (2) that the original designation of the Historic District was *ultra vires* and *void ab initio* because the Town Code did not designate "historic landmarks" as required by both the Town Code and Virginia Code s15.15.2306. Covel sought relief for violation of Equal Protection under the 14th Amendment, and of his substantive due process rights under the Virginia Constitution and United States Constitution. Finally, Covel sought relief under 42 USC 1983. The Covel property is likely the oldest in the district, and is featured in publications on the historic nature of Vienna neighborhoods.

The litigation became dormant until June 7, 2006, when PMY filed suit to appeal the decision denying removal of its property. Again, the litigation became dormant until 2007, due to a discovery dispute which was resolved without Court intervention. In 2008, all three cases were set for trial.

Counsel for the Covels and PMY advised that she intended to depose individuals who "were directly involved in the facts and circumstances associated with the enactment, amendment, and enforcement of Vienna's Historic District ordinance since its inception in 1975." Potential deponents included all members of the Vienna Town Council from 1975 forward, as well as all persons who had served on the Windover Heights Board of Review since 1979. In response, the Town filed for a Motion for a Protective Order for Local Legislators, requesting judicial intervention due to the burden and expense entailed, and that the proposed depositions were in essence appeals of determinations made by Vienna Town Council, and barred by evidentiary rules, and that the proposed deposition would violate the Speech and Debate Clause of the Virginia and United States Constitutions.[43] In pre-trial motions, the Petitioners agreed that their constitutional and 1983 claims were not viable and the Town's Motion to Nonsuit those claims was granted. The court dismissed the claims for reversal as void in the consolidated actions on the basis of subject matter jurisdiction.[44]

In their final claim for declaratory judgment, the Petitioners cited Dillon's Rule, alleging that Vienna Town Code section 18:280.1 is void *ab initio*, as the Virginia General Assembly did not delegate the authority to enact a historic district without designating qualified buildings as "historic." In reviewing the Virginia enabling statute, the court found that local bodies were authorized to adopt local district ordinances setting forth any "historic area," which was defined as "an area containing buildings or places in which historical events occurred or having special public value because of notable or architectural or other features." Given the inclusion of historic places such as Vienna's Salsbury Spring, the Salsbury House, and the first black public school in the town's Planning Commission report issued in 1979, the court found a legal and factual basis for the creation of the district.

Michael Covel next asserted that the ordinance establishing the criteria to be considered in evaluation of Certificates of Appropriateness were unconstitutionally vague as written. The Court found that Petitioner's argument was not grounded in an understanding of traditional legal interpretation of the delegation of legislative authority. Recognizing that legislators cannot possibly address all possible variables which might arise in the administration of such authority, Virginia courts accord discretion where precise standards would not serve the overarching goals of the legislation.[45] The Town Council was tasked with preserving the integrity of the historic district, and diverse designs, arrangements, textures, and materials could serve this goal. Again, Covel tendered no evidence of arbitrariness or caprice.

Petitioners made additional arguments of arbitrary and capricious decisions by the Town Council, but the Court found no probative evidence of unreasonableness. The Town's burden to show sufficient evidence of reasonableness as to "make the question fairly debatable"[46] was met by expert testimony given by an architect familiar with historic preservation who presented evidence as to landscaping, architectural styles dating from1870 to 1920, the effect of the color of new structures, and the age of housing stock found in Windover Heights.

In conclusion to this lengthy and much-contested case, the Court commented that the Petitioner's initial applications and correspondence were likely intended to create a test case as part of a plan to compromise the integrity of Windover Heights.

### Disposition of Historic Properties: Taxes, Sale, and Demolition

**Georgia** The Court of Appeal of Georgia heard an appeal by the Chatham County Board of Tax Assessors (BOA) on a narrow issue of application of state tax exemption for rehabilitated historic properties. Ms. Bock sued the BOA after it refused to apply a county-specific homestead exemption to her property on the grounds that she had already received the benefit of an assessment under the Rehabilitated Historic Property Preferential Assessment Act (RHPPA).

The RHPPA allows a preferential assessment of rehabilitated historic properties for eight years for ad valorem tax purposes at the greater of the acquisition cost or the appraised fair market value. In the ninth year, the fair market value may be increased by one-half of the difference between the initial value as a rehabilitated historic property and the current fair market value. In the tenth year, the property loses any preferential assessment and is assessed at its current fair market value.

Ms. Bock's property was built in 1900 and is listed on the Georgia Register of Historic Places. She purchased it in 1997, and in 2008, the fair market was assessed for ad valorem purposes at $213,000. At the time of the assessment, she was notified by the BOA that it considered the homestead exemption would not be applied to rehabilitated historic properties. Based on this position, the BOA had refused to set the fair market value for the Bock property until the RHPPA preferential assessment had expired in 2007.

Ms. Bock filed an action for declaratory judgment, claiming the BOA had exceeded its authority by refusing to apply the homestead exemption to her property as of 2001. The BOA argued at trial and on appeal that it did not exceed its authority, as the application of both the homestead and the RHPPA would confer an improper double benefit. However, the court reflected that Ms. Bock had requested the benefit of the fair market value assessed under homestead law after the RHPPA had expired. On its face, the homestead exemption excludes the value of improvements Ms. Bock made to the property over time, effectively foreclosing the possibility of a double benefit. The court also noted that the BOA's position would undermine the goals of the RHPPA as expressed by the legislature.

Accordingly, the court held that the property be assessed at its fair market value on January 1, 2001 for the purposes of the homestead exemption, affirming the trial court's judgment.

**New Jersey** *Pansini Custom Design Assocs., LLC v. City of Ocean City*

Property owners Pansini and Parkin filed a motion for declaratory judgment seeking to establish the fair market value of their property so it could be advertised for sale consistent with a city's historic-preservation ordinance as part of procedures required to apply for a demolition permit.[47] Ocean City challenged their determination of value, claiming that the owners were required to use the fair market value of a single family residence rather than the commercial development value. After hearing expert testimony, the Superior Court of New Jersey entered an order determining the property's value by averaging the lowest value proffered by all experts. The City appealed. The Superior Court of New Jersey, Appellate Division, reversed the lower court's decision and remanded the case for proper valuation and for inquiry as to use of gross adjustment. The court reasoned that the lower court's averaging of property values was not a valid technique and that the appraiser's use of gross adjustment on property of high value could not provide comparative figures for sound analysis of property value.

**Application for Project Authorization Under the N.J. Register of Historic Places Act**

Respondent New Jersey Department of Environmental Protection (DEP) granted the application of respondent municipal redevelopment agency to acquire and demolish the Sears, Roebuck and Company building as part of the City of Camden's Gateway Redevelopment Plan.[48] Camden Redevelopment Agency (CRA) entered into a Project Development Agreement with Campbell Soup to participate in the plan by building an office park on the site of the Sears building, acknowledging the project would accomplish a "major public benefit." Demolition of the Sears Building, a historic property on the New Jersey Register of Historic Places, was "an unfortunate consequence of the Project in order to permit a broad array of site improvements . . . . creat[ing] conditions conducive to attracting a variety of purchasers, private developers, and tenants." The CRA, relying on multiple experts, produced evidence reflecting that extensive mold, asbestos, and lead paint remediation costing $1.6 million would make rehabilitation of the property into Class A office space costly. Appellants, manufacturers, and distributors of "urban life-style hip-hop clothing," claiming contractual rights to purchase the building and plans to spend $1 million for use as a warehouse, office, retail, and light manufacturing, asked the DEP to reconsider its approval of the application; it refused. Appellants sought judicial review, alleging that the CRA lacked standing to apply for and receive demolition authorization for the Sears building and that the DEP's grant was arbitrary, capricious, and unsupported by the record. The court found that CRA was not required to own or control the property prior to beginning encroachment authorization. The Gateway plan authorized the CRA to acquire by condemnation any buildings or land required for redevelopment under New Jersey's eminent domain act. Further, the administrative record reflected that the CRA correctly considered the public benefit of the project and feasible alternatives to demolition, and held public meetings for review of the applications related to the project.

## Notes

1. *Friends of Hamilton Grange v. Salazar*, No. 08 Civ. 5220 (DLC), 2009 U.S. Dist. LEXIS 21855 (S.D.N.Y. Mar. 12, 2009).
2. "Friends of the Hamilton Grange" is a group comprised of several members of the HHHA, 141st and 142nd Street Block Associations, historian Michael Henry Adams, and CB 9 member Carolyn Kent. The plaintiffs acknowledge that the group did not meet formally from 1995 to 2006.
3. Public reaction prior to this period was intense. In March 2008, CB 9 voted 27 to 3 to protest "willful violations" of commitments made to the community in the Final GMP. A letter-writing campaign to Charles Rangel was begun in early 2008. A FOIA request was made to the NPS by the HHHA. In May 2008, the Friends sent a letter of appeal alleging these approvals were obtained in the absence of public notice or proceedings. In further meetings with the Friends, the NPS explained the rationale for the orientation on May 15, 2008. In late May 2008, the ACHP reviewed NPS compliance with NHPA at the request of complaining community groups, but after review declined to ask the NPS to revisit its Programmatic Agreement.
4. 16 U.S.C. §470f.
5. 16 U.S.C. §470h-2f.
6. 5 U.S.C. 706(2)(D).
7. Specifically, the plaintiffs claim defendants failed to (1) provide information on the relocation and its effects on historic properties or the Programmatic Agreement; (2) seek public participation by the Friends, who allege they have 'consultant' status under 36 C.F.R. §800.2(c); (3) assess the adverse effects of the development; (4) document their decision-making process related to the Grant; and (5) give notice of the Programmatic Agreement and make available agency procedures implementing the Agreement.
8. At the time the motion to dismiss was filed, the Grange had been affixed to its new foundations.
9. The court held that further consultations could lead to a different outcome, citing *Tyler v. Cuomo*, 236 F.3d 1124 (9th Cir. 2000): "The Ninth Circuit concluded that the plaintiffs did have standing because there was a possibility that further consultations could lead to a different outcome and that the district court should not prejudge the result of the NHPA process by concluding no relief is possible." *Id.* at 1128-9, 1131.
10. *North Idaho Community Action Network v. United States Department of Transportation*, 545 F.3d 1147 (9th Cir. 2008).
11. *See* 49 U.S.C. §303(c); Section 4(f) provides that for federal projects "requiring the use of a historic site" approval may be granted only if "1) there is no prudent

and feasible alternative to using that land; and 2) the program or project includes all possible planning to minimize harm to the park, recreation area, wildlife and waterfowl refuge, or historic site resulting from the use."

12. *Citing Corridor H Alternatives, Inc. v. Slater*, 334 U.S. App. D.C. 240, 166 F.3d 368 (D.C. Cir. 1999).
13. *Concerned Citizens of Chappaqua v. United States Department of Transportation*, 579 F. Supp. 2d 427 (S.D.N.Y. 2008).
14. The plaintiffs attempted to strike the Markunas affidavit, but their motion was denied.
15. *Union Square Community Coalition v. New York City Department of Parks & Recreation*, 2009 NY Slip Op. 50641U, 7 (N.Y. Sup. Ct. 2009) at 3.
16. *California-Nevada Annual Conference et al. v. City and County of San Francisco*, 173 Cal. App. 4th 1559 (Cal. App. 1st Dist. 2009).
17. *CCS Investors, LLC v. Brown, 977 A.2d 301(Del. 2009).*
18. The ZBA cited renovation costs between 9 and 10 million dollars; the deterioration of the existing buildings, including animal invasion and extensive ongoing vandalism; the significant historic value of the premises as an asset to the neighborhood and the city; that the development restrictions, while self-imposed, had been instated to prevent destruction of the property and large-scale redevelopment, and to promise restoration of the house and gardens; that in the event some alternative use would have been required to sustain and fund the restoration; that a use similar in scope had been approved by the BZA in the past, and the number of alternative uses had been considered, and that proposed new structures have been designed to limit their visibility and for compatibility with the surrounding neighborhood; that ample parking and traffic patterns have been designed to lessen impact on residential neighborhood streets; and that there are other commercial and residential spaces in the area, such that the proposed use could not be entirely inconsistent with the character of the neighborhood.
19. *Bowie-McCready v. Morristown Zoning Bd. of Adjustment*, No. A-6071-06T2, 2008 N.J. Super. Unpub. LEXIS 1377 (App. Div. Sept. 12, 2008).
20. Each building would house four three-story units ranging from 2,800 to 3,600 square feet, with two car garages and two outdoor parking spots. Limited roads would be created on the property, and a soil erosion and sediment control plan would be implemented to mitigate the effects of building into the steep slopes.
21. At 18, citing N.J.S.A. 40:55D-70(d).
22. *Philogene v. CPR Holdings, Inc.*, No. A-0156-07T3, 2009 N.J. Super. Unpub. LEXIS 10 (App. Div. 2009).
23. In keeping with the statutory requirements of New Jersey's Municipal Land Use Law ("M.L.U.L.") at N.J.S.A. 40:55D-1 to -99, and the balancing test for granting variances in *Sica v. Board of Adjustment of Township of Wall*, 127 N.J. 152, 603 A. 2d 30 (1992).

24. N.J.S.A. 40:55D-2(b), (j).
25. *Chambers v. Neiffer*, No. A-3692-07T3, 2009 N.J. Super. Unpub. LEXIS 245 (App. Div. Feb. 3, 2009).
26. *Id.* at 2.
27. *Id.* at 7.
28. *Id.* at 13, citing *Sica v. Board of Adj. of Twp. Of Wall*, 127 N.J. 152, 156, 603 A.2d 30 (1992).
29. *Virginia City v. The Estate of Greg Olsen and Philip Mason, Jr.*, 2009 MT 3, 348 Mont. 279, 201 P.3d 115 (2009).
30. *Meares v. Town of Beaufort*, 667 S.E.2d 239 (N.C. Ct. App. 2008).
31. *A-S-P Associates v. Raleigh*, 298 N.C. 207, 222; 258 S.E.2d 444 (1979).
32. NC Gen. Stat. §160A-400.9(a) (2003).
33. *Hanna v. City of Chicago*, 388 Ill. App. 3d 909 (Ill. App. Ct. 1st Dist. 2009).
34. Chicago Municipal Code §§2-120-620 *et seq.* (2000).
35. Chicago Municipal Code §§2-120-705 *et seq.* (1999).
36. *Rocky Hill Citizens for Responsible Growth v. Planning Bd.*, 406 N.J. Super. 384, 967 A.2d 929 (App. Div. 2009).
37. *Id.* at 939.
38. *Ibid.*
39. *Id.* at N.J.S.A. 40:55D-1-163 and D-20.
40. *Stahl York Ave. Co. LLC v. City of New York*, No. 107666/07, 2008 N.Y. Misc. LEXIS 7415 (N.Y. Sup. Ct. 2008).
41. *Covel v. Town of Vienna*, Nos. CH-2003-184618, CH-2003-186629 & CL-2006-7105, 2009 Va. Cir. LEXIS 20 (Va. Cir. Ct. Mar. 14, 2009).
42. A previous Motion for Declaratory Judgment was filed by Covel in relation to his request for a Certificate of Appropriateness to build a fence on two of the contested properties, 130 Pleasant Street and 342 Windower Street, which adjoins the Pleasant Street property. The request to build the fence was made by Covel while the removal request was pending decision by the Town Council. In his application for the COA, Covel responded "N/A" to virtually all the Town's requested information. With the application, Covel submitted sixteen separate inquiries related to the Town Code and the Windover Heights Board of Review process, and the COA application form. During the hearings on his application for COA, Covel declined to supplement the information on his original application, and the COA for the fence was denied by unanimous vote.
43. On the date of trial, Petitioners had issued subpoenas for members of the Town Council and Board of Review, resulting in further argument on the Speech and Debate Clause. In a supplemental memorandum they explained they merely wanted an explanation for "the definition of terms used during hearings" and the basis for rejecting Michael Covel's application for a Certificate of Appropriateness. The Court quashed the subpoenas under the protections of the Speech and Debate clause.

44. Virginia's historic district enabling statute, Va. Code 15.2-2306(A), limits judicial review of such decisions made by a locality to claims that the decision is made in a way that is "arbitrary and constitutes an abuse of discretion" or "is contrary to law."
45. *Gorieb v. Fox*, 145 Va. 554, 134 S.E.2d 914 (1997) and *Helmick v. Town of Warrenton*, 254 Va. 225, 492 S.E. 2d 113 (1997), holding that delegations of legislative authority must be accompanied by guidelines, except "where it is difficult to lay down a definite rule, or where the discretion relates to the administration of a police regulation and is necessary to protect the public morals, health, safety and general welfare. *Gorieb* at 563-564 or 917.
46. *See Bd. of Supervisors v. Stickle Town of Painter*, 239 Va. 343, 389 S.E. 2d 702, 704 (1990).
47. *Pansini Custom Design Assocs., LLC v. City of Ocean City*, 407 N.J. Super. 137, 969 A.2d 1163 (App. Div. 2009).
48. Application for Project Authorization Under the N.J. Register of Historic Places Act., 2009 N.J. Super. LEXIS 174 (App.Div. July 30, 2009).

# Tribes, Tribal Lands, and Indian Arts

• • •

## *Section Editor: Rob Roy Smith*

This section focuses on cultural property issues involving Indian tribes in the courts, the United States Congress, state legislatures, and on a programmatic level, as well as Indian Arts and Crafts Acts matters.

### Tribal Lands, Sacred Sites, and Cultural Properties

#### Religious Freedom and Restoration Act and Sacred Lands

**San Francisco Peaks** For the past two years, *Yearbook* readers have been introduced to the Religious Freedom and Restoration Act of 1993 (RFRA),[1] as well as the so-called San Francisco Peaks Litigation. During this time, the litigation has taken dramatic turns and, despite last year's resounding rejection of the Indian tribes' claims by the Ninth Circuit Court of Appeals, the case continues to have impact on cultural resource protection strategies.

A brief history of the case follows. On March 12, 2007, the Navajo Nation, Hopi Tribe, and other southwest tribes scored a major sacred sites victory before the Ninth Circuit Court of Appeals by stopping certain activities of a ski resort in the San Francisco Peaks of Arizona, including the resort's planned use of reclaimed wastewater for snowmaking at the environmentally sensitive and spiritually important site.[2] The Ninth Circuit panel decision was the first case to hold that RFRA was available to Indian tribes to use religious beliefs to block certain land use practices that threaten Indian sacred sites. However, the victory for the Indian tribes was short lived as, on August 8, 2008, a twelve judge *en banc* panel of the Ninth Circuit issued a 9–3 opinion vacating the prior opinion and reversing the prior holding that RFRA barred use of reclaimed wastewater at the ski resort.[3] The majority opinion found that the Indian tribes failed to show that the government's approval of the use of reclaimed wastewater placed a "substantial burden" on the Indian tribes' exercise of their religion. The Tribes promptly sought review by the United States Supreme Court, which was denied in June 2009. Nevertheless, the dispute over the use of reclaimed wastewater on the San Francisco Peaks has not ended.

On September 21, 2009, a new complaint was filed against the United States Forest Service in Federal District Court in Arizona. The Save the Peaks Coalition and nine individuals sought to enjoin the snowmaking activities based on the U.S. Forest Service's alleged failure to perform an adequate analysis of what impact the ingestion of snow made from reclaimed wastewater would have on the health of children and skiers who use the Peaks. The suit focuses on alleged violations of the National Environmental Policy Act (NEPA)[4] and does not raise cultural resource protection issues because the Indian tribes are not a party to the litigation. The three-judge panel decision of the Ninth Circuit originally found that the Forest Service failed to adequately consider the possibility of human ingestion of snow made from treated sewage effluent, but that holding was vacated when the *en banc* panel issued its decision. This latest iteration of the lawsuit will certainly be of interest to the Indian tribes in the area, most of which consider the Peaks to be of the most sacred nature. The environmental litigation could succeed where the Tribes' RFRA claims could not by blunting the use of treated sewage effluent for snowmaking.

While concerned citizens continue to focus on a judicial remedy, the Navajo Nation, one of the tribes involved in the litigation, is considering a different tack: purchase of the ski resort that is at the center of the sacred site dispute. As of this writing, the Navajo Nation Council has authorized hiring an appraiser to determine the value of the Arizona Snowbowl and to begin to negotiate a purchase. This type of direct involvement by an Indian tribe may be one of the last resorts available for the protection of sacred sites now that RFRA's application to protect Indian tribal sacred sites has been substantially limited by the courts. For tribes that have the financial capacity to acquire sacred lands to prevent culturally offensive private development, the Navajo Nation's approach may mark a watershed moment in tribal sacred site preseveration strategy.

**Western Shoshone Challenge to Barrick Gold Mine** On November 20, 2008, the TeMoak Shoshone Tribe, the East Fork Band Council of theTeMoak Shoshone Tribe and the Timbisha Shoshone Tribe, the Western Shoshone Defense Project, and Great Basin Resource Watch filed a lawsuit against the United States seeking to enjoin the majority of the activities comprising the Barrick Gold Mine "Cortez" project on grounds that it violates the Western Shoshone's rights under the RFRA and the Federal Land Policy and Management Act's prohibition on "unnecessary and undue degradation," and that the Project's Environmental Impact Statement did not meet the requirements NEPA.[5] Plaintiffs' RFRA claim is based on the assertion that the project and adjoining areas are sacred to certain Western Shoshone.

On November 24, 2008, plaintiffs filed a Motion for a Temporary Restraining Order and a Preliminary Injunction seeking to bar work on the project until after trial. After a four day hearing, on January 26, 2009, the Nevada Federal District Court denied Plaintiffs' Motion for a Preliminary Injunction, concluding that plaintiffs had failed to demonstrate a likelihood of success on the merits and that plaintiffs had otherwise failed to satisfy the necessary elements for a preliminary injunction. In a troubling ruling for cultural resource protection advocates looking for a means to reenergize RFRA, the District Court opined that "The effect of the proposed mining project is on the plaintiffs' subjective, emotional experience. It is offensive to their sensibilities and in the mind of some will desecrate a sacred mountain. . . . Nevertheless, the diminishment of that spirituality—as serious as it may be—under the Supreme Court's holdings it is not a substantial burden on religious freedom."[6] This language echoes that of the Ninth Circuit's *en banc* panel in the San Francisco Peaks case. Not surprisingly, before appealing the denial of the injunction to the Ninth Circuit, the tribes dismissed their RFRA claim with prejudice, likely because of the Ninth Circuit's *en banc* decision in the San Francisco Peaks litigation.

Plaintiffs appealed the decision to the United States Court of Appeals for the Ninth Circuit, which heard oral arguments on June 10, 2009, but has not yet issued a decision. The case is progressing towards a final judgment on the merits in the District Court while the Ninth Circuit considers the appeal of the preliminary injunction. Construction of the project is ongoing.

These cases beg the question: what is a spiritual belief if it is not a "subjective emotional experience"? And, if a "subjective emotional experience" is not subject to protection under the RFRA, what legal recourse do tribes have to protect their land-based spiritual practices from adverse Federal actions that threaten their ability to practice their spiritual beliefs? Indeed, the failing here seems not to be of the law, but rather the judiciary's misunderstanding of Indian belief systems and failure to appreciate the importance of "place" to certain practices. It very well may be that, short of a Federal law criminalizing an Indian religious practice, RFRA might not be available to cultural resources advocates to protect a tribal belief system, let alone Indian sacred sites.

## Tribes and the Native American Graves Protection and Repatriation Act

The *Yearbook* editors located two Native American Graves Protection and Repatriation Act (NAGPRA)[7] court actions this year.

### Museum Inventories

The first case was initiated in 2007, but was only resolved on November 13, 2009. In *Brown v. State of Hawai'i*,[8] plaintiff, an archaeologist, sought an injunction alleging, among other things, that certain state historic preservation officials with the Hawaii State Historic Preservation Division (SHPD) violated NAGPRA because the state's inventories of Native Hawaiian human remains were not in compliance with NAGPRA's inventory requirements as the inventories failed to meet NAGPRA's notification and content requirements.[9] Plaintiff alleged that NAGPRA applied to the SHPD because it qualified as a "museum" under NAGPRA.[10] The alleged harm that required the injunction was that plaintiff would have a very difficult time advising clients as to where human remains were located in the absence of an inventory that accurately describes with specificity where human remains were found.

During a bench trial, the Hawai'i state defendants conceded that the SHPD is a "museum" for purposes of NAGPRA and that the human remains in its possession are, therefore, subject to NAGPRA's inventory requirements. The SHPD also acknowledged that, technically, they failed to comply with the NAGPRA notification requirements. The SHPD indicated that, prior to the lawsuit, it believed that NAGPRA's inventory requirements only applied to a museum's holdings that were originally found on federal or tribal lands and that NAGPRA only applied to a museum's holdings that were in its possession prior to NAGPRA's enactment on November 16, 1990. The SHPD further advised the Court during the trial that it was working to come into compliance with NAGPRA and that, therefore, plaintiff's permanent injunction on inventories and reburials should not issue.

The Federal District Court agreed with SHPD officials that an injunction was not warranted. However, while the Court refused the requested injunction, the Court praised the plaintiff for bringing the suit. The Court concluded its order as follows: "Plaintiff should be commended for bringing his NAGPRA claim. As the State Defendants' counsel acknowledged in his opening statement, the claim effectively brought certain issues of noncompliance to light. . . . It appears that, as a direct result of this litigation, SHPD has initiated consultation with the National NAGPRA Program in an effort to come into compliance with the statute."[11]

**Human Remains**

A NAGPRA case was filed in February 2009 in the United States District Court in Washington, D.C., by twenty claimed lineal descendents of the Apache warrior Geronimo seeking relief against various Federal officials as well as Yale University and the infamous Order of Skull and Bones, for alleged NAGPRA violations.[12] Plaintiffs allege that the United States and Yale University have failed to account for the human remains of Geronimo (who passed away in federal custody in 1909) and seek to force the defendants to surrender the remains and associated funerary objects to the lineal descendents. A primary purpose of the suit appears to be to relocate all of Geronimo's remains from federal government property to another burial site in New Mexico near his birthplace. Plaintiffs also seek compensatory and punitive damages in an unspecified amount. The suit was brought against Yale University, which apparently still has not been served with the complaint, because it has been widely claimed that in either 1918 or 1919 a group of Yale University students disturbed Geronimo's grave and retained possession of his remains and associated funerary objects for use in furtive exercises.

The United States responded by filing a motion to dismiss based on the United States' sovereign immunity, which prevents it from being sued without the government's express consent, as well as on the grounds that the NAGPRA claims lack merit. The United States argues that plaintiffs failed to identify any United States final action, or any federal action whatsoever, that contravened NAGPRA. The United States also argued for a reading of NAGPRA that would continue a trend of narrow judicial application of what was once heralded as a "human rights" statute. The United States alleges that there is no NAGPRA cause of action because there was no allegation of an action that triggered NAGPRA, namely inadvertent discovery or intentional excavation from federal land after 1990, and that in the absence of an intentional excavation after 1990, NAGPRA does not apply.[13] Of course a plain reading of NAGPRA would indicate that land situs is not an issue for collections accumulated prior to 1990, or thereafter, and held in museums, that is, federal repositories, or other repositories that receive federal funds. The NAGPRA issue in this case is whether the alleged entity that controls the remains, alleged to be the Order of Skull and Bones, is an organization of Yale University, or a private organization that does not receive federal funds and thus is outside of NAGPRA compliance requirements.

Soon after the case was filed, the Mescalero Apache Tribe sought intervention. In August 2009, the Fort Sill Apache Tribe also sought intervention, effectively tabling further proceedings until an inter-tribe dispute over who may rightfully possess Geronimo's remains can be resolved before the court. The dispute opens a battle of succession for Geronimo's legacy. The Fort Sill Apaches claim they are the chieftain's rightful heirs because Geronimo lived the last years of his life—and is now reportedly buried—in the Fort Sill area of Oklahoma. The Mescalero Apaches claim a blood relation to Geronimo, which they argue supersedes the Fort Sill Tribe's claim of interest. As of this writing, the intervention motions, as well as the United States' motion to dismiss, are still pending before the court.

### Kennewick Man

Thirteen years after the discovery of "Kennewick Man" along the banks of the Columbia River, the ancient remains once claimed to be "Native American" under NAGPRA resurfaced in the media this year. A July 2009 story in the *Seattle Post-Intelligencer* disclosed that after three years of opportunities for studies by the plaintiff academics and scientists involved in the *Bonnichsen* litigation,[14] no results of the studies, if conducted, have been made public. The human remains are still in place at the Burke Museum in Seattle, Washington, where the United States Army Corps of Engineers pays approximately $30,000 annually for storage. The article reports that, much as the Indian tribes involved in the initial litigation feared, there is no intention to move the remains or provide for their final disposition in the foreseeable future. Under an agreement with the plaintiffs and the United States, tribal spiritual leaders have twice been allowed to provide blessing to the remains, which have remained in the boxes in which they were stored during the ceremonies.

### Criminal Enforcement

Theft of Indian artifacts was prosecuted more vigorously in 2009 than in the prior year, perhaps as part of a push by United States Secretary of the Interior Ken Salazar to "crack down" on artifact smugglers and as the culmination of multi-year investigations.

In June 2009, Federal authorities indicted twenty-four individuals on charges of buying, selling, or exchanging archaeological artifacts stolen from Indian lands. The artifacts, stolen from grave sites, included burial and criminal masks, decorated pottery, and a buffalo hide headdress. These items were originally removed from the Four Corners Area—Utah, Colorado, Arizona, and New Mexico. The indictments allege the crimes took place in 2007 and 2008. Federal agents recovered 256 artifacts worth an estimated fair market value of $335,685. The charges carry possible criminal sentences of one to ten years in prison for violating the criminal provisions of the Archaeological Resources Protection Act[15] and NAGPRA.[16] ARPA prohibits the unauthorized excavation and removal of archaeological *resources on federal lands, which are also over 100 years of age*, as well as the unlawful sale, purchase, or exchange of such resources. As of this writing, the criminal case is still pending.

An unanswered question from the criminal cases is, when the cases are over, where will the artifacts go? Are any Indian tribes entitled to them under NAGPRA provisions? The BLM will most likely consult with area tribes to determine whether there is cultural affiliation with the artifacts and to facilitate repatriation under NAGPRA for any "Native American" human remains, funerary objects, objects of cultural patrimony, and sacred objects. For artifacts not subject to NAGPRA, the BLM will likely work with museums to stabilize, identify, and preserve the artifacts under the curation provisions of ARPA regulations.

In another incident, this one made famous because the guilty party posted a video of himself committing the crime to *YouTube*, a California man pled guilty and was sentenced on October 27, 2009, to 30 days in jail, 60 hours of community service, and a $530 fine, for illegally excavating an ancestral village of the Yurok Tribe. The sentence could have reached a maximum of one year in jail and a $10,000 fine. Tribal members had asked the judge to impose the maximum sentence for the grave robberies.

These enforcement actions appear to be part of a more sustained and coordinated federal effort to punish Indian grave robbers. A statement released by the United States Department of Justice at the time of the Four Corners indictments provides two enlightening quotes attributed to Obama Administration officials. First, Assistant Secretary of the Interior for Indian Affairs Larry Echo Hawk was quoted as stating, "The problem American Indian and Alaska Native tribes face of looters robbing them of their cultural patrimony is a major law enforcement issue for federal agencies responsible for enforcing historic preservation laws in Indian Country. Today's action should give tribes reassurance that the Obama Administration is serious in preserving and protecting their cultural property." Secretary of the Interior Salazar was also quoted as stating, "Let this case serve notice to anyone who is considering breaking these laws and trampling our nation's cultural heritage that the BLM, the Department of Justice, and the federal government will track you down and bring you to justice." The enhanced prosecutions should bring some welcome relief to tribal cultural resource protection advocates.

For further review of cultural resources law enforcement, see Practice Area 8.

**NAGPRA Review Committee**

The National NAGPRA Program's report for the fiscal year ending September 30, 2009, indicates that, as of the end of FY 2009, a total of 477 Notices of Intent to Repatriate Cultural Items and 1,295 Notices of Inventory Completion had been published. Of those totals, 50 Notices of Intent to Repatriate Cultural Items and 150 Notices of Inventory Completion were published in FY 2009 alone. The Notices of Intent to Repatriate Cultural Items account for 144,163 unassociated funerary objects, 4,303 sacred objects, 948 objects of cultural patrimony, 822 items that are both sacred objects and objects of cultural patrimony, and 292 "cultural items" not identified as to category. The Notices of Inventory Completion account for the human remains of 38,671 individuals and 998,731 associated funerary objects.

During the calendar year 2009, covered by this *Yearbook* edition, no disputes were considered by the Review Committee. However, in October, the Review Committee was asked to make a finding, which is short of a dispute, and where input from the Review Committee on matters of fact may facilitate the repatriation process. In that matter, the San Carlos Apache Tribe and the White Mountain Apache Tribe asked the Review Committee to find as a matter of fact that items requested by the tribes, and listed in a Notice of Intent to Repatriate by the American Museum of Natural History, in New York, were both cultural patrimony and sacred objects. Although the museum did not dispute the claim and was willing to move forward with repatriation, the notice submitted for publication by the museum indicated that the 35 items were "cultural items," but declined to identify the NAGPRA category of the items. The tribes desired that the National NAGPRA Program require the specification of a NAGPRA category in all notices published, and asked the Review Committee to establish the NAGPRA identity of the items as a precedent. The Review Committee agreed and found all of the items to be both cultural patrimony and sacred objects.

In the absence of a regulation to guide the disposition of culturally unidentifiable Native American human remains to federally recognized tribes, which claim them as co-aboriginal occupants of the land or related culturally, if not identifiable as having a shared group identity to the present-day tribe, the NAGPRA Review Committee hears requests and makes recommendations to the Secretary of the Interior to approve disposition agreements. Since the last report in *Yearbook* 2009, there have been 22 such requests heard and recommended by the Review Committee to the Secretary for approval. In this manner, for 2009 alone, more than 1,000 culturally unidentifiable Native American individuals will leave collections and be available for reburial.

A NAGPRA civil penalty may be assessed against a museum if it fails to comply with the requirements of the Act in one of eight ways. As of the end of FY 2009, a total of 233 counts of failure to comply had been alleged against 43 museums. Of those counts, 65 were alleged in FY 2009 alone. By the end of FY 2009, 111 of the counts had been investigated, and 28 of them had been substantiated. The 28 substantiated counts of failure to comply were comprised of 1 count of sale or transfer of NAGPRA cultural items contrary to NAGPRA (43 C.F.R. 10.12 (b)(1)(i)); 1 count of failure to complete a summary (43 C.F.R. 10.12 (b)(1)(ii)); 17 counts of failure to complete an inventory (43 C.F.R. 10.12 (b)(1)(iii)); 6 counts of refusal to repatriate (43 C.F.R. 10.12 (b)(1)(v)); and 3 counts of failure to consult with tribes (43 C.F.R. 10.12 (b)(1)(vii)). Through the end of FY2009, the percentage of investigated museums that were determined to have failed to comply with the requirements of NAGPRA was 63.2%, whereas the percentage of investigated counts that were substantiated was 25.2%.

The House Committee on Natural Resources, Committee of the Whole on Indian Affairs, held a hearing on NAGPRA in October, but did not discuss amendments to the law.

## Indian Arts and Crafts

Indian arts and crafts are a culturally and commercially important part of the lives of many tribal people. This section discusses efforts pertaining to Indian artisans and their craft, including the Indian Arts and Crafts Act (IACA).[17]

### Congressional Action

Once again, the 111th Congress has seen the introduction of legislation to amend the Indian Arts and Crafts Act to protect Indian arts and crafts through the improvement of applicable criminal proceedings to provide for the investigation and punishment of individuals misrepresenting Indian produced goods and products. Senator John McCain introduced S. 151, "The Indian Arts and Crafts Amendments of 2009" on January 6, 2009.[18]

This bipartisan legislation would amend the IACA to authorize any federal law enforcement officer (not just the Federal Bureau of Investigation as is currently the case), including an officer under the Indian Law Enforcement Reform Act acting in coordination with a federal law enforcement agency on a violation outside Indian Country, to investigate offenses involving the sale of arts and crafts that are misrepresented as Indian products. The bill would also revise the requirements for initiating civil actions for the misrepresentation of Indian produced goods to make it easier for the enforcement of IACA.

Much like its predecessor legislation, on July 24, 2009, the bill was passed by the U.S. Senate by unanimous consent. On August 19, 2009, the bill was referred to the U.S. House Subcommittee on Crime, Terrorism, and Homeland Security. A companion bill, H.R. 725, is pending in the U.S. House of Representatives.[19] At the date of this writing, neither bill had passed the House.

### IACB Enforcement

The Indian Arts and Crafts Board, a federal agency under the U.S. Department of the Interior, established by Congress in 1935 to promote authentic Indian art and craftwork and to implement and to enforce the IACA, recently concluded a three year investigation in conjunction with the New Mexico State Attorney General's Office to shut down sales of fake Indian arts and crafts (jewelry) in New Mexico. The investigation ended with the entry of a consent decree on July 29, 2009, with a Santa Fe company that imposes penalties of more than $12,000. The consent decree halts the fraudulent sales of Indian art and craftwork by Golden Bear Trading. Golden Bear Trading is also required to provide refunds over a four month period to consumers who purchased jewelry under the false assumption it was produced by prominent Navajo jeweler Calvin Begay. This case is an important victory in the ongoing battle against fraudulent Indian art and craftwork in the Southwest.

## Tribal Courts and Tribal Codes

A number of tribes have enacted or are considering enacting tribal code provisions addressing cultural properties. None of the resources available to editors of the *Yearbook* revealed any cases, new tribal code sections enacted, or tribal enforcement actions brought during 2009.

## Conclusion

The past year saw a marked increase in enforcement actions by federal agencies against persons and businesses that have profited from peddling fake Indian arts and crafts and from looting Indian lands. This increase in enforcement activity, in conjunction with the promise by officials at the Obama Administration to both support tribal rights and continue to crack down against those responsible for the discretion of Indian lands may signal an important shift in federal policy towards this important and sensitive issue. However, at this writing, the federal investigation that resulted in search warrants for items in four California museums is still pending.

## Notes

1. 42 U.S.C. §§ 2000bb – 2000bb-4.
2. *Navajo Nation et al. v. U.S. Forest Serv.*, 479 F.2d 1024 (9th Cir. 2007), *vacated by en banc decision*, 535 F.3d 1058 (9th Cir. 2008).
3. *Navajo Nation et al. v. U.S. Forest Serv.*, 535 F.3d 1058 (9th Cir. 2008) (*en banc*).
4. 42 U.S.C. § 4321 *et seq.*
5. *South Fork Band Council of Western Shoshone of NV v. U.S. Department of the Interior*, 643 F. Supp. 2d 1192 (D. Nev. 2009), *aff'd in part, rev'd in part & remanded*, 588 F.3d 718 (9th Cir. 2009).
6. *Id.*
7. 25 U.S.C. § 3001 *et seq.*
8. *Brown v. State of Hawai'i*, Civ. No. 07-00556 ACK-LEK, 2009 U.S. Dist. LEXIS 106418 (D. Haw. Nov. 13, 2009).
9. 25 U.S.C. § 3003; 43 C.F.R. §§ 10.9, 10.13.
10. Under NAGPRA, a "museum" is "any institution or State or local government agency (including any institution of higher learning) that receives Federal funds and has possession of, or control over, Native American cultural items." 25 U.S.C. § 3001(8). NAGPRA provides that "[e]ach museum which has possession or control over holdings or collections of Native American human remains and associated funerary objects shall compile an inventory of such items and, to the extent possible based on information possessed by such museum . . . , identify the geographical and cultural affiliation[5/] of such item[s]." *Id.* § 3003(a).
11. *Brown v. State of Hawai'i*, Civ. No. 07-00556 ACK-LEK, 2009 U.S. Dist. LEXIS 106418 (D. Haw. Nov. 13, 2009).
12. *Geronimo v. Obama*, Case No. 1:09-cv-00303- RWR (D.D.C. filed ___, 2009). This is not the first time a group has sought Geronimo's remains. In 1997, a group of plaintiffs filed suit against the U.S. Army and President Clinton. *See*

*Idrogo v. U.S. Army*, 18 F. Supp. 2d 25 (D.D.C. 1998). That action requested, inter alia, the repatriation of Geronimo's remains pursuant to 25 U.S.C. § 3005 (Section 7) of NAGPRA. *Id.* at 26. The court dismissed the suit, holding that the plaintiffs lacked standing to assert their claims because they were not lineal descendants or an affiliated tribal organization.

13. *Rosales v. United States*, No. 07cv0624, 2007 WL 4233060 (S.D. Cal. 2007) (finding that "NAGPRA creates a private right of action but no waiver of sovereign immunity"); *Hawk v. Danforth*, No. 06-C-223, 2006 U.S. Dist. LEXIS 58104 (E.D. Wis. Aug. 17, 2006) (holding that NAGPRA "applies only to remains or artifacts that are 'excavated or discovered'— not to remains that may still be buried" and that NAGPRA "protects human remains and cultural items found in federal public lands and tribal lands."); *see also Castro Romero v. Becken*, 256 F.3d 349, 354-55 (5th Cir. 2001) (upholding the conclusion that the request for damages under NAGPRA is inappropriate on state land).
14. *Bonnichsen v. United States*, 357 F.3d 962 (9th Cir. 2004), *amended in* 367 F.3d 864 (9th Cir. 2004).
15. 18 U.S.C. § 1361.
16. 18 U.S.C. § 1170.
17. 25 U.S.C. 305 *et seq.*
18. S. 151, 111th Cong. (2009).
19. H.R. 725, 111th Cong. (2009).

# Marine Environment

• • •

## *Section Editor: Nathaniel R. Orpen*

### Introduction

This section addresses updates on litigation, domestic and international law, and noteworthy events concerning cultural property in the marine environment. There have been important developments in two shipwreck cases that were covered in *Yearbook* 2009, the *Black Swan/Mercedes* and the *Griffin*. Also, a long-standing controversy over artifacts recovered from the *Titanic* is nearing a decision, and the wreck of the HMS *Victory*, an eighteenth century British battleship, was discovered. Lastly, an update on the newly effective UNESCO Convention on the Protection of the Underwater Cultural Heritage is included.

### The *Black Swan/Mercedes*

In May 2007, Odyssey Marine Exploration (Odyssey) announced that it had recovered over 500,000 gold and silver coins worth approximately $500 million from a shipwreck site it code-named "The Black Swan."[1] The Spanish government immediately became involved, arguing that the site is the final resting place of the *Nuestra Señora de las Mercedes* (*Mercedes*)—a Spanish frigate that exploded when its powder magazine was hit during a battle with the

British Navy off the coast of Gibraltar in 1804.[2] Since becoming aware of the find, Spain has become an outspoken critic of Odyssey's for-profit business model, accusing the company of modern day piracy.[3]

Spain bases its claim upon the International Convention on Salvage 1989, which declares that state-owned vessels like the *Mercedes* are never considered abandoned, and perpetually remain the property of the sovereign state.[4] Odyssey argues that the identity of the wreck remains unknown, and that it should be granted salvage rights.[5] If, however, the wreck is the *Mercedes*, Odyssey argues that the gold and silver it carried were commercial in nature, and was not the property of Spain.[6]

Odyssey's claim was dealt a blow on June 3, 2009, when U.S. Magistrate Judge Mark Pizzo issued a nonbinding Report and Recommendation (Report) advising the federal district court overseeing the case that the wreck is the *Mercedes*, and Spain's claim should prevail.[7] The Report is currently being reviewed by the U.S. District Court for the Middle District of Florida, where Odyssey's admiralty arrest action is filed.[8] If the court agrees with Judge Pizzo's Report, Odyssey will have to return all 500,000 coins to the government of Spain.

Judge Pizzo's Report dismissed Odyssey's arrest action under the Foreign Sovereign Immunities Act (FSIA) for lack of subject matter jurisdiction.[9] The FSIA states that the property of foreign sovereignties is immune from the jurisdiction of United States courts unless a statutory exemption applies.[10] Judge Pizzo's Report points to historical accounts of the *Mercedes*, dates on the recovered coins, the cannons found at the site, and the geographical location of the wreck as evidence that the site is the final resting place of the *Mercedes* and her crew.[11] The Report concludes that Spain therefore owns all legal rights to the site and its artifacts under the principal of sovereign immunity.[12]

Odyssey disagrees, and has filed objections to Judge Pizzo's Report. Odyssey argues that FSIA does not apply because the coins on the wrecked vessel were commercial cargo belonging to parties other than Spain, and are therefore subject to the jurisdiction of U.S. federal courts because they meet the commercial activity exemption found in the FSIA.[13] Odyssey also argues that the identity of the wreck remains unknown, and that Judge Pizzo failed to distinguish between the exploded vessel itself and the cargo and other property it carried.[14]

Judge Pizzo's Report also denied the claims of the government of Peru, and 25 individual descendents of sailors who perished on the *Mercedes*.[15] Peru had claimed that the coins were minted from gold and silver stolen from its natives, and that they are rightfully the cultural property of the Peruvian people.[16]

On December 22, 2009, the U.S. District Court for the Middle District of Florida issued an opinion that adopted in full Judge Pizzo's Report and granted both Spain's motion to dismiss and motion to vacate Odyssey's arrest warrant.[17] Peru's claim was also dismissed.[18] The court ordered Odyssey to return the 500,000 gold and silver coins and any other recovered items to Spain within ten days. However, the court stayed this order until either the time for appeal has lapsed or an order from an appellate court is issued.[19] Odyssey announced on December 23, 2009, that it has begun preparations to appeal this decision to the Eleventh Circuit Court of Appeals.[20] If a timely appeal is filed, Odyssey will retain custody of the coins during the appellate process.

## The *Griffin*

The addition of a new litigant has complicated the legal battle over a Lake Michigan wreck thought to be the *Griffin*, a small trading vessel built by French explorer Robert de la Salle that sank in the northern waters of Lake Michigan during a violent storm in 1679.[21] On January 30, 2009, France filed a claim in U.S. District Court for the Western District of Michigan to join the five-year-old lawsuit between Great Lakes Exploration Group (GLEG) and the state of Michigan.[22] France asserts that if the wreck is the *Griffin*, it owns the wreck because the *Griffin* was sailing under decree of the King of France when it was lost.[23] France thought it had already established its legal claim through contact it had made with the U.S. Department of State in 2005, but no formal claim had actually been filed in court at that time.[24]

When the *Griffin* sank, it was returning to Niagara Falls from near what is now Green Bay, Wisconsin, with a crew of six men and 6,000 pounds of fur and other goods in stow. While the wreck is not thought to contain treasure, the *Griffin* would offer significant historical value, as it is believed to be the first European trading ship to sail the waters of the northern Great Lakes.

The State of Michigan claims it owns the wreck under the Abandoned Shipwreck Act (ASA), and that the wreck should remain in its resting place at the bottom of Lake Michigan.[25] Under the ASA, the federal government has title to all wrecks located within the waters of the United States, but a state without actual possession of a wreck can establish good title if it proves that the wreck has been "abandoned" and is "embedded in the submerged lands of a state."[26] GLEG and France argue that since the ship sailed on behalf of the French crown it was never abandoned, and therefore still belongs to France.[27]

GLEG has secured France's approval to salvage the wreck if the court holds that France is the legal owner.[28]

Michigan and France have been discussing the possibility of settling the case throughout the past year, but have not made the contents of these negotiations public.[29] Several hearing dates in federal court have been postponed because of these talks. Most recently, a summary judgment hearing scheduled for October 15, 2009, was cancelled because Michigan suddenly withdrew its summary judgment motion.[30] Michigan stated in a court filing that after speaking with France's newly appointed counsel, it had decided to no longer object to France's claim of ownership in the *Griffin*.[31] Michigan then withdrew its motion for summary judgment, in which it had argued that the wreck, if it is the *Griffin*, was abandoned and that Michigan is its rightful owner under the ASA.[32] The October 15, 2009, court date was instead used for a half-hour telephone status conference during which the parties updated the court on the status of the case and answered questions.[33] The substance of this conference is not publicly available, but Michigan's withdrawal of its summary judgment motion may signal that France and Michigan are progressing toward a settlement.

## The *Titanic*

Six days of hearings held in late October and November of 2009 will determine the ownership of 6,000 artifacts salvaged from the wreck of the famous luxury liner, RMS *Titanic*.[34] U.S. District Court Judge Rebecca Beach Smith, sitting in the Eastern District of Virginia, has indicated that the disposition of these artifacts, valued at $110 million, will be decided sometime after January 4, 2010—the filing deadline for follow-up briefs to the recent hearings.[35]

The artifacts at issue include china, currency, ship fittings, and passengers' personal belongings.[36] RMS Titanic Inc. (RMST), the company that discovered the wreck in 1985, is asking for ownership of the artifacts as a salvage award.[37] The case has continued since 1992, when RMST was granted the legal status of salvor-in-possession, giving it the exclusive legal right to salvage the ship.[38] It has collected artifacts during six dives, which it displays for public viewing at touring museum exhibitions.[39] RMST claims that ticket sales to its exhibitions have not covered the costs expended in raising and preserving these artifacts.[40] If the court grants RMST legal title, it will likely include covenants that would restrict RMST's ability to sell off portions of the collection.[41] Judge Smith has described the wreck of the *Titanic* as an "international treasure," and has publicly stated that the artifacts should be kept together as one collection that is accessible to the public.[42]

The battle for ownership of these artifacts has been highly contested because the ship's original owner, White Star Line, no longer exists. White Star Line merged with Cunard Line in 1934, but the agreement did not include the *Titanic* because at that time it was considered lost forever.[43] Since the wreck was found in 1985, numerous claimants have emerged, including insurance companies that had paid out policies on the lives of those who drowned in the April 15, 1912, sinking.[44]

The *Titanic* sank in international waters, and rests two and one-half miles under the North Atlantic.[45] The wreck is both a time capsule and the final resting place of 1,522 passengers and crew who drowned when the ship sank.[46] The wreck is suffering damage not only from the gradual forces of deep oceanic water, but also from submersibles that have collided with and landed on the wreck.[47] According to the National Oceanic and Atmospheric Administration, the wreck of the *Titanic* will likely collapse on itself within the next fifty years.[48] RMST is currently making preliminary plans for a seventh dive to the wreck sometime in 2010.[49]

The last known survivor of the *Titanic* disaster, Elizabeth "Millvina" Gladys Dean, died on May 31, 2009, at the age of ninety-seven.[50] She was only nine weeks old when the liner sank.[51]

### The *Victory*

On February 2, 2009, Gregory P. Stemm, CEO and founder of Odyssey Marine Exploration (Odyssey), announced that Odyssey had found the wreck of the HMS *Victory*, a British warship lost in 1744.[52] The *Victory* sank during a violent storm in the English Channel on October 4, 1744 while returning to England after its fleet broke a French blockade off the coast of Lisbon, Portugal.[53] Admiral Sir John Balchin and his crew of 1,150 sailors drowned with the ship, taking four tons of Portuguese gold coins valued at approximately $1 billion with them to the bottom of the English Channel.[54]

Odyssey discovered the *Victory* in April 2008 while conducting a 5,000 square mile mapping project of the English Channel, which began in 2005.[55] After alerting the British Ministry of Defense, Odyssey was allowed to raise two of the forty-one bronze cannons it found at the site.[56] The royal insignias and dates of manufacture stamped on the cannons convinced experts that the wreck is the *Victory*.[57]

As a Royal Navy ship, the *Victory* remains the property of the British government under the International Convention on Salvage 1989.[58] For this reason, Odyssey has been negotiating with the British Ministry of Defense regarding the salvage of the *Victory*.[59] The British government, however, has informally committed to abide by the principles of the 2001 UNESCO Convention on the Protection of Underwater Cultural Heritage (Convention) and its Annex.[60] The Convention states that underwater cultural heritage should remain *in situ* (in the original place) whenever possible.[61] The Annex of the Convention contains widely used ethical and archaeological guidelines, and regards the commercial exploitation of underwater sites as anathema to careful management and preservation.[62]

Odyssey filed suit in U.S. District Court for the Middle District of Florida on May 29, 2008, to establish its admiralty arrest claim against the *Victory*, and brought a piece of glass from the wreck to the court to obtain constructive *in rem* jurisdiction over the entire site.[63] Odyssey has since been negotiating with Britain and other stakeholders for permission to salvage the *Victory*'s wreck from the English Channel.[64] Odyssey has set forth a proposal under which the entire site would be raised and conserved as a collection.[65] This proposed salvage will only occur if Odyssey can prove that the wreck is in danger of being destroyed if left *in situ*, as the Convention prescribes. The Ministry of Defense has asked English Heritage, the government's official advisor on the historic environment, to analyze the threats to the *Victory* wreck if it remains *in situ*.[66] It is the policy of English Heritage to leave shipwrecks intact and untouched unless there is a definite risk of damage.[67]

According to Odyssey, the *Victory* is presently in danger from the heavy fishing trawler traffic in the English Channel, which Odyssey claims is destroying shipwrecks.[68] Odyssey found that of the 267 wrecks it located in the English Channel, 112 (41 percent) show damage from bottom trawling fishing practices.[69] According to Odyssey, the wreck of the *Victory* lies in the most heavily trawled area of the western English Channel. Nets and cables are snagged across cannons and ballast blocks on the wreck of the *Victory*, and three bronze cannons have been moved by fishing nets dragging across the wreck. One of these cannons, a "42-pounder" that weighs four tons, was dragged 55 meters and turned upside down, and the two cannons that Odyssey has brought up also show scratches and other damage from fishing nets.

Similar damage has occurred elsewhere to other wrecks in the English Channel. Odyssey claims to have located only three pre-1800 wrecks in the English Channel during its mapping project, which represents less than 0.2% of the ships thought to have been lost in the area up until that time. This has bred fears that deep-sea fishing has already destroyed most of the oldest wrecks in the English Channel. Skeptics point out, however, that Odyssey's reports may have been embellished due to its financial interest in salvaging the *Victory*.

In the event that the *Victory* is preserved *in situ*, Britain is negotiating an agreement with Odyssey wherein Odyssey could accept monetary payment as a salvage award instead of artifacts from the wreck.[70] This sort of arrangement would allow the Royal Navy to simultaneously pay Odyssey its salvage award and honor the UNESCO guidelines.[71] Details of this purported agreement, or any other concerning the entire wreck, have not been officially released, but it is rumored that Odyssey will be awarded 40 of the cannons and a sliding scale payment for the remainder of the wreck.[72]

While the fate of the wreck and its gold remains unsettled, a partial agreement regarding the two salvaged cannons has been reached. On September 9, 2009, Odyssey reported that the British government would pay Odyssey a $160,000 salvage award for the two recovered cannons, and in turn Odyssey would file a motion to dismiss and vacate its admiralty arrest action.[73] Odyssey filed its motion to dismiss on September 17, 2009.[74]

## UNESCO Convention on the Protection of the Underwater Cultural Heritage

The 2001 UNESCO[75] Convention on the Protection of the Underwater Cultural Heritage (Convention) entered into force on January 2, 2009.[76] The Convention is intended to safeguard underwater cultural property, and is guided by four main tenets: (1) an obligation to preserve underwater cultural heritage, (2) a preference for *in situ* preservation, (3) prevention of commercial exploitation, and (4) cooperation among States to protect cultural property, promote training in underwater archaeology, and raise awareness and encourage public access to underwater heritage.[77]

The first two meetings of States Parties occurred in 2009, but the business conducted has been exclusively organizational in nature. The first session of the Meeting of States Parties took place at UNESCO Headquarters in Paris, France, on March 26–27, 2009.[78] During this first session, the States Parties adopted procedural rules, determined the functions and responsibilities of the meeting, and established a Scientific and Technical Advisory Body and its governing statutes. The Scientific and Technical Advisory Board is a twelve-member body that will advise the States Parties as they begin to implement the rules of the Convention and its Annex.[79]

The second session of the Meeting of States Parties took place December 1–2, 2009.[80] During this meeting, the States Parties elected members to the Scientific and Technical Advisory Board and established a working group of representatives from 14 States Parties to revise the draft of Operational Guidelines.[81] It was determined that the first meeting of the Scientific and Technical Advisory Board will occur in the second quarter of 2010, and the third meeting of States Parties will take place in the first quarter of 2011.[82]

## Notes

1. Sam Jones, *£254m battle of the Black Swan*, THE GUARDIAN, Mar. 24, 2008, *available at* http://www.guardian.co.uk/world/2008/mar/24/usa.spain (last visited Dec. 3, 2009).
2. Graham Keeley, *Treasure Hunter Gregg Stemm Ordered to Hand Over £300m Shipwreck Coins*, THE TIMES, Jun. 5, 2009, *available at* http://www.timesonline.co.uk/tol/news/world/us_and_americas/article6433155.ece (last visited Nov. 29, 2009).
3. Tim Bouquet, *Gregg Stemm: Is Taking Treasure from Shipwrecks Piracy?* THE TIMES, May 21, 2009, *available at* http://www.timesonline.co.uk/tol/life_and_style/men/article6328172.ece (last visited Nov. 26, 2009).
4. Gordon Rayner, *HMS Victory: Why the Sinking Feeling?* THE DAILY TELEGRAPH, Feb. 3, 2009, *available at* http://www.telegraph.co.uk/news/uknews/4449933/HMS-Victory-why-the-sinking-feeling.html (last visited Nov. 29, 2009); International Convention on Salvage, 1989, International Maritime Organization, April 28, 1989, *available at* http://www.jus.uio.no/lm/imo.salvage.convention.1989/doc.html (last visited 11/30/09) (entered into force Jul. 14, 1996).
5. Mike Celizic, *Sunken Treasure Stirs International Booty Battle*, MSNBC, Mar. 24, 2009, *available at* http://www.msnbc.msn.com/id/29856469/ (last visited Dec. 1, 2009); See Pl. Odyssey Marine Exploration, Inc.'s Objections to the Magistrate Judge's June 3, 2009 Report and Recommendation, 4, Jul. 21, 2009, from *Odyssey Marine Exploration v. The Unidentified, Shipwrecked Vessel*, No. 8:07-CV-614-T-23-MAP (Mid. D. Fla. filed Apr. 9, 2007), *available at* http://docs.justia.com/cases/federal/district-courts/florida/flmdce/8:2007cv00614/197978/230/ (last visited Dec. 3, 2009). All court documents for the Black Swan/Mercedes case are available at: http://dockets.justia.com/docket/court-flmdce/case_no-8:2007cv00614/case_id-197978/.
6. Celizic, *supra* note 5; See Pl. Odyssey's Objections, *supra* note 5, at 4.
7. Report and Recommendation, 1-2, Jun. 3, 2009, from *Odyssey Marine Exploration v. The Unidentified, Shipwrecked Vessel*, No. 8:07-CV-614- T-23-MAP (Mid. D.

Fla. filed Apr. 9, 2007), *available at* http://docs.justia.com/cases/federal/district-courts/florida/flmdce/8:2007cv00614/197978/209/ (last visited Dec. 3, 2009).
8. Brian Baxter, *Covington Helps Spain Sink Salvage Claims in Shipwreck Suit*, THE AMERICAN LAWYER, Jun. 8, 2009, *available at* http://www.law.com/jsp/article.jsp?id=1202431262418 (last visited Dec. 1, 2009).
9. Report and Recommendation, *supra* note 7, at 1-2; Baxter, *supra* note 8.
10. See 28 U.S.C. §§ 1330, 1332(a), 1391(f), 1441(d), 1602-1611 (2009); Report and Recommendation, *supra* note 7, at 16. The exemptions to FSIA's general rule of immunity from jurisdiction are found at 28 U.S.C. § 1610(a)-(b).
11. Baxter, *supra* note 8.
12. *Id.*
13. 28 U.S.C. 1610(a); Pl. Odyssey's Objections, *supra* note 5, at 12-19, 30.
14. Pl. Odyssey's Objections, *supra* note 5, at 9-12; Baxter, *supra* note 8.
15. Pl. Odyssey's Objections, *supra* note 5, at 28-33.
16. Baxter, *supra* note 8.
17. *Odyssey Marine Exploration, Inc. v. Unidentified Shipwrecked Vessel,* No. 8:06-cv-1685-T-23, 2009 U.S. Dist. LEXIS 119086 (M.D. Fla. Dec. 22, 2009).
18. *Id.* at 6-7.
19. *Id.* at 9.
20. Black Swan Project Overview, *available at* http://www.shipwreck.net/blackswan.php (last visited Jan. 14, 2010).
21. Daniel Nasaw, *US and France battle for rights over shipwreck found in Lake Michigan*, THE GUARDIAN, Feb. 16, 2009, *available at* http://www.guardian.co.uk/world/2009/feb/16/france-us-shipwreck-lake-michigan (last visited Dec. 2, 2009).
22. Francis X. Donnelly, *Diver, France fight state over right to salvage historic vessel in Lake Michigan*, THE DETROIT NEWS, Feb. 16, 2009.
23. Nasaw, *supra* note 17.
24. *Id.*
25. 43 U.S.C. §§ 2101-2106 (2009).
26. See 43 U.S.C. § 2105.
27. Nasaw, *supra* note 17.
28. Donnelly, *supra* note 18.
29. Ed White, *Michigan says it is trying to settle the Griffin shipwreck case*, A.P., Jun. 30, 2009, *available at* http://www.petoskeynews.com/news/article_56400106-8c2d-5f18-b494-905f9a7a0c90.html (last visited Dec. 2, 2009).
30. Intervenors' Req. to Withdraw Their Mot. for Summ. J., 2, Oct. 7, 2009, from *Great Lakes Exploration Group, LLC v. The Unidentified, Wrecked, and Abandoned Sailing Vessel*, No. 1:04-CV-375 (W.D. Mich. filed Jun. 7, 2004), *available at* http://docs.justia.com/cases/federal/district-courts/michigan/.

miwdce/1:2004cv00375/5376/169/ (last visited Dec. 3, 2009). All court documents from the *Griffin* case are available at: http://news.justia.com/cases/featured/michigan/miwdce/1:2004cv00375/5376/

31. Intervenors' Req. to Withdraw, *supra* note 26, at 2-3.
32. *Id.*
33. Minutes, Oct. 7, 2009, *supra* note 30.
34. Tim McGlone, *Judge will decide fate of Titanic artifacts after Jan.*, THE VIRGINIAN-PILOT, Nov. 24, 2009, *available at* http://hamptonroads.com/2009/11/judge-will-decide-fate-titanic-artifacts-after-jan (last visited Dec. 2, 2009).
35. *Id.*
36. Steve Szkotak, *Fate of Titanic, its treasures in US judge's hands*, A.P., Mar. 24, 2009, *available at* http://www.foxnews.com/wires/2009Mar24/0,4670,TitanicSalvage,00.html (last visited Dec. 2, 2009); Ray Kelly, *Officials from Titanic Historical Society in Springfield shocked to hear another salvage mission being proposed*, Masslive.com, Oct. 26, 2009, *available at* http://www.masslive.com/news/index.ssf/2009/10/officials_from_titanic_histori.html (last visited Dec. 2, 2009).
37. Szkotak, *supra* note 32. RMST is owned by Premier Exhibitions, Inc., a museum touring exhibitions company responsible for a Star Trek exhibit and the preserved human cadaver exhibit, "Bodies." *Id.*
38. *Id.*; Szkotak, *supra* note 32.
39. Szkotak, *supra* note 32.
40. *Id.*
41. McGlone, *supra* note 30.
42. Szkotak, *supra* note 32.
43. Chris McGreal, *US court aims to establish ownership of over $100m in Titanic artefacts*, THE GUARDIAN, Nov. 26, 2009, *available at* http://www.guardian.co.uk/world/2009/oct/26/titanic-artefact-case (last visited Dec. 2, 2009).
44. *Id.*
45. Szkotak, *supra* note 32.
46. *Id.*
47. McGreal, *supra* note 39.
48. *Id.*
49. Kelly, *supra* note 32.
50. Kelly, *supra* note 32.
51. *Id.*
52. William J. Broad, *Treasure Hunters Say They've Found a 1744 Shipwreck*, N.Y. TIMES, Feb. 2, 2009, *available at* http://www.nytimes.com/2009/02/03/science/03shipwreck.html (last visited Nov. 30, 2009). A later version of the *Victory* was captained by Admiral Horatio Nelson. Lisa Abend, *The HMS Victory, Famed Shipwreck, Is Found*, TIME MAGAZINE, Feb. 2, 2009, *available at* http://

www.time.com/time/world/article/0,8599,1876515,00.html (last visited Nov. 25, 2009).

53. Broad, *supra* note 48. The *Victory* was the largest battleship in the world at the time, and while mystery surrounds the precise cause of its sinking, some have speculated that it was too top heavy. See Bouquet, *supra* note 3.
54. Broad, *supra* note 48; Rayner, *supra* note 4.
55. Broad, *supra* note 48; Interview by Carsten Volkery, *Professional Treasure Hunter Gregg Stemm*, DER SPIEGEL, Feb. 3, 2009, http://www.spiegel.de/international/world/0,1518,605306,00.html (last visited Nov. 27, 2009). As of February of 2009, Odyssey had found 273 wrecks during its mapping project of the English Channel, including the *Victory* and some unidentified German U-boats. *Id.* The mapping exercise is the first deep-sea survey of any European waters. Bouquet, *supra* note 3.
56. Bouquet, *supra* note 3.
57. Broad, *supra* note 48.
58. Rayner, *supra* note 4; International Convention on Salvage, 1989, *supra* note 4. State-owned vessels are never considered to have been abandoned by their sovereigns without express proof of an intent to abandon.
59. Rayner, *supra* note 4. Gregory Stemm was a part of the UNESCO experts' meeting that negotiated the Draft Convention for the Protection of Underwater Cultural Heritage. Bouquet, *supra* note 3.
60. Rayner, *supra* note 4, (The Convention entered into force on January 2, 2009); Position Statement: 2001 UNESCO Convention on the Protection of the Underwater Cultural Heritage, United Kingdom National Commission for UNESCO, Aug. 2008, *available at* http://www.unesco.org.uk/UserFiles/File/Culture/UCH%20Position_082008.pdf (last visited Nov. 30, 2009) (The decision to not formally ratify the Convention is described as a policy decision and not purely a legal matter.).
61. Rayner, *supra* note 4.
62. UNESCO calls for measures to preserve wreck of the British warship HMS Victory, UNESCO, Press Release No. 2009-09, Feb. 5, 2009, available at http://portal.unesco.org/en/ev.php-URL_ID=44506&URL_DO=DO_TOPIC&URL_SECTION=201.html (last visited Dec. 1, 2009).
63. *Odyssey Marine Exploration v. The Unidentified Shipwrecked Vessel*, No. 8:2008-CV-01045 (M.D. Fla. filed May 29, 2008), Verified Complaint in Admiralty *In Rem*, 1, 4, May 29, 2008, *available at* http://docs.justia.com/cases/federal/district-courts/florida/flmdce/8:2008cv01045/214517/1/. All other court documents from the *Victory* case can be found at: http://dockets.justia.com/docket/court-flmdce/case_no-8:2008cv01045/case_id-214517/ (last visited Nov. 30, 2009).
64. *Salvagers want to raise Victory*, The BBC, Nov. 4, 2009, http://news.bbc.co.uk/2/hi/europe/guernsey/8299835.stm (last visited Nov. 26, 2009).

65. *Id.*
66. Frank Pope, *Trawlers are destroying historic wrecks, say explorers*, THE TIMES, May 20, 2009, *available at* http://www.timesonline.co.uk/tol/news/environment/article6322407.ece (last visited Nov. 26, 2009). English Heritage is the British government's statutory advisor on the historical environment. See www.english-heritage.org.uk for more information on English Heritage.
67. *Id.*
68. Bouquet, *supra* note 3.
69. Pope, *supra* note 62.
70. Abend, *supra* note 48.
71. Salvage fees can range from 50 to 80 percent of the value of the wreck. Rayner, *supra* note 4. On February 5, 2009, UNESCO's Director-General, Koïchiro Matsuura, made public his desire that the *Victory* be preserved in accord with the 2001 UNESCO Convention. *UNESCO calls for measures*, *supra* note 58.
72. Rayner, *supra* note 4. Few details of the agreement regarding the *Victory* have been made public, but the specifics of a 2002 agreement between the British government and Odyssey regarding the wreck of the HMS *Sussex* are well known. The overall value of the *Sussex* wreck will be split 80 percent to Odyssey and 20 percent to Britain for the first $45 million, a 50–50 split of the value of the remaining artifacts up to $500 million, and Odyssey gets 60 percent and Britain 40 percent of anything over $500 million. Jim Flannery, *Court Will Decide Who Gets $500m Haul*, SOUNDINGS MAGAZINE, Oct. 28, 2009, *available at* http://www.soundingsonline.com/features/in-depth/243142-court-will-decide-who-gets-500m-haul (last visited December 1, 2009).
73. Tess Stynes, *Odyssey Marine Reaches Salvage-Award Deal; Shares Up*, Dow Jones Newswires, Sept. 18, 2009, *available at* http://online.wsj.com/article/BT-CO-20090918-706138.html (last visited Nov. 26, 2009). This is approximately 80 percent of the value of the two cannons. *Id.* Odyssey plans to donate $75,000 of this salvage award to support the National Museum of the Royal Navy. *Id.*
74. Motion to Dismiss and to Vacate Warrant for Arrest, 2, Sept. 17, 2009, from *Odyssey Marine Exploration v. The Unidentified Shipwrecked Vessel,* No. 8:2008-CV-01045 (M.D. Fla. filed May 29, 2008), available at http://docs.justia.com/cases/federal/district-courts/florida/flmdce/8:2008cv01045/214517/27/ (last visited Dec. 3, 2009).
75. United Nations Educational, Scientific, and Cultural Organization (UNESCO).
76. To date, 27 states have become States Parties; they are Albania, Barbados, Bosnia-Herzegovina, Bulgaria, Cambodia, Croatia, Cuba, Ecuador, Grenada, Haiti, Islamic Republic of Iran, Lebanon, Libyan Arab Jamahiriya, Lithuania, Mexico, Montenegro, Nigeria, Panama, Paraguay, Portugal, Romania, Spain, St. Lucia, Slovakia, Slovenia, Tunisia, and Ukraine.

77. *Convention on the Protection of the Underwater Cultural Heritage will enter into force in January 2009*, UNESCO, Press Release No. 97-2008, *available at* http://portal.unesco.org/culture/en/ev.php-URL_ID=37965&URL_DO=DO_TOPIC&URL_SECTION=201.html (last visited Dec. 6, 2009); Convention on the Protection of the Underwater Cultural Heritage 2001, *available at* http://portal.unesco.org/en/ev.php-URL_ID=13520&URL_DO=DO_TOPIC&URL_SECTION=201.html (last visited Dec. 3, 2009).
78. First session of the Meeting of States Parties to the Convention on the Protection of the Underwater Cultural Heritage, *available at* http://www.unesco.org/en/underwater-cultural-heritage/the-2001-convention/meeting-of-states-parties/first-session-of-the-meeting-of-states-parties/ (last visited Dec. 3, 2009).
79. Statutes of the Scientific and Technical Advisory Body to the Meeting of States Parties to the Convention on the Protection of the Underwater Cultural Heritage, March 27, 2009, *available at* http://unesdoc.unesco.org/images/0018/001821/182130E.pdf (last visited Dec. 3, 2009).
80. Second session of the Meeting of States Parties to the 2001 Convention, *available at* http://www.unesco.org/en/underwater-cultural-heritage/the-2001-convention/meeting-of-states-parties/second-session-of-the-meeting-of-states-parties/ (last visited Dec. 6, 2009).
81. Resolutions of the Meeting, Dec. 1–2, 2009, *available at* http://unesdoc.unesco.org/images/0018/001863/186327E.pdf (last visited Dec. 6, 2009). Eleven members were elected to the Scientific and Technical Advisory Board, they are: Francisco Alves (Portugal), Milton Eric Branford (Saint Lucia), Pilar Luna Erreguerena (Mexico), Andrej Gaspari (Slovenia), Hugo Eliecer Bonilla Mendoza (Panama), Jasen Mesic (Croatia), Kalin Stoynev Porozhnov (Bulgaria), Carmen García Rivera (Spain), Hossein Tofighian (Islamic Republic of Iran), Serhiy Oleksandrovych Voronov (Ukraine), Vladas Zulkus (Lithuania). *Id.* The fourteen members of the working group are: Bulgaria, Cambodia, Croatia, Ecuador, Grenada, the Islamic Republic of Iran, Lebanon, Mexico, Nigeria, Portugal, Romania, Saint Lucia, Spain, and Ukraine. *Id.*
82. *Id.*

# Museum

• • •

## *Section Editor: Lucille A. Roussin*

### Introduction

The year 2009 brought few new issues to light: the arguments pro and con for some clear rules in museum policies regarding both accession and deaccession of works of art continue without any clear resolution. Cases concerning art looted during World War II continue to be litigated or settled with varying results. The one issue that continues to be newsworthy, though not Page 1 worthy, is the restitution of looted antiquities.

The current economic crisis is, not surprisingly, taking a major toll on art museums, galleries, and other businesses that comprise the art trade. "Museums everywhere are having trouble making ends meet, what with the overblown expansions they've made, the decline in investment income and the steep drop-off in contributions from foundations and individuals. Many have cut staff, frozen pay, trimmed exhibition schedules and slowed or stopped acquisitions."[1]

For some museums, the response has been to deaccession artworks. The National Academy of Art did just that in 2008 when it sold two Hudson River School paintings to pay its bills, and was immediately sanctioned by the American Association of Museums (AAM).[2] As reported last year, in response to the AAM's censure, the National Academy voluntarily withdrew its membership in the association. Ms. Branigan said that the National Academy has a chronic operating deficit of about $800,000 on a $3 million budget and may not use any of its $10 million endowment for operating expenses.[3]

Since then a number of museums have at least suggested deaccessioning some of their works. But for many, this goes against the idea that our museums are the keepers of our past and their duty to acquire and preserve art collections for the benefit of future generations through exhibition, interpretation, and research. The deaccession of artworks from a museum or nationally recognized art institution to provide funds for operating expenses runs counter to the Association of Art Museum Directors' two fundamental principles on deaccessioning:

1) The decision to deaccession is made solely to improve the quality, scope, and appropriateness of the collection, and to support the mission and long-term goals of the museum.
2) Proceeds from a deaccessioned work are used *only* to acquire other works of art—the proceeds are never used as operating funds, to build a general endowment, or for any other expenses (italics in the original). Funds from deaccessioning can be invested in an acquisition endowment earmarked to support the long-term growth of a museum's collection.[4]

Among the most contentious cases is that of the Maier Museum of Randolph College, which occurred in 2007, but raised the consciousness of the museum community, the AAM, and the Association of Art Museum Directors (AAMD). In that case the president of the college arrived at the museum unannounced and accompanied by city police officers and an attorney. The director of the museum was taken completely by surprise and had no recourse other than to allow them to remove four important paintings: George Bellows's *Men of the Docks*, Edward Hicks's *The Peaceable Kingdom*, E. Martin Henning's *Through the Arroyo*, and Rufino Tamayo's *Troubador*. Some members of an alumnae group filed suit in Lynchburg Circuit Court to block the sale, but were unable to raise the $1 million bond to stop the sale. A further appeal on the grounds of a "charitable trust," that challenged the college's switch to coeducation was appealed to the Virginia Supreme Court, which affirmed the lower court's original dismissal of the case.[5]

The most recent attempt to avoid the AAMD's requirements goes farther than any other attempt to merely deaccession. Brandeis University announced in February 2009 that the trustees had voted unanimously to "trash the institution by closing it and auctioning off the 6,000 works in its collection. The decision came without consulting either the museum's own board of governors or its director, Michael Rush."[6] The outcry was immediate and virulent. "The decision to close the 48-year-old museum in Waltham, Mass., and disperse the collection as a way to shore up the university's struggling finances was denounced by the museum's board, its director and a wide range of experts, who warned that the university was cannibalizing its cultural heritage to pay its bills."[7] The Massachusetts attorney general's office is planning to conduct a detailed review of the surprise decision to sell off the entire holdings of the Rose Museum, "one of the most important collections of postwar art in New England."[8] The Rose family filed a lawsuit on July 27, 2009, claiming that the university's decision to close the eponymous museum would not only violate museum ethical codes, but would violate the university's commitment to the Rose family to maintain the museum solely as a public museum.[9]

The Fresno Metropolitan Museum of Art and Science was forced to close its doors permanently and its entire collection will be sold at auction. However, the whole collection has been valued at about $2.1 million, while its debt hovers around $4.4 million. Fresno officials "blame the closure on what Stewart Randall, president of its board of trustees, called a perfect storm of ill fortune: the global financial crash, a corresponding drop-off in key long-term donor contributions and a prolonged three year building rehabilitation project that drained away patrons."[10]

There has been wide criticism of the AAMD policy on deaccession of artworks to fund expenses other than purchase of new artworks. The argument centers on the fear that once deaccessioning for any reason other than to purchase new works is permitted, it will become the first resort in times of economic downturns. On the other hand, might it be better to allow museums to sell some works—perhaps those not on permanent view—than to close whole collections permanently or even put the museum out of business?[11] Art writer and critic Judith Dobrzynski has put forth the idea that a museum would have to present its case for deaccessioning before an impartial arbitrator schooled in art, art law, and nonprofit regulations.[12] Her proposal has engendered many comments, pro and con, including that the idea of arbitration is "unreasonably paternalistic," or that if deaccessioning is permitted, it would be the first, rather than the last, option.[13]

The deaccessioning issue has been under discussion by the New York State Legislature for over a year. Assemblyman Richard L. Brodsky submitted a bill in March 2009, but it was tabled pending further discussion. On Thursday,

Jan. 14 representatives from museums in New York City met with lawmakers in the State Assembly Hearing Room in Manhattan in a "round-table meeting billed as the first discussion of deaccessioning among state policy makers and museum professionals in a public setting."[14] The language of the proposed legislation is quite broad and covers even libraries, historical societies, historic houses, and zoos. There was much dissension, especially in the broad range of cultural entities covered by the bill, and there was no unanimity on the basis of the bill—to prevent deaccessioning for any purpose other than to purchase new works of art.

Tangentially related to deaccessioning, there is some lingering criticism of the move of the Barnes Collection into Center City, Philadelphia. Former trustee Richard Feigen, in an article in the ARTNEWSPAPER, has claimed that the institution is not being saved, but rather being stolen.[15] In a response the General Counsel of the Barnes Foundation refutes every single one of Mr. Feigen's allegations, from the notion that the will has been violated, that the public is being "victimized," that the residents of Merion have been ignored, and that the Barnes Foundation is guilty of "insufficient efforts to find alternative approaches." The matter of the Barnes Foundation's move to its new home, because of its inability to survive under the conditions of the will has been litigated for over 20 years. A thorough conservation of the works, along with a promise of similar placement in a suitable environment and the maintenance of the Merion property as a research facility, should indeed be welcomed.[16]

## International

### Claims to Antiquities

Although restitutions from several U.S. museums have been successfully completed due to negotiations, a few claims to objects in both U.S. and European museums linger.

Egypt's claim to an ancient mummy mask unearthed more than 50 years ago at the Saqqara pyramids and now in the St. Louis Art Museum is still in question. The mask, a golden image of a noblewoman named Ka Nefer Nefer, is said to have been deposited by the archaeologist who discovered it in the storeroom at Saqqara and was still there in 1959. The St. Louis Art Museum acquired it in 1998. Zahi Hawass, head of Egypt's Antiquities Authority, claims that there is no record of the mask ever leaving Egypt legally, and its restitution is his number one priority. The museum's director, Brent Benjamin, contends that Egypt does not have sufficient proof that it was stolen and that an inquiry to the Egyptian Museum in Cairo did not say that it was stolen. The museum's provenance, however, is patently false because it puts the mask in the possession of a Belgian art dealer in 1952 when the Egyptians can prove clearly that it was in the Saqqara storeroom in 1959.[17] Despite the lingering claim on the sculpture that is to occupy the new wing, the Saint Louis Art Museum's plan for a major extension of its sculptural wing is progressing, including a 77,000 square foot addition to its existing structure.[18]

Egypt is still assiduously proceeding with a claim to one of the most emblematic objects of Egypt's cultural history, the head of Queen Nefertiti, the wife of Pharaoh Akhenaten, featured in her own stunningly lit display in the Neues Museum in Berlin. According to Zahi Hawass, Egypt's Chief Archaeologist, the bust was hidden from the Egyptian excavation partners of the Berlin team during the "partage" (sharing) at the end of the excavation at el-Amarna in 1912.[19]

On a more positive note, the Louvre Museum in Paris, following two weeks of difficult negotiations, agreed to return five painted fragments to Egypt. German scholars visiting the Louvre recognized the five 3,200-year-old fragments as those they had discovered in 1980 at the tomb of a nobleman in a necropolis on Luxor's west bank. Under the UNESCO 1972 Convention for the Protection of World Cultural and Natural Heritage, artifacts that are the property of their country of origin must be returned to their homeland. When France at first resisted demands for their return, the Egyptians retaliated by halting any French excavations in Egypt, and although the French had acquired the objects in "good faith," Minister of Culture  Frederick Mitterand immediately agreed to return them in a resolution to take action against the "illegal trafficking of cultural goods."[20]

The *Victorious Youth*—better known as the Getty Bronze—which depicts an athlete crowned with an olive wreath, and is thought by some to be an original by Lysippos, remains the object of a court case in Italy. At issue is whether the Getty was acting in good faith when it purchased the statue for somewhat less than $4 million in 1977. The Italians assert that the statue, after being hidden, was smuggled out of Italy without proper export permits, and that the Getty was negligent in its due diligence before purchasing the work.[21] A newly revealed document in the case shows that billionaire J.P.Getty had legal concerns about the statue, and that Metropolitan Museum director Thomas Hoving and antiquities director, Dietrich von Bothmer, also raised questions about the provenance of the statue, and advised further inquiry as to the legality of the purchase. When Getty died in June 1976, the statue was purchased for $4 million without any further questions. The case remains in the Italian court awaiting a decision.[22]

In a most felicitous agreement, the Metropolitan Museum of Art will return a piece of a red granite shrine it purchased from an antiquities collector in New York for the sole purpose of restituting it to Egypt. The piece belongs to a naos honoring the 12th Dynasty King Amenemhat I, who ruled 4,600 years ago, and which is now part of the Ptah temple of Karnak in Luxor. Zahi Hawass, the Egyptian Director of Antiquities said, "It is a kind gesture from the newly appointed Met director Thomas Campbell."[23]

## Holocaust-Era Looted Art

### The Goudstikker Collection

Jacques Goudstikker was among the most renowned Jewish art dealers in Europe in the 1930s. Forced to flee when the Nazis invaded Holland, he died in a tragic accident when he fell through an uncovered hatch on the deck of the ship that was taking him and his wife and young son to freedom in England. But in his pocket was a small notebook inventorying most of his collection of over 1,000 paintings. Marei von Saher filed a claim in the Central District of California to recover Lucas Cranach the Elder's life-size paintings of Adam and Eve from the Norton Simon Museum in Pasadena, California. A motion to dismiss by the museum was granted on the grounds that the statute of limitations had expired. The court held, among other things, that California's statute extending the statute of limitations for the recovery of Holocaust-era looted art was unconstitutional.[24] Oral argument was held before the Ninth Circuit on December 8, 2008, but in a decision filed on August 19, 2009, the U.S. 9th Circuit Court of Appeals refused to rehear an appeal by Marei von Saher.[25] Her only recourse now is to try to successfully appeal the ruling to the U.S. Supreme Court. Her attorney, Lawrence M. Kaye, said that she has not decided whether to do so.[26]

### *Museum of Fine Arts, Boston v. Dr. Claudia Seger-Thomschitz*

This is another peremptory suit filed to quiet title to a painting by Oskar Kokoschka, *Two Nudes* (*Lovers*), which the museum acquired in 1973 by bequest of Sarah Reed Platt, who acquired it from an art gallery in 1948 or 1949.[27] Seger-Thomschitz is the sole heir of Oskar Reichel, a Jewish doctor and art collector/gallerist in Vienna who was forced by the Nazis to file a property declaration in June 1938 and whose assets were confiscated by 1939. The painting was acquired by Viennese art dealer Otto Kallir in or about 1939 in what Seger-Thomschitz characterizes as a forced sale.

Seger-Thomschitz, with no connection to or knowledge of the art world, was unaware of the artworks and other property confiscated from Oskar Reichel until 2003, when she was contacted by a Vienna museum about four paintings that had been confiscated by the Nazis. A number of prominent historians of the Holocaust have criticized the museum for its stance on the claim for restitution. Deborah E. Lipstadt, a prominent historian of the Nazi era, has said, "To suggest, at that period in Vienna, that there was no pressure is ridiculous. . . . It's ludicrous."[28]

In a decision rendered on May 28, 2009, the U.S. District Court for the District of Massachusetts ruled that Seger-Thomschitz's claims are time barred, even if the cause of action were tolled until 2003, the date at which she asserts she learned of the claim. The court granted her motion to file a reply to the Museum of Fine Arts' opposition to amend her claim, but cautioned that it will not change the judge's decision rejecting her motion to amend. The final result, however, is that the court granted the museum's motion for summary judgment.[29]

### *Sarah Blodgett Dunbar v. Dr. Claudia Seger-Thomschitz*

This case arises out of a claim of adverse possession made by Dr. Seger-Thomschitz to a painting by Oskar Kokoschka entitled *Portrait of a Youth*, which is a portrait of Hans Reichel. The defendant is the sole heir of Raimund Reichel's estate, and she claims the painting was sold under duress to Otto Kallir in Vienna in 1938. Plaintiff's mother purchased the painting from Otto Kallir's St. Etienne Gallery in New York in 1946. This case is unusual because it arises under Louisiana law—the only U.S. state to follow the Napoleonic Code. As such, under Louisiana Civil Code, "one who has possessed a movable as owner for ten years acquires ownership by prescription. Neither title nor good faith is required for this prescription." Moreover, the court found that the Reichel family sought compensation for their home, a commercial property, and another art collection that were forcibly sold. The court therefore granted Plaintiff's Motion for Summary Judgment.[30]

### *Westfield v. Federal Republic of Germany*

This case was originally filed in Davidson County [Tennessee] Chancery Court on behalf of the heirs of Walter Westfield, a successful art dealer in Germany in the mid-1930s who was murdered by the Nazis. The defendant removed the action to federal court based on 28 U.S.C. 1330, Actions Against Foreign States and 28 U.S.C. §§ 1602, et seq., The Foreign Sovereign Immunities Act (FSIA). Plaintiffs asserted that the Federal Republic of Germany could be held liable for the seizure of Westfield's major collection of art and tapestries by the Nazi government, much of which was subsequently auctioned off and found its way to the United States. They sought the imposition of a constructive trust and an equitable accounting as to the collection. After a lengthy discussion of the FSIA, the court dismissed the case and denied a Motion for Judicial Notice.[31]

### *Claude Cassirer v. Kingdom of Spain*

After a decision by the District Court of the Central District of California that Cassirer's claim for restitution of a Pissarro painting in the Thyssen-Bornemisza Museum could go forward on Cassirer's claim conversion and replevin for the painting,[32] both defendants appealed. On appeal, Appellants challenged the district court's denial of their respective motions to dismiss for lack of (1) personal jurisdiction, (2) standing, (3) a justiciable case or controversy, and (4) subject matter jurisdiction based on sovereign immunity. The 9th Circuit Court of Appeals dismissed the appeal with regard to the issues of personal jurisdiction, Article III case or controversy and standing. The court affirmed the district court's interpretation on the claims of sovereign immunity, concluding that the Thyssen-Bornemisza Foundation engaged in sufficient commercial activity within the United States to satisfy the requirements of FSIA § 1605(a)(3). However, the court stated that on remand the district court should examine the issue of exhaustion of remedies, "for the limited purpose to determine in the first instance whether to impose an exhaustion requirement on Cassirer."[33]

### *United States of America v. Portrait of Wally, A Painting By Egon Schiele*

After almost twelve years of litigation and numerous decisions by both state and federal courts, Judge Loretta Presca issued a decision that trial is warranted on the issue of whether Dr. Leopold knew *Wally* was stolen when the Museum (Museum of Modern Art) imported it into the United States for exhibition at MOMA. She therefore denied both parties motions for summary judgment and gave them until October 14, 2009, to submit a proposal as to how they will proceed.[34]

## Restitution of Looted Artworks

### The Max Stern Collection

The Max Stern Collection, which last year recovered two of the paintings that were sold in a forced sale at the Lempertz Auction House in Cologne, has recovered another two paintings from this important collection. The U.S. Holocaust Claims Processing Office spotted an old master painting of *Bagpiper* in the inventory of an American art dealer who was en route to the European Fine Art Fair in Maastricht. Upon its return to the United States, U.S. Immigration and Customs Enforcement (ICE) and the U.S. Attorney's Office informed the dealer of the painting's history and he handed it over. It was returned to a representative of the Max Stern Collection on Holocaust Remembrance Day at the Museum of Jewish Heritage.[35]

Another important painting, *St. Jerome*, by famed Italian Baroque artist Ludovico Caracci, was discovered in the possession of art dealer Richard Feigen, who immediately turned it over to ICE representatives when he learned of its provenance. U.S. government officials turned the painting over to representatives of Concordia University, acting on behalf of the Estate of Max Stern.[36]

Upon his death in 1987, Stern bequeathed his art collection, specifically including any works of art that might yet be recovered, to McGill University, Concordia University, and The Hebrew University of Jerusalem. In 2004 the Stern Estate contacted the Art Loss Register and listed the painting with Germany's Lost Art Internet Database.

Camille Pissarro's *Le Quai Malaquais et l'Institut,(Printemps)*,1903, found in a safe deposit box in the Zurich National bank registered to notorious Nazi art dealer Bruno Lohse in 2007, which is still the subject of police investigations, was restituted to the heirs of the original owner, Samuel Fischer.[37] The painting was sold on behalf of the heirs at Christie's on November 3, 2009, where it fetched $2,154,500.

A painting by Franz von Lenbach depicting Otto von Bismarck was discovered in offices in the German parliament by the heirs of Herbert Guttmann. The German government has agreed to return the painting to Gutmann's heirs. As cited in the press release, "the discovery calls into question how many other looted works could be in the parliament's collection, particularly among the 200 pre-war works installed at the Bundestag."[38]

## General Observations for the Year

Holocaust-era looted art remains the major issue in the international art world, and without some sort of international agreement, accompanied by sincere efforts to locate works of art and their owners, it will remain a major issue. Indeed, the legal strategy now practiced by museums, to file to quiet title the minute they become aware of a claim in cases of Holocaust-era art, is in direct contradiction to the Washington Principles.[39]

An international conference to review progress since the Washington Conference of 1998 took place in Prague in June 2008 and published the Terezin Declaration,[40] but thus far no concrete proposals have resulted. As one prominent author has written,

> unless governments are prepared to aggressively investigate the provenance of artworks in public collections, locate owners and heirs, and establish functioning mechanisms to fairly adjudicate art claims, additional conferences will be academic exercises of no meaningful value to Nazi victims the Washington Principles were intended to aid.
>
> The economic crisis continues to affect the art world and the museum community. We have already seen the move to deaccession works of art to make up the loss in operating expenses and the legal consequences of such moves.

In England, the government has enacted legislation that would permit institutions to restitute Nazi-looted art to the families that once owned them or to their heirs. Previously, legislation forbade all national museums and galleries to dispose of any of their works. The Spoliation Advisory Committee, created in 2000, will now have greater authority to advise restitution rather than reparations. The Tate, the British Museum, and the British Library are all known to hold looted art, and experts estimate that several hundred looted artworks may be in British galleries and museums.[41]

## Notes

1. Judith H. Dobrzynski, *The Art of the Deal,* N.Y. TIMES, Jan 2. 2010 at A21.
2. *Id.*
3. AAMD Censures National Academy Museum, Dec. 5, 2008, available at http://www.artinfo.com/news/story/29702/aamd-censures-national-academy-museum.
4. Art Museums and the Practice of Deaccessioning, http://www.aamd.org/papers.
5. Laura R. Katzman and Karol A. Lawson, The (Im)permanent Collection: Lessons from a Deaccession, American Association of Museums, accessible at http://www.aam-us.org/pubs/mn/deaccession.cfm. The court cases are not reported.

6. Roberta Smith, *In the Closing of Brandeis Museum, a Stark Statement of Priorities*, N.Y. TIMES AT C3.
7. *Id.*
8. *Id.*
9. Lawsuit Over Deaccessioning of the Brandeis Rose Art Museum Moves Forward, *http://artlaw.foxrothschild.com/2009/10/articles/litigation-issues/lawsuit-over-deaccessioning.*
10. Reed Johnson, *The Fresno Metropolitan Museum of Art and Science closes its doors*, L.A. TIMES, Jan 12, 2010, available at *http://articles.latimes.com/2010/jan/12/entertainment/la-et-fresno-museum12-2010jan12.*
11. Dobrzynski, *supra* n.2.
12. Id.
13. Judith H. Dobrzynski, "The Aftermath: Responses to My Deaccessioning Op-Ed," Real Clear Arts, http://www.artsjournal.com/realcleararts/2010/01/deaccessioning-aftermath.html; Donn Zaretsky, "More on the Dobrzynski Proposal," The Art Law Blog, Jan.11, 2010, *http://the* artlawblog.blogspot.com/2010/01/more-on-dobrzynski-proposal.html.
14. Robin Pogrebin, *Museums and Lawmakers Mull Sales of Art*, N.Y. TIMES, Jan. 15, 2010 at C31.
15. Richard Feigen, *A Tale of Institutional Morality: The Barnes Collection is not being saved, it is being stolen*, THE ARTNEWSPAPER, Jan., 2010.
16. *See, e.g. In re Barnes Foundation*, 69 Pa. D. & C.4$^{th}$ 129 (Orphan's Ct. 2004).Patty Gerstenblith, *Art, Cultural Heritage and the Law* 289 ff. (2$^{nd}$ ed. 2008).
17. *St. Louis museum proud of its ancient mask purchase but Egypt calls it a steal*, INTERNATIONAL HERALD TRIBUNE, Nov. 24, 2008, available at http://iht.com/articles/2008/11/24/mideast/loot.php ; Tom Finkel, *The Saint Louis Art Museum Ka-Nefer-Nefer Egyptian Mask Saga Continues*, RIVERFRONT TIMES, Nov. 26, 2008.
18. Saint Louis Art Museum sets groundbreaking for $130M expansion (and still refuses to return KaNefer mask to Egypt), *http://groups.google.com/group/museum_security_network/browse_thread/thread447c9fad887e7* , Jan, 17, 2009.
19. Michael Kimmelman, *When Ancient Artifacts Become Political Pawns*, N.Y. TIMES, Oct. 24. 2009 at A1.
20. AL AHRAM, Oct. 15–21, 2009.
21. Elisabetta Polovedo, *Italy Presses its Fight for a Statue at the Getty*, N.Y. TIMES, Jan 15, 2009 at C3.
22. Ellie Bruggeman, A Twist in Getty Museum's Italian Court Saga, http://groups/google.com/group/museum_security-network/browse_thread/thread/249ad7bb4d5ef.
23. THE JERUSALEM POST, Oct. 27, 2009.
24. *Von Saher v. Norton Simon Museum of Art*, No. CV 07-2866-JFW, 2007 U.S. Dist. LEXIS 95757 (C.D. Cal. Oct. 18, 2007); Suzanne Muchnic, *Norton Simon to keep pair of prized paintings*, LA TIMES, Oct. 19, 2007 at B3.

25. *Von Saher v. Norton Simon Museum of Art,* No. CV 07-2866-JFW, 2007 U.S. Dist. LEXIS 95757 (C.D. Cal. Oct. 18, 2007), *aff'd in part & rev'd in part*, 578 F.3d 1016 (9th Cir. 2009). In 2006 Marei and Charlene von Saher recovered from the Dutch government 200 paintings, many of which were exhibited this year at the Bruce Museum in Greenwich, CT, and at the Jewish Museum in New York in the spring.
26. Mike Boehm, *Woman seeking return of looted art from Norton Simon Museum loses appeal*, L.A. TIMES, Jan 16, 2010.
27. *Museum of Fine Arts v. Seger-Thomschitz*, Civil Action No. 08-10097 (D. Mass. filed May 29, 2008).
28. Geoff Edgers, *Holocaust historians blast MFA stance in legal dispute*, THE BOSTON GLOBE, May 28, 2008 at A1.
29. *Museum of Fine Arts v. Seger-Thomschitz,* Civil Action No. 08-10097, 2009 U.S. Dist. LEXIS 58826 (D. Mass. May 28, 2009).
30. *Dunbar v. Seger-Thomschitz*, 638 F. Supp. 2d 659 (E.D. La. 2009).
31. *Westfield v. Federal Republic of Germany*, No. 3:09-0204, 2009 Dist. LEXIS 65133 (M.D. Tenn. July 28, 2009).
32. *Cassirer v. Kingdom of Spain,* 461 F.Supp. 2d 1157 (C.D. Cal., 2006); *See Yearbook of Cultural Property* 2007, 92 passim.
33. *Cassirer v. Kingdom of Spain,* 580 F.3d 1048 (9th Cir. 2009).
34. *United States v. Portrait of Wally*, 105 F. Supp. 2d 288 (S.D.N.Y. 2000), motion for reargument denied, and *motion to alter or amend judgment so as to file an additional amended complaint granted*, 2000 U.S. Dist. LEXIS 18713 (Dec. 28, 2000), *motion to dismiss denied, and motion for summary judgment to dismiss claim of one purported heir granted*, 2002 U.S. Dist. LEXIS 6445 (Apr. 11, 2002), *motions for summary judgment denied*, 2009 U.S. Dist. LEXIS 91464 (Sept. 30, 2009).
35. U.S. Department of Justice and homeland security return rare painting of Bagpiper to Universities in Canada and Israel. http://mediarelations.concordia.ca/pressreleases/archives/2009/04/us_departments_of_justice.
36. Prominent Old Master Dealer Discovers Max Stern Property in His Private Collection. http://mediarealtions.concordia.ca/pressreleases/archives 2009/05/prominent_old_master-dealer.
37. Stefan Koldehoff, Pissarro Lost and Found, ART NEWS, Summer 2007 at 76.
38. *German Parliament to Return Nazi-Looted Portrait*, ARTINFO, Nov. 13, 2009.
39. Marilyn Henry, *Metro Views: Back to Context*, THE JERUSALEM POST, Nov. 16, 2008.
40. The text is available at http://www.holocausteraassets.eu/program/conference-proceedings/.
41. *UK museums can return looted art*. BBC NEWS, Nov. 13, 2009.

# Art Market

• • •

## *Section Editors:*
## *Thomas R. Kline and L. Eden Burgess*

In 2009, two art market issues increasingly dominated legal developments in the United States and Europe: standards for restitution of looted art and antiquities, most of which had passed through the art market at one time or another, and standards for diligence and transparency in art market transactions. As in the past, questions related to the passage of time—statutes of limitation and laches—tracked along with the two predominant issues, further complicating cases coming to light through judicial decision or publicly announced settlement during the course of the year.

With a gradual refocusing of law enforcement priorities over the past few years (most U.S. law enforcement efforts in the cultural property area having fallen victim to the September 11 attacks), cases in 2009 reflected enhanced efforts of federal authorities, particularly U.S. Immigration and Customs Enforcement (ICE) of the Department of Homeland Security.[1] Thus, law enforcement authorities returned works to claimants and their heirs this past year, either through seizure or by obtaining the voluntary agreement of the holder.

### 1998 Washington Conference on Holocaust Assets Reprise with 2009 Prague Conference

The tenth anniversary of the 1998 Washington Conference on Holocaust-Era Assets[2] and the long-anticipated Prague Conference on Holocaust-Era Assets, which was held in June 2009 as a follow-up, dominated much of the dialogue about appropriate handling of claims related to Nazi art looting. The 1998 Conference had established the Washington Principles,[3] which sought greater transparency and reduced contentiousness in claims handling by calling on museums and private individual collectors—but mostly museums—to seek "just and fair" solutions to art restitution claims based on allegations of Nazi confiscation. These principles, nonbinding but endorsed by the more than 40 countries attending, signaled the interest of Western governments in seeing ethical and moral solutions to such art claims, not just legalistic results based on technical arguments and protracted proceedings. The Prague Conference sought to assess the art world's progress in effectuating these principles with regard to market transactions, museum holdings and collecting, and the actions of private collectors and to propose actions to address perceived shortcomings.

The Prague Conference, while recognizing the continued importance of provenance research as the foundation for decision making, focused, perhaps more than expected, on European issues, reflecting the interests of the vast majority of the attendees. Under postwar arrangements, Allied powers returned Nazi-looted artworks to the countries from which each object was initially displaced, including Germany, and those governments continue to hold works never restituted to their original owners, in addition to objects obtained since the beginning of the Nazi era through purchase, donation, or other means. European countries have, since 1998, created research bodies and decision-making tribunals to address claims that may not have been properly or fairly considered after the war. In connection with the Prague Conference, participants issued the Terezin Declaration,[4] approved by 46 countries, renewing their commitment to the Washington Principles of openness and fairness and calling on private collectors to follow the same standards for resolving claims of Nazi art looting.

Since the Prague Conference and the Terezin Declaration failed to address directly those uniquely U.S. restitution issues—this country has no national collection built on unrestituted Nazi-looted art objects and most American museums are private, not government-owned—the State Department has sought to identify the most pressing American issues and brainstorm possible solutions. Beginning in late 2009, after Prague, and stretching into 2010, the State Department has been holding a series of town hall meetings in search of a consensus within the restitution community—that is, law enforcement officials, historians, claimants' representatives, museums, auction houses, collectors, and others—on the formation of a U.S. Art Commission that would in some manner address unresolved issues. The project is still in the discussion phase, so it is too early to predict the form such a commission would take or its likely impact on the art market. The central points of concern appear to be (1) finding increased resources for provenance research to assist claimants and holders alike; (2) facilitating settlements of claims, through mediation or otherwise; and (3) resolving disputed claims openly, consistently, and fairly through a newly created tribunal of disinterested and distinguished experts.

The point of greatest contention now is the demand by claimants' representatives that American museums forswear reliance on statute of limitations and laches defenses related to the passage of time, matched by museum insistence that such defenses represent significant and substantive legal principles and not just technicalities and, additionally, that museums are particularly justified in raising statute of limitations defenses when faced with a doubtful claim of Nazi art looting. Because of the passage of time since World War II and the Holocaust, and because objects of concern in the U.S. have typically moved here through the art market, the outcome of the State Department's town hall meetings and the progress of any U.S. commission will be closely watched for signs of future trends. Artworks subject to a substantial claim of Nazi looting continue to appear on the art market with some regularity, but not so frequently can they move freely through the art market as they once did. Nonetheless, the risk of continued movement of looted objects through the art market and the consequences of past movement seem destined to bring increased levels of diligence and, perhaps, greater transparency to the art market, just as levels of contentiousness remain relatively high between and among the stakeholders in this area.

## War and Restitution

In April 2009, Hearst Castle, part of the California State Parks system (CSP), reached agreement to restitute two oil paintings to the heirs of Jakob and Rosa Oppenheimer, Berlin art dealers whom the Nazis forced to liquidate their galleries, known as the Margraf group, in 1935. Under the agreement, Hearst Castle would retain a third Oppenheimer painting in its collection. The Oppenheimer heirs' attorney had spotted the artworks in a 1976 pamphlet about art at the estate and notified the museum about the claim.[5] William Randolph Hearst had purchased the paintings from a Berlin gallery in 1935 and brought them to the United States. With the donation of the Hearst Castle and its collections to CSP, the paintings came into possession of California, which settled the case with the Oppenheimer heirs. After investigation, CSP accepted the claimants' position; as stated in California's Press Release, "After the Nazis seized power in Germany, the Oppenheimers were subjected to racial and ethnic persecution, ultimately being forced to give up control of their art business and flee to Vichy, France. The Nazis sold the artwork at auction in April 1935, but neither the Oppenheimers nor their heirs benefited from the revenue of the sale. The proceeds went to pay the Reichfluchtsteuer (Reich flight tax) and other related punitive and confiscatory taxes designed to strip Jews of assets."[6]

Two other 2009 Nazi art looting restitutions stem from a major U.S. court decision issued in November 2008 concerning a similar Nazi order under which a Jewish art dealer sold off his inventory without receiving the proceeds. In *Vineberg v. Bissonnette* the First Circuit Court of Appeals in 2008 affirmed a lower court's decision to order return of a disputed work, Franz Xaver Winterhalter's *Girl from the Sabiner Mountains*, because the National Socialist government had improperly ordered Jewish art gallery owner Dr. Max Stern to liquidate his entire inventory in 1937.[7] The defendant inherited the painting from her stepfather, who purchased it at the 1937 auction. *Vineberg* became the first U.S. court decision to hold a Nazi order to sell to be equivalent to a confiscation and, therefore, a theft.[8] The decision strongly suggested, at the very least, that all Stern paintings in the 1937 auction had been ordered sold by the government and were therefore the subject of Nazi confiscation.

The art market felt the implications of the *Vineberg* case more broadly in 2009, when the Stern Estate recovered two artworks as a result of the widely publicized First Circuit decision. In April 2009, ICE restituted a Stern painting entitled *Portrait of a Musician Playing a Bagpipe*, which had also been sold in the 1937 Cologne auction. A former Holocaust Claims Processing Office (HCPO) research assistant located the painting at the Manhattan art gallery Lawrence Steigard Fine Arts. Gallery owner Steigard acquired the painting from a London dealer, who had earlier purchased it from the same Cologne auction house that sold Stern's paintings in 1937. These market transactions occurred openly, even though the Stern Estate had since 2004 listed the painting with a stolen art registry, Art Loss Register (ALR). ALR explained that due to differences in title ("musician" instead of "bagpipe player"), it missed the painting when searching its database. Steigard consented to ICE's seizure of the painting for return to the Stern Estate, and ICE turned the painting over to the Stern Estate representatives in a ceremony at the Museum of Jewish Heritage in New York on April 21, 2009, Holocaust Remembrance Day.[9]

Within a matter of weeks, publicity concerning restitution of *Portrait of a Musician Playing a Bagpipe* led to another return. In 2000, New York art dealer Richard Feigen had purchased a painting—again from the same Cologne auction house—which turned out to be another product of the 1937 Stern auction: a picture of St. Jerome in the wilderness, attributed to Ludovico Carracci. Feigen learned about the Steigard restitution, conducted his own research on the Carracci, determined that it was indeed from the Stern auction, and contacted the Stern Estate. ICE picked up the painting from Feigen and arranged for its return to the estate.[10]

Further fallout from the Stern Estate's recoveries affects Maria-Louise Bissonnette, the defendant in *Vineberg*; ICE investigators searched her apartment in October 2009, presumably looking for evidence of criminal activity connected to *Girl from the Sabiner Mountains*, which Bissonnette had shipped to Germany after learning of the Stern Estate claim, or information concerning other Stern artworks. Although ICE gave no reason for the search, agents apparently gave Bissonnette and her husband a document specifying that they were looking for items, including artwork, related to the sale or transfer of art illegally imported to the United States. They were also in search of evidence that showed the sale or transfer of goods that were taken by forced sale by Maria-Louise's stepfather.[11] It seems that as a result of the earlier court decisions, ICE is pursuing evidence that Bissonnette knew *Girl from the Sabiner Mountains* was stolen when she exported it to Germany or that Bissonnette's stepfather may have purchased other looted objects that the family later brought into the United States.

In 2009, a portrait by Antoine (Anto) Carte was returned to its owner after the Art Loss Register located it at a Long Island gallery owned by Andre Sakhai. The family had fled Brussels to hide in the Belgian countryside during the war; occupation forces looted their abandoned apartment in 1944. The family filed a claim for the stolen Carte portrait and four other paintings in 1946 and, more recently, listed it with ALR. ALR's database of stolen art included the painting, although it is unclear from public reports when the work was entered.[12] ALR located the painting in 2008 and contacted ICE for assistance. When presented with the evidence of looting, Sakhai reportedly cooperated in forfeiting the painting.

Late in the year, ICE also returned a two-volume Rabbinic Bible dating from the 16th century to the Jewish Community in Vienna, known as Israelitische Kultusgemeinde Wien (IKG). Nazi soldiers seized and sealed IKG's library on November 9, 1938 during Kristallnacht, later transferring large portions of the collection to Berlin, Poland, and North Bohemia (now the Czech Republic). The Bible was illegally imported into the United States on March 19, 2009, with a New York City auction house subsequently offering it for sale in June 2009. The auction house withdrew it from sale upon receiving proof of the Bible's provenance and ownership, and ICE returned it to IKG at a ceremony on the 71st anniversary of Kristallnacht.[13]

Emphasizing the importance of issues related to the passage of time, Claudia Seger-Thomschitz, heir of Jewish collector Oskar Reichel, lost two cases, both brought against her by holders to quiet title, one filed by Sarah Blodgett Dunbar in the Eastern District of Louisiana and the other filed by Museum of Fine Arts, Boston, in the District of Massachusetts. MFA had received its contested painting by Oskar Kokoschka entitled *Two Nudes (Lovers)* as a bequest from Dunbar's mother, so the two cases concern the same historical transactions. Seger-Thomschitz argued primarily that each painting had been effectively confiscated by the Nazis when Reichel listed them on an asset registration form that Jews were required to submit. She also claimed that Reichel had been under pressure due to Nazi persecution when he sent the paintings, along with other works, to Austrian art dealer Otto Kallir in 1939.

Both courts voiced skepticism about whether the artworks in question had been the subject of Nazi art looting—Reichel had developed a long-standing relationship with art dealer Kallir, who took steps to protect Reichel's interest by paying sale proceeds to Reichel's sons in New York. The Massachusetts court noted, for example, that although the Reichel family claimed restitution after the war for other artworks it thought had been stolen by the Nazis, it "never claimed compensation for any of the Kokoschka works that had been transferred to Kallir for sale."[14] Each decision thus rested solely on issues related to the passage of time.

In the MFA case, presently on appeal before the First Circuit U.S. Court of Appeals, the district court granted the museum summary judgment because the painting had, without question, been publicly displayed and its location "readily ascertainable" since 1945. In addition, the painting had hung at MFA almost continuously since 1973. Judge Rya Zobel of the U.S. District Court for Massachusetts ruled therefore that the three-year statute of limitations had passed.[15]

Seger-Thomschitz lost the Louisiana case following a similar factual analysis, although the governing legal regime differed. The Court ruled that plaintiff Dunbar had continuous, uninterrupted possession of Kokoschka's *Portrait of a Youth* since she inherited it from her mother in 1973, thus satisfying the Louisiana Civil Code ten-year condition for ownership by prescription. Prescription under the Louisiana Code requires neither title nor good faith, just ten years uninterrupted possession. The Court also considered Seger-Thomschitz's counterclaims, but found that family members had shown no interest in seeking compensation for the Kokoschka work—despite its location being ascertainable—although they had claimed recompense for other losses after the War.[16] Thus, a museum case and one involving a private collector, in jurisdictions with very different legal traditions—the discovery rule in Massachusetts and ownership by prescription in Louisiana—yielded the same result for similar reasons: claim dismissed due to the claimant's lack of diligence in seeking to recover lost art.

*Schoeps v. Museum of Modern Art and Solomon R. Guggenheim Foundation* ended in 2009, in a manner unsatisfactory to many observers: confidential settlement. In 2007, both museums sued Julius Schoeps in response to his demands for restitution of two Picasso paintings, the 1906 *Boy Leading a Horse* at MoMA and the 1900 *Le Moulin de la Galette* at the Guggenheim. Schoeps asserted that both paintings had been sold under duress during the Nazi era and properly belonged to him as an heir to Paul von Mendelssohn-Bartholdy. At the time the museums filed suit, they issued a joint press release asserting: "Evidence from our extensive research makes clear the museums' ownership of these works and also makes clear that Mr. Schoeps has no basis for his claim."[17]

Both MoMA and Guggenheim settled their cases, but under strictly confidential terms. The museums offered to publicize the settlement terms; Schoeps refused. Judge Rakoff, who had entered an interim ruling indicating his view that Schoeps had been forced to sell the paintings and also refusing to dismiss Schoeps' claims for lack of standing,[18] expressed deep dissatisfaction with the lack of transparency, stating in a memorandum issued about two months after the settlement that it "baffles the mind and troubles the conscience" that Schoeps and his relatives would keep the settlement out of the public eye. At this time, the terms remain private,[19] as do the terms of most settlements based on claims of Nazi art looting. This secrecy, perhaps unavoidable, is nevertheless unfortunate. Along the lines of Judge Rakoff's statement, not just claimants and holders of disputed art, but market participants—buyers, sellers, dealers, and auction houses—would benefit from understanding the settlement terms reached in light of the facts of the *MoMA/Guggenheim* case. Only in this way can settlements serve as legitimate precedents; lack of transparency in settlements makes informed decision making difficult for future disputants.

Another Schoeps case was settled at the very beginning of 2010, this one against the Andrew Lloyd Webber Art Foundation for restitution of Picasso's *The Absinthe Drinker* (*Angel Ferdinand de Soto*). In August 2009, the Appellate Division of the New York State Supreme Court, First Department, affirmed dismissal of Schoeps' complaint on the grounds that he lacked standing to represent the heirs. Disagreeing with Judge Rakoff's decision on the exact same point of law, the New York State court ruled that Schoeps could not act on behalf of the heirs without first being appointed representative of the decedent's estate.[20] Just after the start of 2010, Schoeps and the Webber Art Foundation announced a settlement of their lawsuit under terms that would remain "confidential in their entirety."[21]

Several foreign restitution headlines in 2009 concerned Austria. In March 2009, the City of Vienna agreed to return a painting entitled *The Death of Pappenheim* by Austrian artist Hans Makart to the heirs of Herbert Gutmann. After the Nazis came to power in 1933, they forced Gutmann, a German Jewish banker, to sell his possessions; he then fled to Britain. The City Council of Vienna elected unanimously to return the work, even though Austrian restitution law covers only events in Austria after Hitler's annexation in 1938 through the defeat of Nazi Germany in 1945.[22]

Just two months later, Austria announced repatriation to the Czech Republic of more than $600,000 worth of objects looted by the Nazis from the Vyssi Brod Monastery in 1941 and transferred to Linz. Objects to be returned include art, musical instruments, and weapons.[23]

In another European return story, in September Moderna Museet of Stockholm, Sweden, agreed to return the 1917 painting *Blumengarten (Utenwarf)* by German artist Emil Nolde in September, which disappeared in 1939 after Otto Nathan Deutsch fled Germany to the Netherlands to escape persecution. A private collector agreed to purchase the painting, then lend it to the Moderna Museet for up to five years, "after which other seminal expressionist paintings from the early 20th century will be lent to the museum for another five years."[24]

In Germany, a restitution that caught a lot of international attention involved Peter Sachs, son of poster collector and Jewish dentist Hans Sachs.

The Nazi government seized Hans Sachs' collection in 1938; soon thereafter, he fled Germany with his family. A Berlin court ruled in February that a poster by Thomas Theodor Heine was owned by Sachs, not the Museum of German History (Deutsches Historisches Museum), thus setting up potential returns of over 4,000 posters that once belonged to Sachs' father. The case attracted controversy because Sachs had first presented his claim to the German commission specially created to hear claims based on allegations of Nazi looting, but it had been rejected on the grounds that partial compensation had been provided after the war. The attorney who handled the case says there is evidence that many of the seized posters were later sold at auction in West Germany.[25] The museum has said it plans to appeal.

In another World War II–related case, a court effected restitution of artwork taken by an American Army officer. In March 2009, the U.S. District Court for the Southern District of New York ordered Rod Shene, a self-described book scout from St. Louis, to return a rare sixteenth century volume of German prints and drawings known as the *Augsburger Geschlechterbuch* ("Augsburg Book of Genealogy" or "Augsburg Book of Nobles") to the State of Baden-Württemberg.[26] The Staatsgalerie Stuttgart ("Stuttgart State Art Gallery") stored the volume in Waldenburg Castle late in World War II for protection, but vicious fighting occurred in the vicinity of the castle and, after the battle, Staatsgalerie's investigation indicated the volume had been destroyed by fire. In fact, a U.S. Army Captain stationed at Waldenburg had taken the volume home to Missouri, along with other books, where it sat on his home bookshelf for decades until several years after his death. The volume then moved to a St. Louis auctioneer and then on to Shene, who consigned it to Sotheby's in 2004. Sotheby's noticed museum stamps on the volume's pages and contacted the Staatsgalerie, which claimed ownership. The Court found Baden-Württemberg to be the legal owner of the volume, and granted its motion for summary judgment on replevin and conversion.[27]

Thus, Staatsgalerie's *Book of Nobles* passed through the hands of two art market professionals in St. Louis, and was viewed by other dealers at a private auction there, before Sotheby's received the book and noticed museum stamps marked on the back of every page. The case, therefore, appears to reflect a large gap in the diligence exercised by the top echelon of the art market compared to smaller and individual dealers and auction houses, particularly those outside major art market centers—one of the St. Louis transactions with the Staatsgalerie's volume took place at a private auction held in the auctioneer's bedroom. As one reporter noted in the wake of the Prague Conference, "Both Christie's and Sotheby's now have restitution specialists and due diligence programs in place that minimize the risk of selling looted art. . . . Unfortunately, Christie's, Sotheby's and Austria's Dorotheum remain the exception in the art market, and smaller houses and private dealers, lacking either interest or resources, have yet to implement such restitution and provenance mechanisms."[28] How to close that diligence gap is an important question for art market professionals, heirs, governments, and others, since many lost objects are not high value and thus do not necessarily move through Sotheby's, Christie's, or other premier auctioneers or dealers.

Finally, the longest-running Nazi art looting art restitution case, filed in the Southern District of New York in 1999 after several years in New York State court, yielded a 100+ page slip opinion on a pretrial decision: Judge Loretta A. Preska of the Southern District of New York ruled that the forfeiture action *United States of America v. Portrait of Wally, A Painting by Egon Schiele,* would have to be tried.[29] The well-known case concerns a Schiele painting that had been sent to the United States on loan from the Leopold Foundation for an exhibition at the Museum of Modern Art. Just as the painting was about to return to Austria, New York's District Attorney seized it under a criminal investigatory subpoena. Eventually, the New York Court of Appeals ruled the subpoena was invalid under a state law preventing judicial seizure of artwork loaned to museums for exhibition. The United States then initiated federal civil forfeiture proceedings which have themselves dragged on for more than 10 years.

In her comprehensive decision resolving cross motions for summary judgment, Judge Preska rejected most of the Leopold Foundation's arguments, holding that the only question remaining for trial was whether Dr. Rudolph Leopold, predecessor-in-interest to the foundation, knew the painting had been stolen from Lea Bondi Jaray during the period of Nazi rule in Austria. Preska concluded that neither the Act of State doctrine nor the doctrine of International Comity required dismissal of the case based on a balancing of interests of the parties, primarily because Austria, which had been responsible for the allegedly defective restitution of *Portrait* after the War, did not have a significant interest in protecting its postwar restitution decisions from judicial scrutiny in the United States. The heart of Judge Preska's decision addresses the merits of the claims and defenses concerning forfeiture, in particular, considering whether the government had made out a *prima facie* case that a Nazi agent had stolen the painting during the Nazi era. Although the exact facts of Bondi's loss of the painting to a Frederic Welz were hotly contested, Judge Preska found she could rule that there were no material disputed facts that Welz, a Nazi, "stole *Wally* from Bondi by demanding it from her at a time when she could not refuse."[30] The Museum argued, nonetheless, that Leopold did not know the painting had been stolen when he acquired it after the war; however, the presence of suspicious circumstances in its Nazi-era movement requires trial to establish his knowledge or lack thereof.

Conventional wisdom might suggest that the volume of World War II and Holocaust art claims would be dropping as the years and decades pass, but the many restitution decisions and settlements in 2009 clearly show no reduction yet. Improved transparency and increased diligence practiced by some high-level art market participants domestically and internationally can be credited with finding looted art and locating the proper owners—even 65 years after the war. Moreover, 2009's Prague Conference reminded many art market participants—governments, museums, collectors, dealers, galleries, and others—to refocus their efforts not only on defining standards for restitution, but also on applying those standards in a meaningful way to existing collections and market transactions.

### Non-War-Related Thefts and Restitution

This past year's emphasis on standards for restitution, diligence, and transparency was not limited to Holocaust or World War II–related stories. The Cleveland Museum of Art, for example, honoring an agreement reached with Italy in November 2008, announced in April that it will return 14 artworks claimed to have been smuggled out of that country. Italy, in turn, will loan the Cleveland Museum 13 objects of comparable quality for renewable 25-year periods, and will cooperate on future special exhibitions.[31]

Standards for diligence and transparency also affect Native American tribes which rely on similar themes in their efforts to protect their cultural property. In May, the Onondaga nation complained to Sotheby's about two belts scheduled for auction and the auction house removed the objects from the sale. A lawyer for the Onondaga nation explained in a letter to Sotheby's that the belts are community property and not owned by one person. "Therefore, these belts were originally taken out of these communities without proper 'title.'"[32] In addition to title, the Onondaga attorney raised concerns about whether the belts had been properly deaccessioned from the National Museum of the

American Indian in New York. Problems with applying the Anglo-American concept of title to Native American objects are not new, and will continue to present challenges to museums and collectors.

## Dealers and Auction Houses

2009 also saw legal developments concerning commercial issues facing consignors, buyers, auction houses, and dealers. The collapse of Salander-O'Reilly Galleries, which filed for Chapter 11 bankruptcy in November 2007, continued to generate significant legal issues. Lawrence Salander and the galleries were charged in March 2009 with 100 counts of fraud and theft concerning property with a total value of $88 million. The State of New York brought new charges over the summer, bringing the total to $93 million and adding a gallery director as a criminal defendant. Salander allegedly defrauded prominent individuals both in and outside the art world—including the estate of Robert De Niro, Sr. (father of the actor), tennis star John McEnroe, and Earl Davis, son of American modernist painter Stuart Davis—by selling the same artworks to multiple buyers, selling consigned works without informing the owners, and falsifying business documents. For example, in 2006 Earl Davis reportedly asked Salander to account for 96 missing paintings by his father consigned to the gallery and suggested that attorneys resolve the disagreement; Salander refused to cooperate, emailing that "It will not be pretty but believe me Earl I don't think you understand what you would be in for."[33]

The Salander bankruptcy and related fraud claims come as a startling glimpse into the business side of the art world, where some dealers—despite recent improvements in transparency and accountability—continue to operate on a handshake-and-smile basis. The Manhattan district attorney Robert M. Morgenthau remarked that "The moral of [the Salander] case is, be careful who you sign your artwork to,"[34] but the more significant question is how much the average consignor can really do to protect himself in a scenario like Salander-O'Reilly, when artworks are regularly consigned, bought, and sold with little or no documentation.

Just as bankruptcy laws have provided little comfort to consignors trying to recover from Salander in bankruptcy proceedings, transactional laws also provide little protection for consignors, as evidenced by a 2009 decision from the Southern District of New York. In *Brown, as Trustee of Deca Trust v. Mitchell-Innes & Nash*, Deca Trust consigned Edvard Munch's *Mystery of the*

*Beach* to New York art dealer Mitchell-Innes & Nash (MIN) to solicit offers for purchase.[35] A written consignment agreement between Deca Trust and MIN detailed the limitations on MIN's authority—such as the requirement to obtain written permission before moving the painting off MIN's premises or selling it. Nevertheless, MIN shipped the painting to Germany to be viewed by a potential buyer and sold it to that buyer, all without informing Deca Trust personnel. Deca Trust settled its claims against MIN, then sought to recover the painting from the German company that had bought it.

Judge Crotty dismissed the Trust's claims in April, ruling that New York's Uniform Commercial Code protected the buyer, since it purchased the painting from a merchant and no red flags surrounded the purchase that would create doubt in the buyer's mind regarding the propriety of the sale.[36] In short, the dealer disregarded instructions from its consignor, as set forth in a binding contract, yet because the buyer had no apparent warning, the consignor had no means under the law to recover the improperly transferred artwork.

Finally, major auction house Christie's had legal developments on several fronts.[37] In February, Christie's International handled the auction of the Yves Saint Laurent auction in Europe, which raised 373.9 million Euros and sold over 95% of its lots. The refusal of Chinese art dealer Cai Mingchao to pay for two Qing bronzes, however, marred the auction. The bronze sculptures of a rabbit and a rat were taken from the Old Summer Palace in Beijing by invading soldiers in 1860. China tried to stop the auctioning of these pieces, but a Paris court ruled just days before the auction that it could go forward. Cai won the bronzes by bidding $40 million, then declined to pay. Cai claims that he intended to pay at the time he bid, but after hearing that China's State Administration of Cultural Heritage issued a circular requiring Christie's to detail ownership and provenance of artifacts imported into or exported from China, he had second thoughts.[38]

In September, the plaintiffs in *Doss v. Christie's* sued the auction house for various breach of warranty claims and related claims based upon their 1991 purchase of a Marie Laurencin painting entitled *Portrait*. Doss had taken *Portrait* to Sotheby's to sell it in 2006, and Sotheby's told Doss the painting had been stolen from Paul Rosenberg, a well-known prewar Paris art dealer. Plaintiffs' lawsuit sought a full refund of the purchase price and damages. Judge Preska in the Southern District of New York dismissed the claims on New York statute of limitations grounds, eighteen years having passed since the purchase. The Court read literally the Uniform Commercial Code provision, setting a four-year limitations period running from date of sale for breach of warranty claims, declining to find any exceptions or to apply the demand-and-refusal rule to toll the accrual of the claims.[39]

In part as a reaction to Holocaust-looted art continuing to turn up at auction, Christie's is taking steps to provide consignors and buyers with additional guidance and predictability by issuing Guidelines for Dealing with Holocaust Art Restitution Issues. Announced in June,[40] the guidelines concentrate on transparency in claim handling and provide a role for the auction house as intermediary. Under the guidelines, Christie's will work with consignors to establish the provenance of an object that may have Nazi-era issues, conduct its own research if needed, find the potential claimant if possible, and share information and documentation with both sides. The guidelines also stress Christie's offer to help find an amicable, just, and fair resolution in the event potential claimants want to recover the object. Christie's guidelines set out an approach that seeks to reach a merits-based resolution to satisfy both sides, rather than resorting to litigation that sometimes turns on what some consider technicalities. Christie's is the first major auction house to publish its restitution policy.

## Conclusion

Developing standards for what should be considered Nazi art looting or forced sales dominated 2009 restitution cases and the Prague Conference. Issues related to the passage of time also continue to play a central role in legal developments, with claimants frequently on the losing side. In response, claimants' representatives call for decision making on the merits of a claim of Nazi spoliation, but museums reserve the right to argue statute of limitations in appropriate cases. Federal law enforcement, particularly ICE, demonstrated increased involvement and effectiveness in restitution issues in 2009. Against this background of litigiousness, diligence and transparency continue to be the watchwords for self-protection in the art market.

## Notes

1. See Cultural Heritage Investigations and Repatriations, http://www.ice.gov/pi/news/factsheets/cultural-artifacts-repatriation.htm.
2. Available at http://www.state.gov/www/regions/eur/wash_conf_material.html.

3. Available at http://www.state.gov/p/eur/rt/hlcst/122038.htm.
4. Available at http://www. www.holocausteraassets.eu/files/200000215-35d8ef1a36/TEREZIN_DECLARATION_FINAL.pdf.
5. Samantha Young, *Hearst Castle returns art to heirs of German Jewish owners*, THE ASSOCIATED PRESS, April 16, 2009.
6. Press Release, *Gov. Schwarznegger Returns Holocaust-Era Artwork to Heirs of Jewish Family*, April 10, 2009, available at http://gov.ca.gov/press-release/11989/.
7. The authors represented the Trustees of the Max Stern Estate in this case.
8. *Vineberg v. Bissonnette*, 548 F.3d 50 (1st Cir. 2008).
9. Catherine Hickley, *U.S. Seizes Old Master Lost in Nazi-Era Forced Sale*, BLOOMBERG, April 21, 2009; Press Release, *United States Returns Painting, Expropriated by Nazis, to the Estate of Its Rightful Owner, Dr. Max Stern*, April 21, 2009, available at http://www.justice.gov/usao/nys/pressreleases/April09/bagpipeplayerrepatriationpr.pdf.
10. Catherine Hickley, *Dealer Returns Paintings Lost in Nazi-Era Forced Sale*, BLOOMBERG, May 6, 2009.
11. Glenn Osmundson, *Providence couple embroiled in search for Nazi art,* THE PROVIDENCE JOURNAL, Nov. 5, 2009.
12. Press Release, *The Art Loss Register: A Child's Portrait, Looted During the War, is Returned to its Owner; Painting returned with the Help of the Art Loss Register*, Dec. 3, 2009.
13. Press Release, U.S. Immigration and Customs Enforcement, *ICE returns 16th century Hebrew Bible looted by Nazis*, Nov. 9, 2009.
14. *Memorandum of Decision and Order*, *Museum of Fine Arts v. Seger-Thomschitz*, Civil Action No. 08-10097, 2009 U.S. Dist. LEXIS 58826 (D. Mass. May 28, 2009).
15. Geoff Edgers, *MFA wins legal claim to valuable painting*, THE BOSTON GLOBE, May 30, 2009. An appeal of the district court's decision in *Museum of Fine Arts v. Seger-Thomschitz* has been docketed with the United States Court of Appeals for the First Circuit (No. 09-1922).
16. Order and Reasons in *Dunbar v. Seger-Thomschitz,* 638 F. Supp. 2d 659 (E.D. La. 2009).
17. MoMA and Guggenheim Foundation Issue Statement Regarding Two Paintings, artdaily.org, available at http://www.artdaily.com/index.asp?int_sec=11&int_new=22614&int_modo=2.
18. *Schoeps v. The Museum of Modern Art*, 594 F. Supp. 2d 461, 466-67 (S.D.N.Y. 2009).
19. Philip Boroff and Lindsay Pollock, *Judge Slams MoMA, Guggenheim on Secret Holocaust Art Agreement*, BLOOMBERG, June 18, 2009.
20. *Schoeps v. The Andrew Lloyd Weber Art Foundation,* 66 A.D.2d 137, 884 N.Y.S.2d 396 (2009).

21. *Heirs Relinquish Claim to £30 M Holocaust Picasso, Times Online*, January 11,2010, available at http://entertainment.timesonline.co.uk/tol/arts_and_entertainment/visual_arts/article6982955.ece.
22. *City of Vienna gives up art expropriated in Nazi Germany*, REUTERS, April 2, 2009.
23. *Austria returns looted art to Czech monastery*, THE ASSOCIATED PRESS, May 8, 2009.
24. *Press Release in re. settlement Blumengarten*, Moderna Museet, Sept. 14, 2009.
25. Craig Whitlock, *Winning Back a Family Legacy*, WASHINGTON POST FOREIGN SERVICE, Feb. 11, 2009.
26. The authors represented the State of Baden-Württemberg in this case.
27. *Sotheby's v. Shene*, 04 Civ. 10067, 2009 WL 762697 (S.D.N.Y. Mar. 23, 2009).
28. Yael I. Friedman, The Road to Restitution, *ArtInfo, Financial Times*, available at http://www.artinfo.com/news/story/31924/the-road-to-restitution/?printer_friendly=1.
29. *United States v. Portrait of Wally*, No. 99 Civ. 9940 (LAP), 2009 U.S. Dist. LEXIS 91464 (S.D.N.Y. Sept. 30, 2009) (denying motions for summary judgment).
30. *Id.*
31. Steven Litt, *Cleveland Museum of Art will return tainted antiquities to Italy Wednesday*, THE PLAIN DEALER, April 22, 2009.
32. James Barron, *2 Disputed Indian Wampum Belts Pulled from Auction*, NEW YORK TIMES, May 18, 2009. To the authors' knowledge, this dispute remains unresolved at the time of this writing.
33. Karen Zraick, *New Charges Brought in Art Fraud Case*, NEW YORK TIMES, July 14, 2009; Philip Boroff and Lindsay Pollock, *'Broken' Dealer Salander Is Arrested on Fraud Charges*, BLOOMBERG, March 27, 2009.
34. Quoted in Zraick, *New Charges Brought in Art Fraud Case, supra.*
35. The authors represented Nathaniel T. Brown, as Trustee of Deca Trust, in this case.
36. *Brown, as Trustee of Deca Trust v. Mitchell-Innes & Nash*, No. 06 CIV. 7871 (PAC), 2009 WL 1108526 (S.D.N.Y. Apr. 24, 2009).
37. The authors' firm, Andrews Kurth LLP, is a member of Christie's global art panel.
38. Le-Min Lim, *Chinese Art Dealer Weeps After Refusing to Pay for YSL Bronzes*, BLOOMBERG, March 9, 2009.
39. *Doss v. Christie's*, No. 08 Civ. 10577 (LAP), 2009 WL 3053713 (S.D.N.Y. Sept. 23, 2009). The authors represent Christie's in the *Doss* case. The case is still pending; plaintiffs requested leave to file an amended complaint.
40. *See* Remarks of Monica S. Dugot, Restitution and the Art Market: Combining Business and Morals—The Perspective from 2009, available at: http://www.holocausteraassets.eu/files/200000237-a735ff3411/WG_LA_2_4_Dugot.pdf.

# International Cultural Property

• • •

*Section Editor:*
*Patty Gerstenblith*

## Introduction

In 2009, nearly fifty-five years after the United States played a major role in the drafting of the first international convention to address the protection of cultural property exclusively, the United States became a party to the 1954 Hague Convention on the Protection of Cultural Property in the Event of Armed Conflict. New developments concerning the United States' implementation of the 1970 UNESCO Convention on the Means of Prohibiting and Preventing the Illicit Import, Export and Transfer of Ownership of Cultural Property through its legislation, the Convention on Cultural Property Implementation Act, continue to expand and test the parameters of the role of the United States in this international treaty regime. A decision concerning a painting looted during the Holocaust equally tests the extent of foreign sovereign immunity afforded under the Foreign Sovereign Immunities Act. Finally, claims, recoveries, and restitution of looted, smuggled, and stolen cultural artifacts continued.

## International Conventions and Agreements

### The 1954 Hague Convention on the Protection of Cultural Property in the Event of Armed Conflict

On March 13, 2009, the United States deposited its instrument of ratification of the 1954 Hague Convention on the Protection of Cultural Property in the Event of Armed Conflict, thus becoming the Convention's 123rd High Contracting Party.[1] The United States ratification became effective immediately under Article 33(3), as a State currently engaged in armed conflict with or occupation of another State Party. The United States was the only nation to ratify or otherwise join the main Convention during this year. There were no new States Parties to the First Protocol, which addresses movable cultural objects removed from occupied territory, but five nations, Germany, Italy, Jordan, Bosnia and Herzegovina, and the Dominican Republic, ratified the Second Protocol, which expands upon and strengthens the main Convention.[2]

New Zealand, which ratified the main Convention in July 2008, continued to consider implementing legislation, the Cultural Property (Protection in Armed Conflict) Bill, for the First and Second Protocols.[3] The revised bill was given a second reading in Parliament in August 2009. The original legislation was amended to clarify that there would not be universal jurisdiction for grave violation offenses; rather, a person who commits an offense in the territory of a Party to the Second Protocol and then comes to New Zealand may be prosecuted.[4]

### 1970 UNESCO Convention on the Means of Prohibiting and Preventing the Illicit Import, Export and Transfer of Ownership of Cultural Property

Two nations joined the 1970 UNESCO Convention—Belgium and the Netherlands.[5] While the number of new States Parties is small, both of these nations are international art market nations and so their joining of the international treaty regime to regulate the flow of artworks is significant.

There were several developments concerning the United States' implementation of the 1970 UNESCO Convention through its legislation, the Convention on Cultural Property Implementation Act (CPIA).[6] The first development, which caused little reaction, was the renewal and extension of its memorandum of understanding (MOU) with Honduras.[7] Such agreements, which impose restrictions on the importation of archaeological and/or ethnographic materials into the United States, last for a maximum of five years but may be renewed an unlimited number of times. This was the second renewal for the agreement with Honduras and continues import restrictions on pre-Columbian archaeological materials.

In a far more controversial move, the United States concluded a memorandum of understanding with China,[8] which had been under consideration for four years.[9] Items subject to import restriction include archaeological materials of the Paleolithic (beginning c. 75,000 B.C.) through the Tang Dynasty (ending A.D. 907),[10] such as ceramic vessels, sculpture, architectural decoration, and molds; stone, such as jade ornaments and jewelry, vessels and weapons, relief sculpture, cave and grotto temple art, stelae, and architectural elements; metal, including vessels, sculpture and coins; silks and textiles; lacquer and wood. The agreement also covers monumental sculpture and wall art that is at least 250 years old, the minimum age requirement for archaeological materials to be subject to import restriction under the CPIA.[11]

In addition to listing the designated categories of archaeological and ethnological materials that will be subject to import restriction, the bilateral agreements in Article II set out actions that both nations are expected to take during the five years of the agreement. The provisions of Article II are important in delineating mutual actions and collaborative efforts that make the bilateral agreements a positive force for improving cultural relations as well as for ensuring better protection of cultural heritage.

Article II in the U.S.–China agreement encourages both nations to improve effectiveness of their customs officers in interdicting illegal import and export of Chinese archaeological materials and training them in recognizing Chinese archaeological material. In addition, China is expected to make greater efforts to educate its citizens about the importance of safeguarding its rich cultural heritage; broaden archaeological research; prevent archaeological material looted or stolen from the Mainland from entering Hong Kong Special Administrative Region and the Macao Special Administrative Region; promote additional long-term loans of Chinese archaeological objects to a broad cross-section of American museums for public exhibition, education, and research purposes; increase collaboration among and exchange of students and professionals; facilitate the grant of permits for archaeological research in China; improve regulation of China's internal market for antiquities; prevent museums in Mainland China from acquiring those archaeological objects subject to import restriction into the United States unless the objects left China legally or before the date of the U.S. import restrictions; and explore ways of making the legal export of antiquities more available.

In the first reported decision to interpret the import restrictions imposed under the CPIA and the procedures for forfeiture under this statute,[12] a federal court ordered the forfeiture of two paintings that were illegally imported into the United States in violation of the memorandum of understanding between the United States and Peru.[13] Noting that forfeitures under Title 19 of the United States Code, including those under the CPIA, are exempted from the procedural requirements of the Civil Asset Forfeiture Reform Act,[14] the court set out the procedural steps for forfeiture under the CPIA.[15] The government has the initial burden of showing that the imported materials are designated ethnological materials under the CPIA pursuant to a bilateral agreement. Once the government makes its prima facie case for forfeiture by meeting this initial burden, the burden shifts to the claimant to rebut this showing, which in this case the claimant failed to do.[16]

The claimant's primary argument in rebuttal was that the paintings originated in Bolivia rather than in Peru. Art experts were of the opinion that both paintings originated in the Cuzco School of Art in Peru. The court concluded that any question as to whether one or both paintings originated in Peru or Bolivia was not relevant because both MOUs (the one with Bolivia and the one with Peru) impose import restrictions on Spanish colonial period religious art. This conclusion is important for future forfeitures under the CPIA because many ancient cultures do not coincide with modern national boundaries. The task of enforcing import restrictions under the CPIA should be simplified by the fact that the government does not have to prove the exact country of origin so long as the type of object at issue is subject to import restriction from all of the possible countries of origin.

The Ancient Coin Collectors Guild (ACCG), an organization committed to promoting the free and independent collecting of ancient coins,[17] arranged for the importation of coins originating from Cyprus and China, apparently in violation of the import restrictions imposed under the United States' bilateral agreements with Cyprus and China. Ancient coins first became subject to import restriction when the MOU between Cyprus and the United States was extended and amended in 2007[18] and were also included in the MOU between China and the United States in January 2009.[19] In response to the inclusion of coins in the U.S.–Cyprus agreement, the ACCG had previously filed a suit against the Department of State under the Freedom of Information Act in an attempt to obtain documents concerning the decision-making process. This case was recently decided, however, and the ACCG's request for the release of additional documents was rejected.[20]

The ACCG arranged for the import of the coins in April 2009 in order to test the validity of the inclusion of coins in a bilateral agreement. The Department of Homeland Security, which enforces the import restrictions, seized the coins in September 2009,[21] and litigation is expected. It is interesting to contemplate the possible bases on which the legitimacy of these import restrictions might be challenged. Based on the FOIA suit, it seems that the ACCG and other numismatics organizations believe that the State Department did not follow the appropriate procedures in promulgating these regulations. Given the discretion that is vested in the State Department official who makes the decision whether to enter into a bilateral agreement, this would seem to be a difficult argument to make. A second route for attacking the regulation would be to argue that coins do not fit the statutory definition of "archaeological material" as required under the CPIA.[22] However, this may also be a difficult argument to make.

**Foreign Sovereign Immunity**

Claude Cassirer sued the Kingdom of Spain and the Thyssen-Bornemisza Collection Foundation[23] to recover a painting, *Rue Saint-Honoré, après midi, effet de pluie*, by Camille Pissarro. While the Ninth Circuit dismissed the appeal as to personal jurisdiction, standing, and the existence of a justiciable case or controversy, because there had been no final judgment on these issues, the court considered the question of whether the Foreign Sovereign Immunities Act (FSIA)[24] permitted a suit against a foreign state under the FSIA's expropriation exception[25] even when the foreign state being sued did not effect the expropriation.

Claude Cassirer's grandmother, Lilly Cassirer, owned the painting. In 1939, when she sought to leave Germany because of Nazi persecution, she was forced to sell the painting, for which she never received payment. The painting was ultimately confiscated by the Gestapo, later sold through several hands (including a New York gallery), and finally purchased by Baron Thyssen-Bornemisza some time after 1976. In an arrangement between the Baron and Spain, his collection is displayed at the Thyssen-Bornemisza Museum in Madrid. In 2000, Cassirer learned the location of the painting and requested its return. In 2005, without having pursued any judicial proceedings in Spain, Cassirer, a United States citizen and resident of California, filed suit in federal district court in California against the Foundation and Spain. In 2006, the district court denied motions to dismiss brought by Spain and the Foundation.[26]

Because all parties agreed that Spain had not been involved in the expropriation of the painting, the main question on appeal was whether the FSIA's expropriation exception applied in this situation. Relying on both the language of the statute and Congressional intent as expressed in the legislative history, the Ninth Circuit held that "the plain language of § 1605(a)(3) does not require that the foreign state (against whom the claim is made) be the entity who expropriated the property in violation of international law."[27]

Noting that the FSIA's requirement of commercial activity is determined by the "nature of the course of conduct or particular transaction or act, rather than by reference to its purpose" and that the question is whether the activity is of a kind in which private individuals might engage,[28] the Ninth Circuit also affirmed the District Court's holding that the Foundation had engaged in commercial activity in the United States.[29] Among those activities that the court cited as commercial in nature were: transacting in business as both a purchaser and seller of goods and services; advertising and distributing marketing and other commercial promotional materials; purchasing books, posters, post cards, and related materials; purchasing books about Nazi expropriation of artworks, Pissarro, and museum acquisition policies; licensing reproduction of images to U.S. businesses; purchasing of goods to be sold in the Museum gift shop; sale of a poster of the painting at issue to individuals in California; assisting in the production of a film featuring the painting, which would be presented in-flight on Iberia Airlines flights to and from the United States; lending its artworks to U.S. institutions and borrowing artworks from U.S. institutions to display in the Foundation museum.[30]

On the final issue—the question of whether Cassirer is required to exhaust local remedies by bringing an action in Spain—the Ninth Circuit held that Congress did not impose an absolute requirement to exhaust remedies in the FSIA. However, the District Court needs, on remand, to conduct a prudential exhaustion analysis.[31]

Another decision, *Westfield v. Federal Republic of Germany*,[32] addressed the FSIA but focused on the commercial activity exception to sovereign immunity.[33] The plaintiff is the estate representative of Walter Westfield, the owner of a significant art collection in Germany before World War II. Beginning in 1933, he was persecuted as a Jew, forced to sell his collection, and ultimately killed. The plaintiff alleged that the collection was wrongfully converted and sought to impose a constructive trust.

The plaintiff asserted that the conversion and subsequent sale of artworks that had been intended by Westfield for transfer to the United States fit the statutory criterion of commercial activity having a "direct effect in the United

States."[34] The court rejected this characterization of Nazi Germany's actions as commercial in nature and held that acts of expropriation or nationalization are uniquely sovereign. Subsequent commercial use of the property, after its expropriation, does not render the expropriation itself a commercial act.[35]

## Recoveries, Restitutions, and Claims

### Claims

**Peru's Efforts to Recover Machu Picchu Artifacts from Yale** In late 2008, after the failure of negotiations to reach an agreement,[36] Peru filed a claim to recover ancient artifacts that were excavated by Hiram Bingham in 1912 and 1915 at the Inca site of Machu Picchu and have been housed at Yale since that time. Peru is seeking the return of these artifacts.[37] In October 2009, Yale filed its answer to Peru's complaint.[38] Both parties agree that Bingham removed the artifacts from Peru with permission. The dispute centers on whether the artifacts were given to Yale as owner or whether they were on loan. However, Yale asserts that even if the artifacts were on loan to Yale, Peru's attempt to recover the artifacts is barred by the statute of limitations. Yale claims that it rejected Peru's request to return all of the artifacts as early as 1920 (at the time that it returned some of the artifacts but not all) and that it has consistently asserted dominion and held itself out as the owner of the artifacts since that time.[39] Because Yale's possession of the artifacts initiated as a loan and its possession was therefore permissive, the statute of limitations would seem to run on a claim for conversion from the time that Yale communicated its assertion of ownership to Peru.

**Russian Heir Attempts to Recover van Gogh Painting from Yale** Yale filed suit to quiet title to Vincent van Gogh's painting, *The Night Café*, in anticipation of a claim by Pierre Konowaloff. Konowaloff counterclaimed and Yale filed a motion to dismiss the counterclaims.[40] The painting had been in the collection of Konowaloff's great-grandfather, Ivan Morozov, and was nationalized in 1918, following the 1917 Russian Revolution.[41] The painting was originally placed in the Museum of Modern Western Art in Moscow. It was sold in 1933 and eventually purchased by Stephen C. Clark. The Yale University Art Gallery received the painting as a bequest from Clark in 1960. According to Yale, the painting was widely publicized, exhibited and published while it was owned by Clark and subsequently by Yale.[42]

The first issue in the case is whether the statute of limitations has run on the several claims asserted by Konowaloff, including claims for conversion, replevin, statutory theft, declaratory judgment, and quiet title. Yale asserts that none of the doctrines that might delay the running of the statute of limitations, such as fraudulent concealment or equitable estoppel, apply in this situation.[43] The more interesting issue from an international law perspective is whether Konowaloff's claims are barred under the act of state doctrine.[44] This doctrine states that U.S. courts will not examine the acts of another sovereign, including the nationalization of property, so long as the act is carried out against its own nationals, within its own territory, and by a state that is recognized by the United States, and the act was not in violation of an international treaty obligation.[45] Yale finally alleges that even if the act of state doctrine did not preclude a U.S. court's examination of Russia's title to the painting, the Russian nationalization of the painting was not in violation of an international law.[46] A nation's expropriation of the property of its own citizens, even without the payment of compensation, does not violate international law, while the 1907 Hague Convention (IV) Respecting the Laws and Customs of War on Land applies only to conflicts between nations and would not have applied to an internal revolution.

**China's Claim to Zodiac Animals** In February 2009, Christie's auctioned the estate of the designer Yves Saint Laurent. Included in the auction were two of the twelve animal figures, the rat and the rabbit, from the zodiac fountain at Emperor Qianlong's Summer Palace in Beijing that were looted by British and French forces in 1860. The two bronze figures, made in the 18th century, were sold over strenuous objection from China and a suit to prevent the sale brought by Chinese citizens living in France. The winning bidder was a Chinese dealer, Cai Mingchao, who bid approximately $18 million for each figure, but then later refused to pay.[47] This case illustrates the difficulty of finding a viable legal basis for the restitution of artworks stolen, looted, or otherwise taken before the advent of the current legal and treaty regime. Nonetheless, Chinese officials are beginning to review the collections of major museums throughout the world to locate other artifacts stolen from China during the Opium Wars.

**Seizure of Egyptian Sarcophagus** In October 2009, the United States filed a forfeiture complaint to forfeit an ancient Egyptian sarcophagus, dating between 1070 and 946 B.C.[48] In late 2008, a Spanish dealer sold the sarcophagus to an importer and shipped the sarcophagus from Barcelona, Spain, to Dublin, Ireland, to Orlando, Florida and finally to Miami, Florida. The complaint indicates some discrepancies as to the provenance history of the sarcophagus and as to when the sarcophagus left Egypt.

Citing a succession of Egyptian laws dating back to 1835, the United States alleges that these laws indicate that Egypt owned antiquities found in Egypt since at least 1874. The sarcophagus is therefore stolen property and left Egypt without an export license, in violation of Egyptian law. Its import into the United States would have violated 19 U.S.C. § 1595(c)(1)(A), which states that "[m]erchandise which is introduced or attempted to be introduced into the United States contrary to law . . . shall be seized and forfeited if it (A) is stolen, smuggled, or clandestinely imported or introduced."

**Restitutions and Recoveries**

In January 2009, the FBI returned a collection of more than 100 ancient artifacts to Panama that had been recovered in Portland, Oregon. The artifacts included a number of pottery pieces and gold works, including jewelry. Experts date many of the objects to the pre-Columbian period of 1100–1500 A.D. The objects were removed from Panama and brought to the United States in the late 1980s. The 1972 Panama Constitution and a 1982 law make it illegal for anyone to own antiquities.[49]

In June 2009, the FBI announced the return of approximately 1,600 objects that were found in the home of a collector, John Sisto, in a suburb of Chicago. The objects included books, parchments, manuscripts, artworks, and antiquities, which were voluntarily turned over by the collector's heirs and subsequently returned to Italy.[50] The FBI also returned to the Government of Anguilla more than 100 bronze religious medallions which originally belonged to Franciscan friars.[51]

In February 2009, the Department of Homeland Security Immigration and Customs Enforcement (ICE) and Customs and Border Protection in Laredo, Texas, returned 334 pre-Columbian artifacts to Peru that had been seized in 2007.[52] The artifacts included ceramic figures, wood sculptures, textiles, and metal and stone art. The seller pled guilty to one count of fraudulently importing goods and selling stolen property; he received three years of probation and paid a $2,000 fine. In addition, the FBI returned to Peru and Ecuador 153 pre-Columbian artifacts that had been seized in Miami.[53] The artifacts, including pottery, baskets, jewelry, carvings, figurines, and sculptures, were found in the home of a deceased resident of a retirement community near Miami, Florida.

British authorities repatriated approximately 1,500 artifacts to Afghanistan. Approximately half of the artifacts date to the pre-Islamic period and the other half to the Islamic up to the modern era. They were confiscated at Heathrow Airport, having passed through other countries including Pakistan and the United Arab Emirates, over the past six years and were returned to the Afghan National Museum.[54]

At the time of the June auction sales in New York, ICE agents recovered a Corinthian column krater, dating to 580–570 B.C., from Christie's auction house.[55] A few months later, ICE retrieved two additional pots, an Apulian situla and an Attic pelike, stolen from Italy and apparently sold by Christie's in June.[56] All three pieces seem to be connected to the operations of the Italian dealer Giacomo Medici, who has been the subject of investigations and prosecutions by Italian authorities for several years. In addition, Medici's conviction for receiving stolen antiquities and conspiracy was upheld, although his sentence was reduced to eight years when his conviction for smuggling antiquities was reversed as falling outside the statute of limitations; he is still required to pay a fine of $14 million.[57]

The Cleveland Museum of Art returned thirteen antiquities and a Gothic processional cross to Italy that had been illegally excavated or exported, apparently as part of the Medici conspiracy.[58] Italy and the museum will form a joint commission to research the Apollo *Sauroktonos*, which the museum acquired in 2004, and a small bronze winged chariot ornament. Finally, Italy will lend thirteen objects comparable to those returned beginning in 2010 for renewable 25-year terms.[59]

At the time of the June New York auction sales, with the help of the Art Loss Register, ICE recovered seven Egyptian artifacts from Christie's that had been stolen from the Bijbels Museum in Amsterdam in 2007.[60] ICE agents also recovered a wall fresco fragment that was reported stolen from the site of Pompeii twelve years ago and identified by the Art Loss Register.[61] Finally, it was revealed that Christie's sold, at its December 2008 sale and later, Egyptian artifacts that had been stolen from Long Island University's Hillwood Museum by its former director.[62]

Both the Louvre and the Metropolitan Museum of Art agreed to return archaeological objects to Egypt. In the case of the Louvre, four painted wall fragments from a tomb had been looted in the 1980s and were acquired in 2000 and 2003.[63] Under pressure from Dr. Zahi Hawass, the head of the Egyptian Supreme Council of Antiquities, the Louvre agreed to return the fragments. In contrast, two curators at the Metropolitan Museum of Art identified a fragment from a pharaonic shrine that had been on loan from a private collector for many years. The Metropolitan acquired the fragment from the owner and voluntarily returned it to Egypt.[64]

Sweden's Museum of National Antiquities in Stockholm returned twenty-two skulls taken from Native Hawaiian cemeteries in Hawaii in the nineteenth century. In 2005, the Swedish government directed the return of looted human remains. Bones have already been repatriated to Australian aborigines and a totem pole was returned to a tribe in Canada.[65]

## Museum Registry of New Acquisitions

It was previously reported that the Association of Art Museum Directors, in adopting new guidelines for the acquisition of antiquities, established a website registry where museums would place information concerning acquired antiquities whose provenance history did not conform with the AAMD Guidelines promulgated in 2008.[66] While a year ago only one object had been placed on the registry,[67] today the Metropolitan Museum of Art has placed three objects on the registry and the Boston Museum of Fine Arts (BMFA) has placed six objects, all of them coins. In the case of the Metropolitan Museum acquisitions, the provenance histories can be traced back to 1972, 1982, and 1984.[68] The provenance histories of these objects seem to indicate a good faith effort to comply with the AAMD 1970 guideline to a substantial compliance standard, unlike the case of the Portland Art Museum acquisition. The Boston Museum of Fine Arts coin acquisitions,[69] several of which seem to have Italy as their likely country of origin, were made with the consent of the Italian Ministry of Culture, apparently as part of the 2006 agreement between the BMFA and Italy.[70]

### Schoyen Collection

Two years ago, it was reported that an investigation was initiated into a collection of 654 Aramaic incantation bowls on loan since 1995 to University College London from the Schoyen Collection.[71] When the report was completed in 2007, the results were suppressed. However, the report was recently placed in the House of Lords Library[72] during a debate on amendments to the British Treasure Trove Act.[73] The report concluded that "on the balance of probabilities," the bowls were removed illegally from Iraq, probably some time after August 1990, when sanctions were imposed on the import of goods from Iraq.[74] The bowls are therefore likely subject to the Statutory Instrument 2003 No. 1519,[75] which, in section 8, prohibits the import or export of illegally removed Iraqi cultural property and created a criminal offense for "[a]ny person who holds or controls any item of illegally removed Iraqi cultural property . . . unless he proves that he did not know and had no reason to suppose that the item in question was illegally removed Iraqi cultural property." While it seems appropriate for legal action to be taken in light of these conclusions, no action has been taken.

## Notes

1. For the administrative and legislative developments leading up to this ratification, see Patty Gerstenblith & Laina Lopez, *International Cultural Property*, in YEARBOOK OF CULTURAL PROPERTY LAW 2009, 159-62 (Sherry Hutt & David Tarler eds., 2009).
2. List of States Parties, available at http://portal.unesco.org/la/convention.asp?KO=15207&language=E.
3. Gerstenblith & Lopez, *supra* note 1, at 161.
4. Cultural Property (Protection in Armed Conflict) Bill—Second Reading, 656 Hansard (debates) 5783 (20 Aug. 2009), available at http://www.parliament.nz/en-NZ/PB/Debates/Debates/2/0/d/49HansD_20090820_00000896-Cultural-Property-Protection-in-Armed-Conflict.htm.
5. List of States Parties available at http://portal.unesco.org/la/convention.asp?KO=13039&language=E.
6. 19 U.S.C. §§ 2601-13.
7. Honduras, Cultural Property Agreement with the U.S., http://exchanges.state.gov/heritage/culprop/hnfact.html. For the text of the 2004 agreement, see Memorandum of Understanding between the Government of the United States and the Government of the Republic of Honduras concerning the Imposition of Import Restrictions on Archaeological Materials from the Pre-Columbian Cultures of Honduras, available at http://exchanges.state.gov/heritage/culprop/hnfact/pdfs/hn2004mou.pdf. For the text of revised Article II of the agreement, see Honduras-U.S.A. MOU, Article II (revised as of 12 March 2009), available at http://exchanges.state.gov/heritage/culprop/hnfact/pdfs/hn2009mouext.pdf.
8. Memorandum of Understanding between the Government of the United States of America and the Government of the People's Republic of China concerning the Imposition of Import Restrictions on Categories of Archaeological Material from the Paleolithic Period through the Tang Dynasty and Monumental Sculpture and Wall Art at least 250 Years Old, available at http://exchanges.state.gov/heritage/culprop/chfact/pdfs/ch2009mou.pdf.
9. Patty Gerstenblith, *International Cultural Property*, in YEARBOOK OF CULTURAL PROPERTY LAW 2006, 91, 93 (Sherry Hutt & David Tarler eds., 2006).

10. Import Restrictions Imposed on Certain Archaeological Material from China, 74:11 Fed. Reg. 2838-2844 (Jan. 16, 2009), available at http://exchanges.state.gov/heritage/culprop/chfact/pdfs/ch2009dlfrn.pdf.
11. 19 U.S.C. § 2601(2)(C)(i).
12. *United States v. Eighteenth Century Peruvian Oil*, 597 F. Supp. 2d 618 (E.D. Va. 2009).
13. Memorandum of Understanding between the Government of the United States of America and the Government of the Republic of Peru concerning the Imposition of Import Restrictions on Archaeological Material from the Prehispanic Cultures and Certain Ethnological Material from the Colonial Period of Peru, available at http://exchanges.state.gov/heritage/culprop/pefact/pdfs/pe1997mou.pdf.
14. 18 U.S.C. § 983. CAFRA increases the government's burden of proof in forfeiture cases and provides for an innocent owner defense. However, forfeitures under any provision of Title 19 are exempted from CAFRA.
15. 597 F. Supp. 2d at 622-25.
16. *Id.* at 621, 624-25.
17. ACCG Home Page, available at http://www.accg.us.
18. Cyprus 2007 Revised Designated List 72:134 Fed. Reg. 38470-38474 (July 13, 2007), available at http://exchanges.state.gov/heritage/culprop/cyfact/pdfs/cy2007dlfrn.pdf.
19. *Supra* note 10.
20. *Ancient Coin Collectors Guild v. U.S. Dep't of State*, Civ. Case No. 07-2074, 2009 U.S. Dist. LEXIS 109303 (D.D.C. Nov. 20, 2009) (granting defendant's motion for summary judgment). It is not clear at this point whether the ACCG will appeal this decision.
21. Press Release, *Collectors Challenge U.S. State Department Bureaucrats After Baltimore Seizure*, WSJ MARKET WATCH (Sept. 15, 2009), available at http://www.marketwatch.com/story/collectors-challenge-us-state-department-bureaucrats-after-baltimore-seizure-2009-09-15.
22. The CPIA states that "no object may be considered to be an object of archaeological interest unless such object—
    — is of cultural significance;
    — is at least two hundred and fifty years old; and
    — was normally discovered as a result of scientific excavation, clandestine or accidental digging, or exploration on land or under water. . . ." 19 U.S.C. § 2601(2).
23. *Cassirer v. Kingdom of Spain*, 461 F. Supp. 2d 1157 (C.D. Cal. 2006), *aff'd in part, rev'd in part and remanded*, 580 F.3d 1048 (9th Cir. 2009).
24. 28 U.S.C. §§ 1602 *et seq.*

25. 28 U.S.C. § 1605(a)(3) provides, in part, that a "foreign state shall not be immune from the jurisdiction of courts of the United States . . . in any case . . . in which rights in property taken in violation of international law are in issue and . . . that property . . . is owned or operated by an agency or instrumentality of the foreign state and that agency or instrumentality is engaged in a commercial activity in the United States."
26. 461 F. Supp. 2d at 1162-63.
27. 580 F.3d at 1056.
28. *Id.* at 1058 (quoting 28 U.S.C. § 1603(d)).
29. *Id.* at 1057-1059.
30. *Id.*
31. *Id.* at 1062.
32. *Westfield v. Federal Republic of Germany*, No. 3:09-0204, 2009 Dist. LEXIS 65133 (M.D. Tenn. July 28, 2009).
33. This exception provides "A foreign state shall not be immune from the jurisdiction of courts of the United States . . . (2) in which an action is based . . . upon an act outside the territory of the United States in connection with a commercial activity of the foreign state elsewhere and that act causes a direct effect in the United States." 28 U.S.C. § 1605(a)(2).
34. 2009 Dist. LEXIS 65133, at *8.
35. *Id.* at *16-*17.
36. Patty Gerstenblith, *International Cultural Property*, in YEARBOOK OF CULTURAL PROPERTY 2008 119, 123-34 (Sherry Hutt & David Tarler eds, 2008).
37. Original Complaint, *Republic of Peru v. Yale University*, No. 1:08-cv-02109-HHK (D.D.C. Dec. 5, 2008).
38. Yale University's Memorandum in Support of Motion to Dismiss Peru's Amended Complaint for Failure to State a Claim, Case No. 3:09-cv-01332 (AWT) (D. Conn, filed Oct. 16, 2009).
39. *Id.* at 1-3. The Connecticut statute of limitations for contract-based claims is six years and for tort-based claims is three years. *Id.* at 7-8.
40. Yale University and *The Night Café*, a Painting, v. Konowaloff, Plaintiff-Counterclaim Defendant Yale University's Motion to Dismiss Amended Counterclaims, Case No. 3:09-CV-00466 (AWT) (D. Conn., filed Oct. 5, 2009).
41. Yale University and *The Night Café*, a Painting, v. Konowaloff, Memorandum in Support of Motion to Dismiss Amended Counterclaims by Plaintiff-Counterclaim Defendant Yale University, Case No. 3:09-CV-00466 (AWT) (D. Conn., filed Oct. 5, 2009), at 1-5 [hereinafter cited as Memorandum].
42. *Id.* at 5-8.
43. *Id.* at 9-25.
44. *Id.* at 25-34. The act of state doctrine "reflect[s] 'the strong sense of the Judicial Branch that its engagement in the task of passing on the validity of foreign acts

of state may hinder' the conduct of foreign affairs." *W.S. Kirkpatrick & Co., Inc. v. Envtl. Tectonics Corp., Int'l*, 493 U.S. 400, 404 (1990)(quoting *Banco Nacional de Cuba v. Sabbatino*, 376 U.S. 398, 428 (1964).

45. The Supreme Court stated the requirements of the doctrine as:

> the Judicial Branch will not examine the validity of a taking of property within its own territory by a foreign sovereign government, extant and recognized by this country at the time of suit, in the absence of a treaty or other unambiguous agreement regarding controlling legal principles, even if the complaint alleges that the taking violates customary international law. *Sabbatino,* 376 U.S. at 428.

46. Memorandum, *supra* note 41, at 34-40.
47. Nazanin Lankarani, *Saint Laurent Auction Rich in Sentimental Value*, INT'L HER. TRIB., Nov. 14, 2009, at 5.
48. *United States v. One Ancient Egyptian, Yellow Background, Wooden Sarcophagus, dating to the Third Intermediate Period*, 09-23030 CIV (S.D. Fla., filed Oct. 8, 2009).
49. FBI, "Recoveries—Panamanian Artifacts," available at http://www.fbi.gov/hq/cid/arttheft/northamerica/us/panama/panamaartifacts.htm.
50. FBI, "Arrivederci—Recovered Italian Artifacts Headed Home" (June 11, 2009), available at http://www.fbi.gov/page2/june09/artifacts061109.html.
51. FBI, "Cultural Artifacts Returned to Anguilla" (June 2, 2009), available at http://www.fbi.gov/pressrel/pressrel09/anguilla_060209.htm.
52. ICE, "334 pre-Columbian Artifacts Returned to Peru," available at http://www.ice.gov/pi/news/factsheets/cultural-artifacts-repatriation.htm.
53. FBI Press Release, "FBI Announces Return of Pre-Columbian Artifacts to Peru and Columbia" (Dec. 1, 2009), available at http://miami.fbi.gov/pressrel/pressrel09/mm120109.htm.
54. Gloria Galloway, *Hundreds of Afghan antiquities repatriated from Britain*, GLOBE AND MAIL, April 7, 2009.
55. ICE Press Release, Stolen Italian Artifact Smuggled into the United States Found at Auction House (June 1, 2009), available at http://www.ice.gov/pi/nr/0906/090601newyork.htm.
56. ICE Agents Recover Stolen Italian Artifacts Smuggled into the United States (Oct. 29, 2009),availableathttp://209.85.229.132/search?q=cache:Ia7M64KSMXQJ:www.art-daily.com/index.asp%3Fint_new%3D34189%26int_sec%3D2+apulian+situla+attic+pelike+artdaily&cd=2&hl=en&ct=clnk&gl=uk&client=firefox-a; Pots seized in NYC: comment from Christie's, Looting matters, Nov. 4, 2009, available at http://lootingmatters.blogspot.com/.
57. Steve Scherer, *Rome Court Upholds Conviction of Antiquities Dealer*, BLOOMBERG, July 15, 2009.
58. Steven Litt, *Cleveland Museum of Art Will Return Tainted Antiquities to Italy Wednesday*, PLAIN DEALER, Apr. 21, 2009.

59. *Id.*
60. ICE Recovers Egyptian Artifacts Stolen from a Museum in the Netherlands, artdaily.org (May 29, 2009), available at http://www.artdaily.org/index.asp?int_sec=2&int_new=31133.
61. ICE Press Release, ICE Seizes a Cultural Artifact Reported Stolen in Italy almost 12 Years Ago (June 1, 2009), available at http://www.ice.gov/pi/nr/0906/090601newyorkcity.htm.
62. Kati Cornell and Joe Mollica, *LI's Pharaoh 'Phraudster'*, N.Y. POST, Sept. 16, 2009, available at http://www.nypost.com/p/news/local/li_pharaoh_phraudster_6M0V9X3dvSWivSV8PuWcpL.
63. *The Met Returns Egyptian Artifact*, DAILY NEWS EGYPT, Oct. 28, 2009.
64. Metropolitan Museum of Art, Press Release, Metropolitan Museum of Art Returns a Granite Fragment to Egypt, Oct. 28, 2009, available at http://www.metmuseum.org/press_room/full_release.asp?prid=%7B768AF8B3-20A5-4EB6-820F-2DECCBC8854D%7D.
65. BBC News, Sweden returns skulls to Hawaii, Nov. 14, 2009.
66. Gerstenblith & Lopez, *supra* note 1, at 167-68.
67. This object is a *ganesh* stele purchased by the Portland Art Museum and with a provenance history consisting solely of a 2000 sale at Sotheby's and the subsequent 2008 sale at Christie's where the museum purchased it. *See* http://aamdobjectregistry.org/node/28.
68. The acquisitions are an Olmec sculpture from Mexico (1972), see http://aamdobjectregistry.org/node/29); a Gujarat sculpture from India (1982); and a Han Dynasty jade sculpture from China (1984).
69. *See* http://aamdobjectregistry.org/A-Browse.
70. *See, e.g.*, http://aamdobjectregistry.org/node/67.
71. Patty Gerstenblith, *International Cultural Property*, in YEARBOOK OF CULTURAL PROPERTY LAW 2008, 119, 124-25 (Sherry Hutt & David Tarler eds., 2008).
72. "An Inquiry into the provenance of 654 Aramaic incantation bowls delivered into the possession of UCL by, or on the instruction of, Mr Martin Schoyen." Report by David John Freeman, Salley MacDonald, Lord Renfrew of Kaimsthorn (27 July 2006), available at http://88.80.16.63/leak/schoyen-ucl-inquiry.pdf.
73. Amendment 37, Amendment of Treasure Act 1996, 26 Oct 2009, Cols. 981-83, Lords Hansard Report, available at http://www.publications.parliament.uk/pa/ld200809/ldhansrd/text/91026-0002.htm. The purpose of these proposed amendments is to strengthen the Treasure Act by increasing the requirements to report treasure finds.
74. Report, *supra* note 72, at 2.
75. Available at http://www.hmso.gov.uk/si/si2003/20031519.htm.

# Enforcement Actions

• • •

## *Section Editor: David Tarler*[1]

### Introduction

Over Memorial Day weekend in 1991, David Lane Woolsey and Jimmy Barney were discovered and photographed by hikers as they dug for archaeological artifacts at a 2,000 year-old, Native American rock shelter along Boulder Creek, on Bureau of Land Management land near Escalante, Utah. A year later, Woolsey and Barney became the first defendants in Utah to be convicted of a felony violation of the Archaeological Resources Protection Act.[2] In Salt Lake City, then-U.S. Attorney David Jordan stated that the case illustrated the "significant damage" being done to archaeological resources, and that he would pursue a "get tough policy to aggressively prosecute this crime, which is ravaging archaeological sites on public lands." He added, "This is not an isolated case. It's a crime that occurs every weekend in Utah. . . . I'm trying to send a message to looters: they have to stop this."

In December 2008, as his administration was ending, President George W. Bush granted a pardon to Woolsey. Woolsey had sought the pardon—he had filled out an application on the Internet—but, nonetheless, he was surprised. "I don't know what got him [President Bush] to do it," he said. Woolsey sought the pardon in order to be able to possess a weapon. He had lost that precious right when he was convicted of the felony violation of ARPA. President Bush's pardon restored that right.

In June 2009, with a new administration overseeing the Executive Branch, Secretary of the Interior Ken Salazar, Assistant Secretary of the Interior for Indian Affairs Larry Echo Hawk, Deputy Attorney General David Ogden, U.S. Attorney for the District of Utah Brett Tolman, and Special Agent-in-Charge of the FBI's Salt Lake City Field Office Timothy Furman announced in Salt Lake City, that an undercover operation begun two and a half years earlier, "Cerberus Action" (In ancient Greek mythology, Cerberus is a multi-headed dog that guards the underworld), had exposed a vast network of illegal excavation and commercial trafficking in cultural heritage resources located on public and Indian lands in the Four Corners area of the American Southwest, and had already resulted in numerous arrests, indictments, searches, and seizures involving diggers, dealers, and collectors. The great majority of those indicted for these alleged crimes, which involved Native American cultural heritage resources—human remains, funerary objects, sacred objects, objects of cultural patrimony, and other cultural items—were residents of San Juan County, Utah.

At the announcement of the indictments, Secretary Salazar remarked, "There is a priceless value to these items in terms of the legacy and the culture of Native Americans, but also the United States of America. . . . The time for the United States government's simply looking the other way and allowing this conduct to occur is over. This is a new chapter in terms of what we will do to protect these very important national assets and cultural resources that are priceless in nature. . . . Let this case serve notice to anyone who is considering breaking these laws and trampling our nation's cultural heritage that the BLM, the Department of Justice, and the federal government will track you down and bring you to justice." His statement meshed with that of Deputy Attorney General Ogden, who said, "These archaeological treasures are precious, and protecting them preserves a rich history and heritage. That is why the Department of Justice will use all its tools to vigorously enforce the laws designed to safeguard the cultural heritage of Native Americans."

In Salt Lake City, Deputy Attorney General Ogden also announced that, in "recommitting resources and focus to criminal justice in Indian Country," the Department of Justice and the Department of the Interior would be conducting training for Assistant U.S. Attorneys on cultural heritage resources protection law. In fact, this training, cosponsored by the Executive Office for United States Attorneys at the Department of Justice through their Office of Legal Education, and by the National NAGPRA Program of the National Park Service and the Department of the Interior's Indian Arts and Crafts Board, was conducted in September 2009. The training had been presented yearly, beginning in 1992, but was stopped after 2003.

In light of the foregoing accounts and statements, one might be challenged to periodically address the following question during the next several years: Did 2009 begin a new chapter in terms of what the Government of the United States will do to protect both Native American cultural heritage and cultural heritage resources generally? Answering the subset of questions below might be relevant to an overall determination:

- Will the percentage of declinations to prosecute alleged cultural heritage resources crimes referred to U.S. Attorney offices decrease? Between 1996 and 2005, about one third of the referrals were declined.[3]
- Will the percentage of convicted defendants sentenced to some period of incarceration for a crime involving a cultural heritage resource increase? Between 1996 and 2005, about 24% of the sentences included a term of incarceration.[4]
- Will the percentage of convicted defendants sentenced to more than one year of incarceration for a crime involving a cultural heritage resource increase? Between 1996 and 2005, about 35% of convicted defendants sentenced to a term of incarceration received 12 months or more, or about 8.4% of all those sentenced for a crime involving a cultural heritage resource.[5]
- Will the Department of the Interior –Department of Justice training program for Assistant U.S. Attorneys on cultural property protection law be revived and offered regularly? Between 1992 and 2003, this training program had been presented at least once a year, but it was discontinued.

As for the Judicial Branch, in 2009, sentences were imposed on the first two defendants to be prosecuted as a result of "Cerebus Action" (*Jeanne Redd* and *Jerrica Redd*). In at least one of the sentences, the judge departed downward from the sentence that would have been indicated by advisory U.S. Sentencing Guideline 2B1.5, which applies to crimes involving a cultural heritage resource.[6] The reasons for his downward departure are under seal. Nonetheless, based on the judge's courtroom statements, one must ask whether a downward departure in sentence should be warranted because the crime in question was committed in "a community where this kind of conduct . . . has been justified for a number of years." Going forward, another question might be asked, too:

- Will the percentage of sentences imposing an advisory U.S. Sentencing Guideline range and using all the 2B1.5 Guideline-specific offense characteristics increase?

Already, it is clear that 2010 will see numerous sentences being imposed on defendants convicted of crimes involving a cultural heritage resource. It should be an interesting year.

## The Archaeological Resources Protection Act

The Archaeological Resources Protection Act (ARPA; 16 U.S.C. §§ 470aa-mm) prescribes criminal punishment (at 16 U.S.C. § 470ee) for persons who:

(a) excavate, remove, damage, or otherwise alter or deface any archaeological resource located on public lands or Indian lands, or attempt to do so, without a permit (16 U.S.C. § 470ee (a));

(b) sell, purchase, exchange, transport, or receive, or offer to sell, purchase, or exchange any archaeological resource removed from public lands or Indian lands in violation of (a), or any provision, rule, regulation, ordinance, or permit in effect under any other provision of federal law (16 U.S.C. § 470ee (b));

(c) sell, purchase, exchange, transport, receive, or offer to sell, purchase, or exchange, in interstate or foreign commerce, any archaeological resource excavated, removed, sold, purchased, exchanged, transported, or received in violation of any provision, rule, regulation, ordinance, or permit in effect under state or local law (16 U.S.C. § 470ee (c)); or

(d) counsel, procure, solicit, or employ another to violate (a), (b), or (c) (16 U.S.C. § 470ee (d)).

An ARPA offense is a general intent crime. The government must prove that the defendant knowingly committed the offense conduct.[7]

ARPA also provides for the assessment of civil penalties for violations on public lands and Indian lands (16 U.S.C. § 470ff). In the case of a second or subsequent violation of ARPA, the amount of a civil penalty may be double the amount which would have been assessed if such violation were the first violation (16 U.S.C. § 470ff (a); 43 C.F.R. § 7.16 (a)(2); 36 C.F.R. § 296.16 (a)(2); 32 C.F.R. § 229.16 (a)(2); and 18 C.F.R. § 1312.16 (a)(2)). Intent is not an element of a civil violation of ARPA.[8]

### *United States v. Dawn Laate and Preston A. Waggoner*[9]

Dawn Laate and Preston A. Waggoner each pled guilty to one misdemeanor count of violation of ARPA (16 U.S.C. 470ee (a)). Each of them was ordered to pay a fine in the amount of $2,500, of which $2,000 would be suspended if they refrained from entering Canyon of the Ancients National Monument for a period of one year and, at their own expense, published in local newspapers—after review and approval by Bureau of Land Management personnel—letters of apology regarding their crimes. The United States Attorney recommended that Laate and Waggoner receive a two-level reduction in the advisory sentencing guideline offense level for acceptance of responsibility.

On August 18, 2009, a member of the public visiting Canyons of the Ancients National Monument, in Colorado, observed two individuals picking up what he believed to be artifacts, and contacted the Bureau of Land Management Ranger on duty. The Ranger responded, and contacted Laate and Waggoner, who admitted to having picked up artifacts off the ground in Lowry Ruin that they believed to be at least 100 years old. Lowry Ruin is listed on the National Register of Historic Places. The BLM's Anasazi Heritage Center subsequently confirmed that the more than 40 items collected by Laate and Waggoner were archaeological resources belonging to Native American cultural heritage.

Neither the archaeological value nor the commercial value of the archaeological resources involved in the offense conduct is known. The cost of restoration and repair of the archaeological resources involved in the offense, likewise, is unknown.

### *United States v. Patricia Doyle*[10]

Patricia Doyle pled guilty to one felony count of conspiracy to violate ARPA (18 U.S.C. 371 and 16 U.S.C. 470ee (a) & (b)). She was sentenced to eight months of imprisonment, to be served concurrently with a 57-month federal prison sentence for an international drug trafficking offense, followed by 36 months of supervised release. As a condition of her probation, Doyle will be banned from entering public lands managed by the Bureau of Land Management, Forest Service, National Park Service, Bureau of Indian Affairs, and Fish & Wildlife Service without advance permission from her probation officer. Doyle also was ordered to pay restitution to the Bureau of Land Management in the amount of $27,292, and to forfeit all the archaeological resources she removed from public lands, along with the equipment she used to commit the offense conduct.

In January 2005, Doyle was awaiting sentencing on the drug trafficking offense when, pursuant to a search warrant, BLM law enforcement personnel seized from her residence several hundred archaeological resources belonging to Native American cultural heritage. Doyle admitted that, during a period of some 20 years, she and several other co-conspirators had looted numerous archaeological sites on public lands in central and eastern Oregon, and had collected the archaeological resources.

Doyle belongs to the group of defendants prosecuted as part of "Operation Bring'em Back." Begun in 2000 to target the illegal excavation and trafficking in Native American human remains and cultural items and archaeological resources, Operation Bring'em Back was a joint investigation involving law enforcement personnel and archaeologists from the Bureau of Land Management; U.S. Forest Service; Internal Revenue Service; Bureau of Alcohol, Tobacco, and Firearms; Oregon State Police Wildlife Division; and Central Oregon Drug Enforcement Team. The Operation yielded the seizure of over 100,000 cultural heritage resources; the recovery of two skulls of Native American children; the discovery of illegal excavation at over 100 cultural sites on public lands in Oregon managed by the BLM, Forest Service, and Fish & Wildlife Service; a determination of damages in excess of $1 million; and the execution of numerous search warrants. Several of the Operation Bring'em Back defendants were methamphetamine addicts and traffickers (search warrants yielded four meth labs, including one at Doyle's residence), and six of them (including Doyle) have been convicted of drug trafficking in federal or state court.[11]

### *United States v. Gregory Truesdell*[12]

Gregory Joseph Truesdell pled guilty to one felony count of violation of ARPA (16 U.S.C. 470ee (b)). He was sentenced to 24 months of probation, and ordered to pay a fine in the amount of $20,000. The United States Attorney recommended that Truesdell receive a three-level reduction in the advisory sentencing guideline offense level for acceptance of responsibility, which resulted in a total offense level of 13. Even though the advisory sentencing guidelines prescribe a sentence of 12–18 months of imprisonment, and even though the United States Probation Officer recommended that the sentence include six months of home detention, nonetheless, the court departed downward from the guideline sentence and the Probation Officer's recommendation.

In October 2007, Truesdell purchased an olla and a ceramic bowl for $100 during a meeting with an undercover special agent in Woodland Hills, California. At the time of the purchase, Truesdell knew that the two items were archaeological resources, and that they had been removed illegally from Lake Mead National Recreation Area, in Arizona (Truesdell did not remove the items). In fact, the archaeological resources had been removed from the Spiderman Rockshelters area of the Park. The archaeological value of the two archaeological resources involved in the theft was determined to be $16,818.

### *United States v. Oscar Ortega-Moreno and Sergio Corona-Venzor*[13]

Oscar Ortega-Moreno and Sergio Corona-Venzor each pled guilty to one misdemeanor count of violation of ARPA (16 U.S.C. 470ee (a)). Each of them was ordered to pay a fine in the amount of $1,100, and they were ordered, jointly and severally, to pay restitution to the Bureau of Land Management in the amount of $5,250. At sentencing, Magistrate Gudrun Rice increased the amount of the fine from the $500 that had been stipulated in the plea agreements. The United States Attorney recommended that Ortega-Moreno and Corona-Venznor receive a two-level reduction in the advisory sentencing guideline offense level for acceptance of responsibility, and determined their total offense level to be 8.

On March 8, 2007, the defendants carved their first names and dates of birth on petroglyphs known as Roc Creek Art Panel #1, located on lands administered by the Bureau of Land Management near the Dolores River, south of Gateway, Colorado. The petroglyphs, which are believed to have been created by the Ancestral Puebloan culture, date to the period 1000–1200 A.D. Working with local ranchers, BLM law enforcement personnel discovered the identities of the defendants, who at the time were employed on a ranch adjacent to the petroglyph site. When contacted, the defendants admitted to having committed the offense conduct, but stated that this type of activity was not a crime in their home country of Mexico.

The archaeological value of the archaeological resources involved in the offense conduct is not known. The Bureau of Land Management has contracted to repair and restore the petroglyph panel at a cost of $5,250.

### *United States v. William A. Graves and Misty D. Graves*[14]

William A. Graves pled guilty to one felony count of violation of ARPA, and Misty D. Graves pled guilty to one misdemeanor count of violation of ARPA (16 U.S.C. 470ee (a)). William Graves was sentenced to six months of imprisonment, followed by 12 months of supervised release, and his wife, Misty Graves, was sentenced to 12 months of probation. In addition, the defendants were ordered, jointly and severally, to pay restitution to Buffalo National River (managed by the

National Park Service) in the amount of $4,610. The archaeological value of the archaeological resources involved in the offense conduct, together with the cost of their restoration and repair, was calculated to be $40,000.

In January 2008, National Park Service rangers at Buffalo National River, in Arkansas, were alerted to the recent looting of a known archaeological site in the park's upper district. After a two-day stakeout yielded no results, surveillance equipment was installed near the site. While installing the equipment, rangers contacted William Graves and a nine-year-old juvenile approaching the site. When asked what they were doing, Graves replied, "Digging for worms." Graves was in possession of digging tools and boots that the Arkansas Crime Lab subsequently determined were a match with the impressions left in the recently disturbed site. Misty Graves remained at a trailhead area with their vehicle. When contacted by the rangers and asked what was happening, she replied "You know what is going on" and that she "knew this was going to happen." Misty Graves was found to be in possession of archaeological resources that were consistent with other artifacts at the disturbed site, along with gloves that matched a hang tag discovered at the site and a pick. A search warrant was executed on the Graves' home, yielding photographs of past digging by the defendants and others at the disturbed site and on nearby private land, as well as numerous items associated with collecting artifacts. During the course of the investigation, which was assisted by the NPS Midwest Region's Cultural and Archeological Response Team (CART), William Graves admitted to digging in the park, and surrendered 71 stone tools, projectile points, and other artifacts that he claimed originated from the disturbed site.

### *United States v. Charles Penn Lindsey*[15]

Charles Penn Lindsey pled guilty to one misdemeanor count of violation of ARPA (16 U.S.C. 470ee (b)). He was sentenced to 6 months of unsupervised probation. The United States Attorney recommended that Lindsey receive a two-level reduction in the advisory sentencing guideline offense level for acceptance of responsibility, and determined his total offense level to be 8. Neither the archaeological value of the archaeological resources involved in the offense conduct nor their restoration/repair cost is known.

In March 2005, Charles Lindsey removed archaeological resources, as well as dinosaur bones, fish fossils, petrified wood, and lava rock from Glen Canyon National Recreation Area (managed by the National Park Service), in Utah, and transported them to his home in Colorado. In 2009, Lindsey's ex-wife reported the stolen items to National Park Service investigators because, she said, she was afraid that Lindsey would teach their son to loot. In addition to the Glen Canyon items, a pottery vessel identified as coming from Mesa Verde was forfeited to the United States as part of the plea agreement.

### *United States v. Dino Harrison and John Oliver Darby*[16]

Dino Harrison and John Oliver Darby each pled guilty to one misdemeanor count of violation of ARPA (16 U.S.C. 470ee (a)). Harrison was sentenced to 12 months of probation, and was ordered to participate in, and successfully complete, a substance abuse treatment program. Darby will be sentenced in 2010.

In April 2006, an Acoma conservation officer spotted a suspicious vehicle near the El Malpais area south of Grants, in western New Mexico. After scanning the badlands, he spotted Harrison and Darby walking out of the El Malpais lava fields, and noticed that Darby was carrying a large object in his arms. The El Malpais lava fields are public land managed by the Bureau of Land Management. By the time the officer approached Harrison and Darby—they had been trying to hide—they no longer were carrying anything. Subsequently, the defendants admitted to having removed a pot from the lava fields, intending to sell it and share the proceeds. The pot turned out to be an olla belonging to the Ancestral Puebloan culture and dating to the period 900–1250 A.D. According to archaeologists, it might have served as a vessel for food left for travelers along the Zuni-Acoma trail.

At sentencing, the judge affirmed that the Mandatory Victim Restitution Act of 1996 applied to the case, but found no need to order restitution, as the stolen olla had been turned over to BLM. Based on this finding, presumably no (restitutionary) restoration and repair costs were offered by the United States for the archaeological site from which the olla had been removed.

### *United States v. John M. Sheild, Brian E. Ekrem, and Richard D. Geffre*[17]

John M. Sheild pled guilty to one misdemeanor count of violation of ARPA (16 U.S.C. 470ee (b)). He had been charged with a felony violation of ARPA. Sheild was ordered to pay a fine in the amount of $10,000. Brian E. Ekrem pled guilty to one felony count of violation of ARPA (16 U.S.C. 470ee (b)). In addition to the count to which he pled, Ekrem had been charged with a second felony count of violation of ARPA (16 U.S.C. 470ee (a)) and a misdemeanor count of trafficking in Native American cultural items obtained in violation of the Native American Graves Protection and Repatriation Act (18 U.S.C. 1170 (b)). Ekrem was sentenced to 10 months of imprisonment, to be followed by 12 months of supervised release. Richard D. Geffre pled guilty to one felony count of violation of ARPA (16 U.S.C. 470ee (b)). In addition to the count to which he pled, Geffre, too, had been charged with a second felony count of violation of ARPA (16 U.S.C. 470ee (b)) and a misdemeanor count of trafficking in Native American cultural items obtained in violation of NAGPRA (18 U.S.C. 1170 (b)). Geffre was sentenced to 6 months of home confinement, to be followed by 36 months of probation, and was ordered to pay a fine in the amount of $20,000. As part of their sentences, the three defendants also were ordered to forfeit, together, more than 8,000 archaeological resources in their possession, including military items; necklaces; shell pendants; copper arm bands; shell, copper, and glass beads; rings; catlinite pipes, effigies, pendants, and a decorated plate; celts; a ceremonial blade; pottery; gaming pieces; projectile points; and bone and stone tools. Along with these three defendants, two others, Elliot D. Hook and Scott A. Matteson, have been charged with violations of ARPA (16 U.S.C. 470ee (b)). Hook has pled guilty to one felony count of violation of ARPA and has agreed to forfeit more than 4,300 archaeological resources. He will be sentenced in 2010. Matteson has pled not guilty to the ARPA charge. His trial is scheduled for January 2010.

Between 2004 and 2008, with the help of research materials that reference and provide maps of archaeological sites, the defendants were involved, variously, in removing, transporting, or trafficking in thousands of archaeological resources from multiple sites on public and Indian lands, including burial grounds and military sites. These sites have been undergoing erosion ever since the Missouri River was dammed, in the 1950s and 1960s.

According to Richard Harnois, a senior field archaeologist for the U.S. Army Corps of Engineers, in Pierre, "there isn't anywhere else in the country that is like this. You have a huge drainage system populated by people for 12,000 years and banks that are eroding." As a result, says Harnois, the Missouri River's banks are "supplying the rest of the country the artifacts they want for their collections." Sheild, a former pastor, in fact was listed as a co-host of the annual Stoughton Native American Artifact Show.

## Theft of Major Artwork

The offense of Theft of Major Artwork (18 U.S.C. 668) is the act of obtaining from a "museum" by theft or fraud an "object of cultural heritage," or receiving, concealing, exhibiting, or disposing of such an object, knowing that the object has been stolen or obtained by fraud. An "object of cultural heritage" is an object that either is over 100 years old and worth in excess of $5,000 or is of any age and worth at least $100,000. A "museum" is an organized and permanent institution situated in the United States whose activities affect interstate or foreign commerce and whose essential purpose is educational or aesthetic, has a professional staff, and owns, utilizes, and cares for tangible objects that are exhibited to the public on a regular schedule. Theft of major artwork is a general intent crime. The government must prove that the stolen property came from a museum and that the defendant knew the item was stolen (or obtained by fraud), but need not prove that the defendant knew the item came from a museum.

***United States v. Joshua T. McCarty, Zachary Scranton, and Angela K. Bays*[18]**

Joshua Troy McCarty pled guilty to two counts of theft of major artwork. He was sentenced to 46 months of imprisonment, to be followed by 36 months of supervised release. During his supervised release, McCarty will be required to participate in an approved substance abuse treatment program and an outpatient mental health treatment program. Zachary A. Scranton pled guilty to one count of theft of major artwork. He was sentenced to five months of imprisonment, to be followed by 36 months of supervised release. In addition, McCarty and Scranton were ordered, jointly and severally, to pay restitution to the Rutherford B. Hayes Presidential Center in the amount of $285. Angela K. Bays, McCarty's girlfriend, originally was charged with one count of theft of major artwork, but that charge subsequently was dismissed.

In June 2008, McCarty and Bays entered the library at the Rutherford B. Hayes Presidential Center, in Fremont, Ohio, and asked to see *Laws of the Territory of the United States North West of the Ohio*, also known as the "Maxwell Code." They were given that book, along with a second book with which it was boxed, *Laws of the Territory of the United States North West of the River Ohio*, also known as the "Freeman Code." The Maxwell Code, published in 1796, was one of the first books ever published in the territory that would become Ohio, and less than 10 copies are known to exist. In 2007, a similar copy of the Maxwell Code had sold for $103,000. The Freeman Code, published in 1798, would later be sold for $35,000.

At the library, McCarty somehow was able to sneak both books into the women's restroom. On emerging from the restroom, he was confronted by a library employee. Confiscating what the employee believed to be both books, the employee reshelved them. In fact, McCarty had taken the Freeman Code from between its covers, leaving behind the approximately 150 blank pages with which the 32-page pamphlet had been bound.

In July 2008, McCarty attempted to sell the Freeman Code. A bookseller in Chicago contacted by McCarty was not interested in buying or brokering the sale of the book, but referred McCarty to other book dealers. Contacting one of them, a rare book dealer in Philadelphia, McCarty claimed he had inherited copies of both the Freeman Code and the Maxwell Code, and stated that he was interested in the immediate sale of the Freeman Code, and that he might be interested in selling the Maxwell Code at some later time. After receiving and authenticating the book, the dealer brokered its sale to an individual in England for $35,000. The dealer took a commission of $3,500, and sent the remaining $31,500 to McCarty in care of McCarty's mother.

In August 2008, McCarty approached Scranton and offered him $300 to steal the Maxwell Code. Scranton agreed. On August 25, Scranton went to the Hayes Presidential Center's library and, using an alias, asked to look at the Maxwell Code. When the head librarian found out that Scranton had been given the book without a showing of identification, she asked him to present some form of identification. He replied that he had none with him. Scranton then was asked to allow the library staff to hold his book bag as collateral while he looked at the book, and he agreed.

At one point, Scranton left the library, but returned shortly thereafter. Subsequently, he told a library employee that he needed to take a call on his cell phone, and left the library a second time. Becoming suspicious of Scranton's activity, the employee checked Scranton's work area and discovered that the Maxwell Code was missing. Scranton's book bag, which he had abandoned at the library, was found to contain only paper towels.

After discovering the theft, the library advised various book dealers and auction houses of the Maxwell Code theft. Responding to the library's advisory, dealers alerted the library that an individual named Joshua McCarty had recently sold a copy of the Freeman Code through the Philadelphia dealer, and that McCarty had indicated he also had a copy of the Maxwell Code. Upon checking to confirm that its own copy of the Freeman Code was intact, the library discovered that the book had been removed from its cover and was missing.

An investigation of McCarty revealed prior arrests, including a 2007 arrest, in Illinois, in connection with the theft of $20,000 worth of antique maps from a bookstore in Harrisburg, Pennsylvania. A review of McCarty's cell phone activity on the date of the Maxwell Code theft led to Scranton, who, in turn, was identified by library staff as the person who had stolen the Maxwell Code. A check of Scranton's cell phone activity, moreover, placed him within one mile of the library on the day of the theft. Following his arrest, Scranton admitted his theft of the Maxwell Code, and provided information that linked McCarty to the theft of the Freeman Code.

The Freeman Code was recovered in Dallas, Texas, and the Maxwell Code was recovered in Columbus, Ohio. On April 1, 2009, the two books were returned to the Rutherford B. Hayes Presidential Center.

## Illegal Trafficking in Native American Human Remains and Cultural Items

The Native American Graves Protection and Repatriation Act (NAGPRA) includes a criminal enforcement section (Pub. L. No. 101-601, § 4, 80 Stat. 3048, 3052 (1990)). Codified at 18 U.S.C. §1170, the law contains two subsections. One subsection (18 U.S.C. § 1170 (a)) criminalizes the knowing sale, purchase, use for profit, or transportation for sale or profit of the human remains of a "Native American" (per the definition at 25 U.S.C. § 3001 (9)) without the "right of possession" (per 25 U.S.C. § 3001 (13)). The other subsection (18 U.S.C. § 1170 (b)) criminalizes the knowing sale, purchase, use for profit, or transportation for sale or profit of other NAGPRA-defined "cultural items" (per 25 U.S.C. §§ 3001 (3) (A), (B) & (C)) obtained in violation of NAGPRA. Regardless of value or loss, a first violation is a misdemeanor, and a second or subsequent violation is a felony. Illegal trafficking in Native American human remains and cultural items is a general intent crime.

### *United States v. Kenneth L. Milette*[19]

Kenneth Lee Milette pled guilty to one misdemeanor count of trafficking in Native American human remains (18 U.S. C. 1170 (a)), two felony counts of violation of ARPA (one count each of 16 U.S.C. 470ee (b) & (c)), and one count of unlawful sale of migratory birds (16 U.S.C. 703 (a) & 707 (b)(2)), which is a Class E felony. In addition to these four counts, Milette had been charged in an indictment with one count of unlawful possession of a golden eagle (16 U.S.C. 668 (a)) and one count of unlawful sale of a golden eagle (16 U.S.C. 3372 (a)(1) & (4), 16 U.S.C. 3372 (d)(1)(B), and 16 U.S.C. 668)). He was sentenced to 36 months of supervised probation, to include six months of electronically monitored home detention. During his probation, Milette will be prohibited from incurring new debt, opening additional lines of credit, entering into any contracts, or having access to any checking account, ATM card, or credit card without the approval of his probation officer. Also, he must pay the costs for an advertisement designed to educate the public on the unlawful removal of archaeological resources from public lands, to be published in three regional newspapers. In addition, Milette was ordered to pay restitution to the National Park Foundation in the amount of $10,000, and to return to the National Park Service the $7,000 in earnest money he had received as part of a sting operation. Further, he must forfeit almost 1,500 archaeological resources that had been removed illegally from Indian lands belonging to the Nez Perce, Coeur d'Alene, Spokane, and Little Blackfeet reservations, and from public lands belonging to Little Bighorn Battlefield National Park, Glacier National Park, and Lake Roosevelt National Recreation Area, as well as archaeological resources that had been removed illegally from the Lindenmeier Site—a National Historic Landmark located on private land, where artifacts from the prehistoric "Folsom Culture" were first found—and were trafficked interstate, in violation of Colorado state law.

In early 2003, a joint investigation was begun by the National Park Service, FBI, Bureau of Indian Affairs, Bureau of Alcohol, Tobacco and Firearms, Fish and Wildlife Service, and the Confederated Tribes of the Colville Reservation, after Milette had advertised the sale of archaeological items in the want ad section of a local paper and on Internet sites such as eBay. The investigation revealed that Milette possessed archaeological resources from graves and other sites located on public and Indian lands, including Native American human remains. He also possessed and was offering for sale contraband wildlife. In November 2003, in a buy/bust operation, the defendant agreed to sell nearly 1,500 items—about 5% of his collection—to an undercover National Park Service law enforcement agent for $750,000, and received $7,000 in earnest money. The value of the archaeological resources that had been removed from public and Indian lands later was determined to be $58,500.

In a plea agreement, the United States and Milette determined that Milette's final adjusted offense level would be 17, which, if Milette's criminal history category were determined to be I, would result in an advisory guideline sentence (under Guideline 2B1.5) of 24 to 30 months of imprisonment. Nonetheless, the United States agreed to request a downward departure from the advisory guideline range. The judge agreed, and imposed the requested sentence.

On September 24, 2009, the archaeological resources that been removed illegally from Indian lands were returned to tribal representatives during a ceremony held at the Federal courthouse in Spokane, Washington.

## Theft of Property Belonging to an Indian Tribal Organization and Unlawful Receipt of Property Stolen from an Indian Tribal Organization

The first paragraph of 18 U.S.C. § 1163 creates the crime of theft of property belonging to an Indian tribal organization or in the custody of a tribal organization official. The second paragraph of the statute concerns the unlawful receipt or possession of that property after it has been stolen. The statute defines "Indian tribal organization" as any tribe, band, or community of Indians that is subject to the laws of the United States relating to Indian affairs, or any corporation or other group that is organized under any such laws.

In order to prove unlawful receipt of property stolen from an Indian tribal organization, the Government must prove that, at the time of the alleged unlawful act, the property in question "belonged" to an Indian tribal organization or was in the custody of a tribal organization official; that the defendant received, concealed, or retained that property; that the defendant knew the property was stolen; and that the defendant intended to deprive the Indian tribal organization of the use of that property. The law provides for both a Class D felony and a Class A misdemeanor offense, depending on the value of the property stolen, with the dividing line between a misdemeanor and a felony offense being $1,000. Thus, in order to prove felony receipt of stolen property from an Indian tribal organization, the Government also must prove that the value of the property in question was greater than $1,000. Interestingly, while "value" is defined in the theft and embezzlement of Government property statute, the term has been left undefined in the embezzlement and theft from Indian tribal organizations statute.

A defendant who has been found guilty of embezzlement and theft from an Indian tribal organization also may be sentenced to pay a fine. For a felony offense, an individual may be fined up to $250,000 and an organization may be fined up to $500,000. If the offense is a misdemeanor, the maximum fine is $100,000 for an individual and $200,000 for an organization.

### *United States v. Jeanne H. Redd and Jerrica Redd*[20]

Jeanne H. Redd pled guilty to three felony counts of unlawful receipt of property stolen from an Indian tribal organization (18 U.S.C. 1163), two felony counts of violation of ARPA (16 U.S.C. 470ee (b)), and two felony counts of theft of Government property (18 U.S.C. 641).[21] She was sentenced to 36 months of supervised probation, during which she has been prohibited from entering all tribal lands and public lands managed by the Bureau of Land

Management, Forest Service, National Park Service, and Fish and Wildlife Service. During the term of her probation, she also is prohibited from purchasing, selling, exchanging, excavating, or removing archaeological resources, regardless of their legality or origin, and from associating with persons involved in such activities. She also was ordered to pay a fine in the amount of $2,000. Indicted with Jeanne Redd was her husband James D. Redd. He was charged with one felony count of unlawful receipt of property stolen from an Indian tribal organization (18 U.S.C. 1163), but committed suicide in June 2009, shortly after he was indicted. Jerrica Redd, the daughter of Jeanne and James Redd, pled guilty to one felony count of unlawful receipt of property stolen from an Indian tribal organization (18 U.S.C. 1163) and two felony counts of violation of ARPA (one count each of 16 U.S.C. 470ee (a) and (b)). She was sentenced to 24 months of supervised probation, during which she, too, has been prohibited from entering all tribal lands and public lands managed by the Bureau of Land Management, Forest Service, National Park Service, and Fish and Wildlife Service, and from purchasing, selling, exchanging, excavating, or removing archaeological resources, regardless of their legality or origin, and from associating with persons involved in such activities. Both Jeanne and Jerrica Redd were further ordered to forfeit their interests in computer equipment, a global positioning unit, and 812 archaeological resources—including human remains—in their possession.

Jeanne Redd admitted to having possessed, sold, or exchanged Ancestral Puebloan cultural items that she knew had been taken from public lands managed by the Bureau of Land Management and the Forest Service, and from the Navajo Indian Reservation. Jerrica Redd admitted to traveling to an area of the Navajo Indian Reservation known as Hoskinnini in April 2008, in order to look for Native American artifacts, excavating and removing three ceramic vessels from Reservation land, and transporting the vessels to her home in Blanding, Utah.

The United States had recommended probation for Jerrica Redd, but had recommended that Jeanne Redd be sentenced to 18 months of imprisonment. Each Statement of Reasons for Judge Clark Waddoups' sentences was ordered docketed separately as a sealed document. The judge did state, though, that "this [Blanding, Utah] is a community where this kind of conduct . . . has been justified for a number of years," that Jeanne Redd "is a woman who has spent her life as a member of her community," and that "prosecution in this case provides sufficient deterrence."

Jeanne Redd has a history of misconduct involving cultural heritage resources. In 1996, she and James Redd, together with several children, were found by a San Juan County sheriff's deputy digging at an Ancestral Puebloan midden containing human remains, located on State land in Cottonwood Wash, near Bluff, Utah. As a result, in 1997, Jeanne and James Redd were criminally charged with desecration of a corpse, a felony. Three times district court judges dismissed the charges, but they were reinstated by courts of appeal. In 2002, Jeanne Redd pled no contest to a reduced misdemeanor count of attempted abuse or desecration of a body, and was placed on unsupervised court probation for six months. The charge against James Redd was dismissed because, according to Utah Assistant Attorney General Joanne Slotnick, Jeanne Redd "was the prime mover and the one most interested in these sorts of relics." In 2003, Jeanne and James Redd settled a $250,000 civil suit against them by the Utah School and Institutional Tribal Lands Administration for their having injured the grave site, and agreed to pay the State $10,000.

Jeanne and Jerrica Redd are the first defendants to be sentenced as the result of a two and a half year undercover operation begun in 2006, known as "Cerberus Action." As part of the operation, an antiquities dealer operating as a paid informant for a team of FBI and Bureau of Land Management law enforcement agents, who is called "the Source" in court documents—he has been identified as Ted Gardiner—infiltrated a network of diggers and dealers in Utah, New Mexico, and Colorado, and spent more than $335,000 in the course of purchasing, selling, and exchanging Ancestral Puebloan archaeological resources known to have been illegally removed from public and Indian lands in the Four Corners area of the Southwest.

Some of the suspects described their methods of looting to "the Source." They discussed digging in camouflage or by moonlight; knowing when a park ranger takes his days off; and looting in the spring, when the earth softens. One suspect said he scouted for ruins in a fly-over, and followed up the flight with a 10-mile hike to a site. A second suspect said he dug fresh holes on his property in case "someone comes asking" about the origin of his artifacts. A third revealed to "the Source" that, in a 1986 search, federal agents seized 32 ceramic vessels, but overlooked a hidden safe and a ledger documenting his trade in archaeological resources and naming his clientele. "The Source" also was told by a suspect that the suspect would die in a gunfight with federal agents rather than be arrested for his crimes.

Beginning in June 2009, 26 suspects, 17 of them residents of San Juan County, Utah, were arrested and indicted, and additional parties were the subject of search warrants. As of August 2009, the investigation was not yet over, according to Brett Tolman, the United States Attorney for the District of Utah. Added Carlie Christensen, First Assistant U.S. Attorney, "It's fair to say the investigation is looking at all levels, from diggers and dealers to high-end collectors."

Two of the suspects have committed suicide. One week after James Redd committed suicide, Steven Shrader, a Santa Fe, New Mexico resident, killed himself in Illinois. On March 1, 2010, Ted Gardiner died during a confrontation with local police officers. The Utah state medical examiner's preliminary report listed the probable cause of death as a self-inflicted gunshot wound.

## National Stolen Property Act

### Interstate Transportation of Stolen Property

Part of the National Stolen Property Act is codified at 18 U.S.C. § 2314. Some of the prohibited acts in this section include the transportation or transfer in interstate or foreign commerce of stolen goods having a value of $5,000 or more. In addition, the Government must prove that the defendant knew the goods had been stolen or obtained by fraud. Interstate transportation of stolen property is a Class C felony.

### *United States v. Bernard Jean Ternus*[22]

Bernard Jean Ternus pled guilty to one count of conspiracy to transport or transfer in interstate or foreign commerce stolen goods having a value of $5,000 or more (18 U.S.C. § 371, 18 U.S.C. § 2314). He was sentenced to 60 months of imprisonment, to run consecutively to a two-month prison term for his conviction on one count of fraud in procuring a visa (18 U.S.C. 1546 (a)).[23] Upon release, Ternus will be on 36 months of supervised release that will run concurrently with the 36-month term of supervised release he received for the visa fraud conviction. During the term of supervised release, Ternus must participate in an approved substance abuse treatment program. Also, following his release from imprisonment, Ternus will be placed in the custody of U.S. Immigration and Customs Enforcement for removal proceedings consistent with the Immigration and Nationality Act. A determination of restitution was deferred until a later date and, at the time of this writing, such a determination is unknown. Ternus has filed an appeal from his sentence with the United States Court of Appeals for the Eleventh Circuit.

Ternus entered the United States in July 2007, and settled in Florida. Between August 2007 and June 2008, he and his co-conspirators tried to broker the sale of four paintings, valued at $6.3 million, which had been stolen on August 5, 2007, during an armed robbery at the Musée des Beaux-Arts, in Nice, France. The paintings were *Cliffs Near Dieppe*, by Claude Monet; *The Lane of Poplars at Moret*, by Alfred Sisley; and *Allegory of Water* and *Allegory of Earth*, both by Jan Breughel the Elder.

In Florida, Ternus held several meetings with a group of would-be buyers, during which he revealed to them that his associates had stolen the paintings, that the paintings were located in southern France, and that he needed to find a buyer for them. The would-be buyers were, in fact, undercover agents from the Federal Bureau of Investigation and the French National Police.

In a later meeting with the undercover agents in Spain, Ternus and a coconspirator negotiated a two-part, 3 million-euro (about $4.7 million) transaction involving the paintings. The two-part transfer was structured in order to create leverage with law enforcement officials in the event anyone was arrested upon the sale of the first two paintings. Should anyone be arrested, the remaining two paintings could be used to bargain for their release.

Following the meeting in Spain, further meetings involving Ternus and the undercover agents took place in Florida. The parties were joined by two of Ternus's co-conspirators who had arrived from France via Madrid. After these meetings and the return of the co-conspirators to France, arrangements were made for the transfer of the stolen paintings and the purchase money, to occur in southern France.

In June 2008, the sting operation culminated in the arrest by the French National Police of Ternus's co-conspirators in southern France, and the arrest of Ternus in Florida by FBI and Immigration and Customs Enforcement agents. The French National Police recovered all four stolen paintings from a van in Marseilles, France.

## Sale or Receipt of Stolen Property Which Has Crossed a State or United States Boundary

Another part of the National Stolen Property Act is codified at 18 U.S.C. § 2315. Some of the prohibited acts in this section include possessing, concealing, storing, bartering, selling, or disposing of stolen goods having a value of $5,000 or more, or pledging or accepting as security for a loan stolen goods having a value of $500 or more. In addition, the Government must prove that the goods crossed a State or United States boundary after being stolen or unlawfully converted, and that the defendant knew the goods had been stolen or unlawfully converted. Sale or receipt of stolen property is a Class C felony.

### *United States v. Christian Popescu*[24]

Christian Popescu pled guilty to one count of sale or receipt of stolen property that has crossed a State or United States boundary after having been stolen (18 U.S.C. § 2315). He was sentenced to 30 days of imprisonment with credit for time served, to be followed by 36 months of supervised release, of which 3 months must be spent, at Popescu's cost, in the home confinement program, with electronic monitoring. During the term of supervised release, Popescu must participate in an approved substance abuse treatment program, and he will be prohibited from incurring new credit charges, opening additional lines of credit, or obtaining a loan without the approval of his probation officer. The court found that Popescu would be unable to pay a fine and, accordingly, waived the imposition of one.

In November 2008, at a Starbucks coffee shop, Popescu agreed to sell a would-be buyer a six-inch long, 18-carat gold bookmark for $100,000 that he knew had been stolen in Spain. The buyer was an undercover agent for Immigration and Customs Enforcement (ICE), and Popescu was arrested in the coffee shop's parking lot during the transaction.

The bookmark is believed to have been a gift from Eva Braun to Adolph Hitler to reassure him after the German Army's defeat at Stalingrad, in 1943. It bears Hitler's image, is topped by an imperial eagle and a swastika, and is inscribed with the message "My Adolph, don't worry . . . [the defeat] . . . was only an inconvenience that will not break your certainty of victory. My love for you will be eternal, as our Reich will be eternal. Always yours, Eva. 3-2-43." After the deaths of Hitler and Braun, the bookmark is believed to have been in the possession of the family of Field Marshal Wilhelm Keitel, an armed forces chief under Hitler who was tried for war crimes in Nuremberg and executed.

In October 2002, the bookmark was set to be auctioned in Madrid, Spain, when it, along with several pieces of jewelry, was stolen from the auction house by three Eastern Europeans. Most of the jewelry was recovered, but not the bookmark. Following the theft, the auction house paid the bookmark's owner 10,000 euros in compensation (at the time, approximately $9,800). An insurance company later paid the auction house 10,000 euros for the loss. Spanish authorities have determined that, today, the value of the bookmark is $13,000–17,000.

Popescu, a Romanian national, purportedly obtained the bookmark for $3,500, and had been seeking a buyer for about three years before U.S. law enforcement agents entered the case. ICE was joined in the investigation by the Spanish National Police, Interpol, the Seattle Police Department, the Port of Seattle Police Department, the Bellevue Police Department, and the ICE attaché in Madrid.

In a news release, the special agent-in-charge of ICE's Office of Investigations identified the bookmark as a "historical artifact." Yet, Popescu was not sentenced under advisory sentencing guideline 2B1.5 for crimes involving a cultural heritage resource. Likely, the United States could not fit the bookmark under the meaning of "cultural heritage resource" for purposes of applying 2B1.5, so, instead, 2B1.1, the generic property crimes guideline, was used to sentence him. If Popescu's sentence had fallen under 2B1.5, which has a higher base offense level and more apposite specific offense characteristics, perhaps his sentence of imprisonment would have been greater.

## Mail Fraud

Whoever uses the U.S. Postal Service or any private or commercial interstate carrier in order to further a scheme to defraud, or obtain money or property by means of false pretenses, representations, or promises is guilty of mail fraud (18 U.S.C. §1341). Mail fraud is a specific intent crime, and a Class C felony.

A defendant who has been found guilty of mail fraud also may be sentenced to pay a fine. For a felony offense, an individual may be fined up to $250,000 and an organization may be fined up to $500,000.

### *United States v. Constance "Connie" Breithoff and Christopher Breithoff*[25]

Constance Chapman Breithoff and Christopher Barrett Breithoff each pled guilty to one count of conspiracy to commit mail fraud (18 U.S.C. § 371, 18 U.S.C. § 1341). Constance Breithoff was sentenced to 18 months of imprisonment, to be followed by 36 months of supervised release. Her son, Christopher Breithoff, was sentenced to 21 months of imprisonment, to be followed by 36 months of supervised release. During their supervised release, both defendants have been ordered to participate in an approved program of orientation and life skills. Also, they will be prohibited from incurring new credit charges, opening additional lines of credit, or obtaining a loan without the approval of their probation officer(s). In addition, the defendants were ordered to pay, jointly and severally, restitution in the amount of $924,023 to the persons injured by their offenses.

The Breithoffs, who, since 1999, owned and operated the Barlow Art Gallery and Transitions, in Louisiana, devised a scheme to defraud customers through misrepresentations. They would purchase from wholesale distributors, in bulk, paintings from China, knowing that Barlow would resell them as original works by local and emerging artists. Constance Breithoff concocted fictional artist identities, biographies, and unique signatures to mask the true nature and origin of the Chinese paintings. In some instances, she would paint over an existing signature on the Chinese artwork with a bogus artist's signature. The defendants would misrepresent the true artist's identity to Barlow's customers, and would provide them with fictional written biographies of the nonexistent artists. In advertisements on their website and in person they would represent that artwork sold at Barlow was painted by "hand-picked local and regional artists" and by "emerging artists." Using the U.S. Postal Service and United Parcel Service, they sent customers certificates of authenticity, along with descriptions of such fictional artists as "Falgot," "S.A.M.," "Shanta," or "Michel."

In January 2008, the FBI seized gallery records that included documentation of the fake artists' biographies and the unique signatures. Other records showed that the Breithoffs charged customers significantly more for a painting once they had assigned it a bogus artist's identity and signature.

## Notes

1. The section editor wishes to thank Elise Foster, Attorney, for her technical assistance.
2. *United States v. Jimmy Barney and David Woolsey*, No. 2:91-CR-00263-JTG (D. Utah sentence Oct. 6, 1992).
3. *See* Robert Palmer, *Federal Prosecutions under the Archaeological Resources Protection Act of 1979: A Ten-Year Review (1996-2005)*, YEARBOOK OF CULTURAL PROPERTY LAW 2007 221-235 (Sherry Hutt ed., 2007).
4. *Id.*
5. *Id.*
6. For a complete and reader-friendly history, presentation, and explanation of U.S. Sentencing Guideline § 2B1.5, see Paula J. Desio, *Crimes and Punishment: Developing Sentencing Guidelines for Cultural Heritage Resources Crimes*, in LEGAL PERSPECTIVES ON CULTURAL RESOURCES 61–84 (Jennifer R. Richman & Marion P. Forsyth eds., 2004).
7. For a discussion of the intent, or *mens rea*, required to be proved in an ARPA criminal prosecution, see Marion P. Forsyth & David Tarler, *Model Jury Instructions in ARPA Prosecutions: Removing the "Lynch-Pins,"* in PRESENTING ARCHAEOLOGY IN COURT 127-142 (Sherry Hutt, Marion P. Forsyth & David Tarler eds., 2006).

8. For a detailed treatment of ARPA civil penalties, see Elise Foster, U.S. Dept. of Agric., USING ARPA CIVIL PENALTIES TO PROTECT ARCHEOLOGICAL RESOURCES ON PUBLIC AND INDIAN LANDS (Sherry Hutt & David Tarler, Nat'l Park Serv., eds., 2007).
9. *United States v. Dawn Laate*, No. 09-MJ-00146-DLW and *United States v. Preston A. Waggoner*, No. 09-MJ-00147-DLW (D. Colo. sentence Nov. 10, 2009).
10. *United States v. Patricia Doyle*, No. CR 08-60043-1-AA (D. Or. sentence Feb. 12, 2009).
11. For reports on other prosecutions of "Operation Bring'em Back" defendants, see *Enforcement Actions*, YEARBOOK OF CULTURAL PROPERTY LAW 2007, at 123-126, and *Enforcement Actions*, YEARBOOK OF CULTURAL PROPERTY LAW 2008, at 140 and 143-145.
12. *United States v. Gregory Truesdell*, No. CR06-735-CAS (C.D. Cal. sentence Sept. 11, 2009, amended Sept. 14, 2009).
13. *United States v. Oscar Ortega-Moreno and Sergio Corona-Venzor*, No. 08-MJ-00032-GJR (D. Colo. sentence Feb. 2, 2009).
14. *United States v. William A. Graves and Misty D. Graves*, No. 3:08CR30005 (W.D. Ark. sentence June 24, 2009).
15. *United States v. Charles Penn Lindsey*, No. 09-mj-01080-MEH (D. Colo. sentence June 17, 2009).
16. *United States v. Dino Harrison*, No. 1:08CR00838-001WDS, and *United States v. John Oliver Darby*, No. 1:08CR01833WDS (D.N.M. sentence Sept. 29, 2008 (Harrison), guilty plea Sept. 14, 2009 (Darby)).
17. *United States v. John M. Sheild*, No. 3:08CR30127, *United States v. Brian R. Ekrem*, No. 1:08CR10073-001, and *United States v. Richard D. Geffre*, No. 3:08CR30124-001 (D.S.D. sentence Aug. 4, 2009 (Sheild), Aug. 12, 2009 (Ekrem), and Aug. 21, 2009 (Geffre)).
18. *United States v. Joshua T. McCarty and Zachary Scranton*, No. 3:08cr409, and *United States v. Angela K. Bays*, No. 3:08crMJ7091 (N.D. Ohio sentence Mar. 30, 2009 (McCarty and Scranton), complaint dismissed Oct. 7, 2008 (Bays)).
19. *United States v. Kenneth L. Milette*, No. 08CR00134-001 (E.D. Wash. sentence Dec. 16, 2008).
20. *United States v. Jeanne H. Redd*, No. DUTX2:09-CR-00044-001-CW and *United States v. Jerrica Redd*, No. DUTX2:09-CR-000467-001-CW (D. Utah sentence Sept. 16, 2009).
21. The first paragraph of 18 U.S.C. § 641 creates the crime of theft of Government property, which is the unlawful taking of "a thing of value of the United States." The second paragraph of the statute concerns the unlawful possession of that property after it has been stolen.

    In order to prove theft of Government property, the Government must prove that, at the time of the alleged unlawful act, the United States owned, or had possession of and control over, the property in question; that the defendant stole that property; and that the defendant intended to deprive the Government of the use and benefit of that property. See Leonard Sand, John S. Siffert, Walter P. Loughton, Steven A. Reiss, & Nancy Batterman, MODERN FEDERAL JURY INSTRUCTIONS—CRIMINAL VOLUMES § P 23A.01 (Theft of Government Property) (2005).

The law provides for both a felony and a misdemeanor offense, depending on the value of the property stolen, with the dividing line between a misdemeanor and a felony offense being $1,000. Thus, in order to prove felony theft of Government property, the Government also must prove that the value of the property in question was greater than $1,000. "Value" is defined in the statute. It means "face, par, or market value, or cost price, either wholesale or retail, whichever is greater" (18 U.S.C. § 641).

22. *United States v. Bernard Jean Ternus*, No. 08-20586-CR-SEITZ/001 (S.D. Fla. sentence Sept. 24, 2009), *appeal docketed*, No. 08-15687-EE (11th Cir. Sept. 28, 2009).
23. Ternus, a French citizen, falsely stated in a visa application that he had no criminal history when, in fact, he had been arrested in France on at least seven separate occasions between 1966 and 2002, and had been convicted on a charge of assault with a deadly weapon in 2006. He pled guilty to the charge.
24. *United States v. Christian Popescu*, No. 2:08CR00400RSM-001 (W.D. Wash. sentence June 19, 2009).
25. *United States v. Constance "Connie" Breithoff and Christopher Breithoff*, No. 08-cr-249-L-EEF (E.D. La. Sentence Nov. 19, 2009).

# New Jurisdictional Tools for Displaced Cultural Property in Russia

## *From "Twice Saved" to "Twice Taken"*

*Amelia Borrego Sargent*[*]
*1st Place Winner 2009 LCCHP/Andrews Kurth LLP Law School Writing Competition*

The D.C. Circuit Court's recent opinion in *Agudas Chasidei Chabad v. Russian Federation* allowed jurisdiction under the expropriation exception of the Foreign Sovereign Immunities Act (FSIA) over Russia and its agencies by employing an expansive interpretation of a "taking in violation of international law."[1] The court held that a governmental "frustration" of an owner's effort to physically recover property, when recovery had been secured through a final judicial judgment, may effect a "retaking" sufficient for jurisdiction.[2] This template for a "retaking" or "second taking" of property has potentially broad consequences for cultural property displaced during and after World War II, particularly in Russia. It also severely limits one of the most effective defenses customarily employed by nations drawn into litigation, the Act of State Doctrine.

This paper examines the implications of *Chabad* for art and antiquities restitution cases in the United States with a particular eye toward Russia, whose museums hold enormous collections of so-called "trophy art" collected after World War II. First, I provide a short historical introduction to the problem of trophy art in Russia, followed by an examination of the FSIA and how it has been

* J.D. Candidate, Stanford Law School; Ph.D. Candidate, University of California, Berkeley. I would like to thank Professor Jenny Martinez, Professor John Merryman, and Matthew Sargent for their valuable comments and support.

expansively applied in Holocaust art restitution cases in the United States. Then I discuss the *Chabad* decision regarding the FSIA's burden of proof standard and template for "twice taken" cultural property, and its implications for the FSIA expropriation exception and the Act of State Doctrine. Finally, I consider how the "twice taken" template may interact with Russia's Federal Law on Displaced Cultural Valuables, and discuss some of the policy implications and likely efficacy of this judicial expansion of the FSIA. Ultimately, I conclude that, although this judicial innovation will make it much easier for individuals to press claims for restitution of Holocaust art, U.S. judicial orders will only exacerbate tensions with reticent countries like Russia. One may hope that such increased tension will spur diplomatic efforts from both sides toward a solution.

## "Twice Saved" Trophy Art

### Art Looting During World War II

Millions of cultural objects were looted or displaced during World War II, including artworks, antiquities, religious objects, sculpture, monuments, and artifacts.[3] Hitler first began realizing his ideological policy of a "pure" and "Germanic" Europe when he rose to power in 1933.[4] Among other things, achieving this involved the systematic wholesale appropriation and purging of so-called "degenerate" or "depraved" art within Germany, which included works by abstract contemporary artists such as Kandinsky or Franz Marc, works by Jewish artists, and works in Jewish collections.[5] Many such works were exhibited for ridicule in "Degenerate Art" shows around Germany, while others were appropriated from their owners or museums and sold on the open market to raise funds for the Third Reich.[6] Some works ended up in the private collections of Nazi officials.[7] "Worthless" paintings were burned.[8]

When war broke out, no fewer than four agencies backed by the Nazi police and military dealt with art matters.[9] Two of these were particularly dedicated. Hitler envisioned a vast museum complex in his hometown of Linz, and established a personal agency to build up a collection with works from newly conquered territories, focusing on the finest examples of art Europe's museums had to offer.[10] The Einsatzstab Reichsleiter Rosenberg [ERR] was a much larger operation. Created under the direction of Albert Rosenberg to loot Jewish books, archives, and religious objects for the purposes of setting up an anti-Semitic think tank, it eventually expanded its activities to include the indiscriminate taking of art from occupied territories that Nazi party officials directed to be seized.[11]

Nazi art looting on the Eastern front was particularly brutal. Slavic culture was to be eliminated completely; only works with "Germanic" connections were preserved.[12] Both the ERR and the Schutzstaffel [SS] engaged in art plunder, with the SS "using methods so brutal that they drew criticism from Reichsleiter Rosenberg himself."[13] The ERR had looting divisions in Minsk, Riga, Tallinn, and Kiev.[14] Many cultural and religious institutions were simply destroyed; the Nuremberg war crimes indictment lists the destruction of over 427 museums, 1,670 Russian Orthodox churches, 237 Roman Catholic churches, and 532 synagogues in the occupied territory of the USSR.[15] The palaces at Pushkin (Tsarskoye Selo), Peterhof (Petrodvorets), Pavlosk, Gatchina, and Oranienbaum (Lomonosov) were also plundered or burned.[16] Buildings in the medieval cities of Novgorod and Gdov were damaged or destroyed by bombs and fire.[17] The famous eighteenth-century Amber Room from the Catherine Palace at Pushkin was dismantled and taken to Königsberg.[18] Never recovered and presumably destroyed, it remains a symbol to the Russians of the cultural treasures lost during World War II.[19]

Albert Rosenberg's conviction at Nuremberg was the first time plunder of cultural property was held to be a war crime.[20] The indictment listed the plunder and destruction of cities, cultural monuments, and "property of all types" as contrary to the Hague Convention (1907), and listed particular museums, private collections, and cities plundered and destroyed in both Western and Eastern countries.[21] The final judgment summed up only a portion of Rosenberg's activity:

> Acting under Hitler's orders of January 1940 to set up the "Hohe Schule," he organized and directed the "Einsatzstab Rosenberg," which plundered museums and libraries, confiscated art treasures and collections, and pillaged private houses.
>
> His own reports show the extent of the confiscations. In "Aktion-M" (Möbel), instituted in December 1941 at Rosenberg's suggestion, 69,619 Jewish homes were plundered in the West, 38,000 of them in Paris alone, and it took 26,984 railroad cars to transport the confiscated furnishings to Germany. As of July 14, 1944, more than 21,903 art objects, including famous paintings and museum pieces, had been seized by the Einsatzstab in the West. . . . The Tribunal finds that Rosenberg is guilty on all four Counts.[22]

He was sentenced to death by hanging.[23]

## Art Looting After World War II

While the Allies jointly considered looting and pillage of cultural property *during* wartime to constitute a crime, the legality of similar activities *after* wartime was more complex. "[S]everal million" objects of art were gathered by U.S. MFA&A officers (Monuments, Fine Arts & Archives Section) at Collecting Points, artworks that the Nazis scattered and dispersed, hid in caves and mines, and walled up in underground bunkers as Allied troops advanced.[24] The Allies had never formulated a coherent policy on restitution-in-kind or using cultural assets as reparations.[25] Ultimately, U.S. and British policy became to return a work to the nation from which it had been taken.[26] German state collections presented a different problem. Initially, several top officials at the U.S. Treasury and State Departments felt certain works should be taken to the United States for "safekeeping," and regarded as reparations.[27] Two hundred and two paintings were taken under protest by MFA&A officers, who felt that "safeguarding" the pictures—"a favorite Hitlerian euphemism"—was directly comparable with Nazi actions during the war.[28] The paintings were exhibited at the National Gallery in Washington, D.C., but ultimately returned to Germany in 1949.[29]

The Soviet approach was much different. As opposed to the Western Allies, whose stationing of art-specialist officers within their ranks was at first "not thought . . . necessary" and in hindsight considered "something of a miracle,"[30] the Soviet government began plans for restitution with Nazi artworks in 1943.[31] In August of that year, Russian art historian Igor Grabar suggested to Nikolai Shvernik, the head of the Extraordinary State Commission, that Soviet museums should be compensated for damage and loss in the form of artworks "equivalent to their losses from enemy collections."[32] The Commission ordered that lists be drawn up of valuable objects in German museums that would be "equivalent" to those lost.[33] What exactly was lost, however, was unknown; destroyed or looted Soviet museums were located in territory still under Nazi occupation.[34] "Equivalent" art thus became a euphemism for "masterpieces in enemy collections that . . . should be brought to the USSR after the war."[35] Experts drew up detailed lists of objects with short descriptions and their locations not only from museums in Germany, but also from Austria, Italy, Hungary, Romania, and Finland.[36] Plans circulated among official circles for a Museum of World Art in Moscow, envisioned as a repository for Axis countries' "wonderful masterpieces, which must be given to the Soviet Union as compensation," and "concentrated in one place . . . [to] play the role of a perfect memorial dedicated to the glory of Russian arms."[37]

Trophy brigades were created on each front to organize the collection of cultural objects.[38] These brigades were made up of thousands of civilian officials from Soviet cultural agencies and organizations: artists, scholars, museum curators and directors, art historians, theater directors, and musicians.[39] They wore military uniforms in order to appear inconspicuous, as the mission was kept secret from both Allied and Soviet forces.[40] Over the course of 1945, a single brigade sent twelve trainloads and three cargo planes of looted art to the USSR.[41] Among the treasures collected were the Bronze-Age Treasure of Priam and the Pergamon altar, which had been in Berlin, and Raphael's *Sistine Madonna* from the Dresden Gallery.[42] As it became clear that the Western Allies were collecting Nazi art to return to the nations of origin, the Soviet trophy brigades' work was expedited to ensure the works did not fall into U.S. or British hands.[43]

Plans for the "supermuseum" never materialized, and total secrecy was imposed on the trophy art.[44] In 1955, however, the Soviet Union began discussing the return of the Dresden Gallery to the newly created German Democratic Republic (GDR).[45] On May 2, 1955, an exhibition of the Dresden masterpieces opened at the Pushkin, which were portrayed as "rescued" from destruction during World War II. In his opening speech, the Soviet Minister of Culture Nikolai Mikhailov described the artwork as having been saved twice: first by the Soviet army, and second by museum officials and conservators.[46] The collection was returned to the GDR after the exhibit.[47] Under Khrushchev, a further 1.5 million works of art and 121 boxes of books and photographs were returned to the GDR,[48] though an official count had revealed 2.6 million objects and 534 crates of archaeological material in Russian hands.[49] In 1960, the Soviet government publically denied the existence of any more trophy art.[50]

### "Twice Saved" or Twice Stolen?

The actions of the Soviet trophy brigade were unknown in the West until 1991, when two Russian journalists reported the existence of "hidden treasures" in the Soviet Union.[51] In 1995, they published a book documenting for the first time the systematic looting of German sites by Soviet trophy brigades just after World War II.[52] Their allegations were confirmed when, in 1995, two Russian museums shocked the art world by staging exhibits of art and artifacts long thought lost or destroyed.[53] On February 27, 1995, the Pushkin Museum opened an exhibit of 63 works that including the artists El Greco and Goya.[54] The name of the exhibit was "Twice Saved," parroting the propaganda surrounding the Dresden exhibit in the 1950s that the masterpieces had been saved from destruction first by the Soviet trophy brigades and then by the Russian museums.[55] This was followed by the Hermitage Museum's "Hidden Treasures Revealed" on March 25, 1995, which featured 74 paintings, including Degas' famous *Place de la Concorde*, Gauguin's *Two Sisters*, and Van Gogh's *White House at Night*.[56]

Obviously, the works displayed were only a small portion of the cultural property remaining in Russia; a current estimate puts the number of artworks and antiquities still in Russia at over 1.2 million, books at well over 10 to 12 million volumes, and 870 trophy archival finds.[57] Their presence had been concealed behind the Iron Curtain for nearly 50 years.

Many of the works were recognized as having belonged to private collections or museums in Germany prior to World War II, leading Germany to immediately seek their return, but its claim for restitution has been fraught with questions about reparations for war damages.[58] Germany's claims are pursuant to international laws of war against plunder, as well as a bilateral treaty that stipulates "missing or unlawfully removed art treasures which are located in [German or Russian] territory will be returned to the owners or their legal successors."[59] Russia insists that its treasures are compensatory restitution, and that historical precedent stemming from Napoleon is evidence of a customary international law norm.[60]

Claims for restitution are not limited to Germany, however. The trophy brigades took cultural property indiscriminately, and much of it had been plundered or "coercively acquired" by the Nazi art-looting machine.[61] Many items were owned by Jewish art collectors who had been forced to flee or were victims of the Holocaust.[62] Others are from the museum collections of occupied nations. Many have yet to be traced; Poland, Belgium, France, and the Netherlands list losses of art taken by the Nazis which still have not been recovered, and could be in Russia's possession.[63] For example, a collection of over 100 Old Master drawings from the Koenigs Collection in the Netherlands surfaced in Kiev in 2003 and was returned by Ukraine.[64] Vast state archives from France, Belgium, the Netherlands, and Luxembourg, as well as French Jewish and Masonic holdings, have been located in the Russian Central State Special Archive and returned, though more undoubtedly exist.[65]

The problem of displaced and looted art from World War II is not Russia's alone,[66] but Russia's reluctance to engage in restitution efforts has led many to consider Russia's trophy art not "twice saved," but "twice stolen," first by the Nazis and then by the Soviets.[67] Overwhelming Russian sentiment, however, views the trophy art as compensation for enormous losses suffered during World War II.[68] In 1995, the Duma enacted a moratorium on restitution of foreign cultural property,[69] and in 1998 passed a law nationalizing most of the "displaced cultural property" located on Russian territory.[70] Russia's Federal Law on Displaced Cultural Valuables is widely considered to be contrary to international law norms and treaties; Yeltsin himself refused to sign it until forced by the Russian Constitutional Court.[71] This law and how it may interact with the recent ruling in *Agudas Chasidei Chabad v. Russian Federation* will be discussed below.

## The FSIA and Art Restitution Cases in the United States

### Art Restitution Cases before the 1990s

Prior to the FSIA's enactment, no cases involving Holocaust art restitution were brought against foreign nations.[72] Until 1952, the United States adhered to a theory of absolute sovereign immunity, meaning that no foreign sovereign could be haled into U.S. court. As states began acting in private commercial capacities, however, more and more governments embraced exceptions to absolute sovereign immunity. In 1952, the Department of Justice issued the Tate Letter, which recognized that absolute immunity was no longer a tenable policy and adopted a restrictive theory of immunity.[73] This theory allowed jurisdiction over foreign sovereigns with respect to their commercial acts.[74]

Even with restricted immunity, foreign sovereigns were still well protected from U.S. courts. The Act of State doctrine precludes courts adjudicating claims involving actions of foreign states, even if the conduct would be illegal in the forum nation.[75] This can include the taking of property.[76] The one art restitution case that arose prior to the FSIA, *Menzel v. List*, was between two individuals.[77] The plaintiff had fled her Brussels apartment in 1941, and returned to find her Chagall painting gone. In its place was a receipt, informing her that it had been confiscated by the Einsatzstab Rosenberg (ERR).[78] When the painting appeared in New York several years later, she sued the good faith purchaser for its return. The defendant argued that the Act of State doctrine precluded the court's inquiry into the Nazi ERR's confiscation of the painting.[79] Because sovereign acts were granted immunity under the

Act of State doctrine, the court found that the paintings were seized by "an organ of the Nazi party" and not by a foreign sovereign recognized by the United States.[80]

Only three other cases involving Holocaust art arose in the 1970s and 1980s, all of which involved artwork located in the United States.[81] In the 1990s, however, there was renewed interest in Nazi-era looted art.[82] Two influential historical accounts were published documenting the extent of Nazi looting, one of which identified over 1,000 looted paintings in French museums.[83] As discussed above, the Iron Curtain fell, and the "hidden treasures" of the Soviet Union were discovered and exposed.[84] The first international academic symposium was convened, featuring art historians, legal scholars, and representatives from nearly a dozen countries identifying losses and damage during World War II and discussing restitution and reparations.[85] Widespread attention was given to the problem of restitution of artwork to the heirs and survivors of victims of the Holocaust. U.S. commissions and task forces to aid in the return and restitution of despoiled art were established.[86]

### The FSIA's Expropriation Exception

Importantly, between *Menzel* and the resurgence of interest in the 1990s, Congress had passed the FSIA. The FSIA was passed in 1976 to clarify the U.S. position on restrictive sovereign immunity and provide a formal procedure for gaining jurisdiction over foreign states in U.S. courts.[87] The purpose was set out at 28 U.S.C. § 1602:

> The Congress finds that the determination by United States courts of the claims of foreign states to immunity from the jurisdiction of such courts would serve the interests of justice and would protect the rights of both foreign states and litigants in United States courts. Under international law, states are not immune from the jurisdiction of foreign courts insofar as their commercial activities are concerned, and their commercial property may be levied upon for the satisfaction of judgments rendered against them in connection with their commercial activities. Claims of foreign states to immunity should henceforth be decided by courts of the United States and of the States in conformity with the principles set forth in this chapter.[88]

Under the FSIA, general immunity was offered to foreign sovereigns subject only to certain listed exceptions.[89] If the exception applied, a federal U.S. court could exert jurisdiction over a foreign sovereign.[90] Crucially, where subject matter jurisdiction is found, personal jurisdiction automatically follows as long as the defendant has been properly served.[91] The Act of State doctrine may still preclude a court from adjudicating the merits of a case, but the FSIA allows foreign sovereigns to be haled into U.S. courts.[92]

Of the exceptions listed in § 1605, the most important for art restitution claims is the expropriation exception. This reads:

(a) A foreign state shall not be immune from the jurisdiction of courts of the United States or of the States in any case—

(3) in which rights in property taken in violation of international law are in issue and that property or any property exchanged for such property is present in the United States in connection with a commercial activity carried on in the United States by the foreign state; or that property or any property exchanged for such property is owned or operated by an agency or instrumentality of the foreign state and that agency or instrumentality is engaged in a commercial activity in the United States.[93]

In order to raise a claim under this exception, the plaintiff must allege that 1) "rights in property" are at issue and that 2) property was "taken in violation of international law," and then satisfy one of two cases outlined in the two clauses of § 1605(a)(3). The first clause covers property (or property exchanged for that property) present in the United States in connection with a commercial activity carried on by the foreign state. The second clause covers property (or property exchanged for that property) owned by an agent or instrumentality of the foreign state that is engaged in commercial activity in the United States.

In the cases falling under this exception, "property taken in violation of international law" has been interpreted to mean property taken in one of three ways: First, valid expropriations of property must always be for a public purpose.[94] Second, "aliens [must] not be discriminated against or singled out for regulation by the state."[95] Third, "An otherwise valid taking is illegal without the payment of just compensation."[96] In order to be "taken in violation of international law," the taking has to be done by a foreign sovereign, though not necessarily the same one over which jurisdiction is sought.[97] The question of whether or not a taking exists for the purposes of jurisdiction does not have to be determined on the merits prior to adjudication, but is merely held to a "substantial and non-frivolous claim" standard.[98]

### The FSIA Expanded I: *Republic of Austria v. Altmann*

A key expansion of the FSIA's expropriation exception was required to make it applicable to the art restitution cases: the exception had to cover takings that occurred prior to the FSIA's enactment in 1976.[99] This question was resolved in *Republic of Austria v. Altmann*, the only art restitution case to this date to go before the Supreme Court.[100]

The case concerned six Gustav Klimt paintings that had belonged to the wealthy Czech sugar magnate Ferdinand Bloch, a Jew who had been forced to flee Germany just before World War II.[101] His wife, Adele Bloch-Bauer, who was the subject of two of the paintings, had died in 1925, and left a will leaving the paintings to Ferdinand and requesting that he donate them to the Austrian Gallery upon his death.[102] Ferdinand died in exile in 1945, leaving his estate to his nieces and nephew.[103] Nazi officials had "Aryanized" his company, and his collections of art and porcelain were divided and sold.[104] The Nazi lawyer liquidating the estate, Dr. Erich Führer, donated two of the Klimt paintings to the Austrian Gallery, claiming in a letter to fulfill Adele's will.[105]

Despite the Republic of Austria's 1946 declaration that transactions carried out by the Nazis were null and void, the heirs were unsuccessful in recovering the Klimt paintings.[106] In 1948, Austria's Federal Monument Agency offered to grant export permits to the family's other recovered artworks in exchange for the "donation" of the six Klimt paintings, even though museum officials knew they had no grounds for legally claiming the paintings.[107] The family reluctantly accepted the deal.[108] In 1998, a journalist examining the Gallery's files found documents revealing that the Gallery officials knew neither Adele nor Ferdinand had donated the paintings, and noting that the portrait of Adele, "which all the [Gallery] publications represented as having been donated to the museum in 1936, had actually been received in 1941, accompanied by a letter from Dr. Führer signed 'Heil Hitler.'"[109] The remaining heir attempted first to bring suit in Austria, and then commenced an action in the United States under the second clause of the FSIA's appropriation exception.[110]

The sole question before the Supreme Court was whether the FSIA allowed jurisdiction over expropriations that occurred prior to its enactment, and even more specifically, to those occurring before the U.S. adoption of the restrictive theory of sovereign immunity in the Tate Letter of 1952.[111] After examining the history of the doctrine of sovereign immunity and distinguishing the "anti-retroactivity presumption" established by prior Supreme Court decision in *Landgraf v. USI Film Products*, the Court determined that the structure of the FSIA and Congress's intent both allowed it to be applied to the taking at issue in the case.[112]

The decision turned on the preamble's phrase, "*Claims* of foreign states to immunity should *henceforth* be decided by courts of the United States and of the States in conformity with the principles set forth in this chapter."[113] The

Court determined that immunity "claims," not the underlying actions triggering the FSIA exceptions, were the "relevant conduct regulated by the Act."[114] Regardless of when the taking occurred, then, a claim filed "henceforth" for litigation is to be decided only under the FSIA.[115] The decision ensured that all illegal takings—in this case, either the Nazi seizure during World War II or the museum's actions in 1948—could be litigated under the expropriation exception of the FSIA.

After the Supreme Court decision, Austria and Maria Altmann agreed to end litigation and submit the dispute to arbitration, which resulted in return of five of the Klimt paintings.[116] They were placed on temporary exhibition at the Los Angeles County Museum of Art.[117]

### The FSIA Expanded II: *Malewicz v. City of Amsterdam and Cassirer v. Kingdom of Spain*

The success of the *Altmann* case prompted additional Holocaust art litigation, which continued the trend of judicial expansion of the FSIA.[118] In *Malewicz v. City of Amsterdam*, the heirs of Kazimir Malewicz, an abstract Russian artist, sued the City of Amsterdam, alleging the expropriation of 84 of his paintings by the City.[119] More than 100 of Malewicz's paintings had been entrusted to a German friend in 1927 for an exhibition in Berlin. When the Nazis suddenly banned such "degenerate art,"[120] the collection was divided; part was sent to the United States and part to Amsterdam's Stedelijk Museum.[121] In 1958 the German friend sold the works in Amsterdam to the City, though he arguably had no authority to pass title to them.[122]

In 2003, fourteen of the works were loaned to two art museums in the United States.[123] While they were in the United States, Malewicz's heirs filed suit under the first clause of the FSIA's expropriation exception, allowing jurisdiction when the expropriated "property . . . is present in the United States in connection with a commercial activity carried on in the United States by the foreign state."[124] Before process was served on the City of Amsterdam, the paintings returned to the Netherlands.[125] The court determined, however, that jurisdiction attached if the conditions were met at the time of filing, and that the fact the lawsuit was filed while the paintings were in the United States was "sufficient to meet the 'present in the United States' factor . . . without regard to later service of the complaint."[126] The court denied the City's motion to dismiss, but required more information to determine whether the City carried on sufficient "commercial activity" in the United States to satisfy the requirements of the FSIA.[127]

In 2007, the court issued a second opinion finding sufficient commercial contacts between the City and the United States, and denying the defenses the City had raised.[128] The contracts were related to the loan of the artworks themselves: the contract for the loan, the 25,000 Euro consideration provided by the U.S. museums, and the exchange of Stedelijk staff to oversee the safety of the paintings.[129] The court also addressed the application of the Act of State doctrine, holding first that, as the Act of State doctrine defense was properly a Rule 12(b)(6) defense, a court must be satisfied that there is "no set of facts" favorable to the plaintiff in the complaint that could negate an alleged "act of state."[130] The court determined that a museum's acquisition of artworks was simply not an act of state pursuant to *jure imperii*, and moreover that adjudicating the matter would not imperil U.S. foreign relations with the Netherlands.[131] The court again denied the City's motion to dismiss.[132]

Though only a district-level court opinion, the implications of this holding are far-reaching. Most museums in Europe are public institutions, and are thus included in the definition of a "foreign state" under the FSIA.[133] Since according to the court's reasoning, contract terms, consideration paid, and staff accompaniment in the course of a loan of art or artifacts to a U.S. museum constitute sufficient "commercial activity" for the expropriation exception, any such museum's art or artifacts of uncertain title could be subject to suit as soon as they are "present in the United States." Any state museum's loan of a painting of uncertain title is essentially guaranteed to fall under the expropriation exception of the FSIA. This possibility could have a serious "chilling effect" on the loan of artwork to the United States, as occurred following the infamous *Portrait of Wally* scandal, where a painting on loan from Austria to the New York Museum of Modern Art was seized by U.S. officials as illegally imported stolen property.[134]

Another district-level opinion further clarified and expanded the reach of the FSIA, though appellate rehearing *en banc* is currently pending. In *Cassirer v. Kingdom of Spain*, the plaintiff sought to recover a Pissarro painting that a Nazi art dealer in Munich, Jakob Scheidwimmer, had coerced Lily Cassirer Neubauer (plaintiff's grandmother) into relinquishing in exchange for an exit visa in 1939.[135] The Kingdom of Spain purchased the painting in 1993 along with a collection of works owned by Baron Thyssen-Bornemisza.[136] This claim was brought pursuant to the second clause of the expropriation exception, which allows jurisdiction when the expropriated property "is owned or operated by an agency or instrumentality of the foreign state and that agency or instrumentality is engaged in a commercial activity in the United States."[137]

Unlike the previous cases, the Kingdom of Spain was not the "taking" party, but rather a good faith purchaser.[138] As a preliminary matter, then, the court had to determine explicitly whether Scheidwimmer's actions constituted a "taking in violation of international law."[139] The first issue was whether the art dealer was an agent of a "sovereign," since the act of a "taking in violation of international law" must be by a foreign state.[140] The court determined that Scheidwimmer was "an agent of the Nazi German regime" based on expert testimony asserting that he was a "member of the Nazi Party, implemented state policies and can be viewed as an agent of the state."[141] Interestingly, this approach directly contradicts the New York court's 1966 decision in *Menzel v. List*, which refused to consider the Nazi party a sovereign (and the ERR an agent of that sovereign) because sovereign actions at the time were almost totally immune to suit under the Act of State doctrine.[142]

The second question was whether a "taking in violation of international law" could have occurred, since Lily Cassirer Neubauer was a German national and the Nazi party was in control of Germany.[143] Takings between citizens and the sovereign of the same state are considered domestic acts, and do not implicate international law.[144] However, the court determined that Ms. Neubauer was not actually a citizen of Germany, because "according to the Nazis' citizenship laws at that time, '[a] Jew cannot be a citizen of the Reich' and '[a] citizen of the Reich is that subject only who is of German or kindred blood.'"[145]

The *Cassirer* court's two innovations, first, that an individual Nazi art dealer is an "agent of a foreign state" for the purposes of FSIA, and second, that a Jewish person *per se* cannot be considered a German citizen under the Third Reich, have immense implications for applying the FSIA to future Holocaust art cases and indeed, to all property cases arising from Nazi expropriation. By this reasoning, *any* Nazi party member who appropriates property, whether acting as part of a systematic looting scheme or simply for individual gain, may be an "agent" of a foreign state sufficient under the FSIA's definitions at § 1603.[146] Moreover, *any* Jewish person may bring a claim, even if he or she was German, because no Jewish person may be "a citizen of the Reich." Finding that such an appropriation was substantively a "taking in violation of international law," i.e., that it was not for a public purpose, or it was discriminatory against aliens, or for which just compensation was not paid,[147] is subsequently a very simple task.

## Is an "Expansive Reading" of the FSIA Appropriate?

In her study on the topic, Lauren Redman summarizes the FSIA's applications in *Altmann*, *Malewicz*, and *Cassirer* and questions whether such an "expansive" reading is appropriate.[148] She identifies cases where the Supreme Court has upheld the general constitutionality of the FSIA as well within the ceiling of judicial power granted by Article III, and within Congress's power to enact pursuant to both the Commerce and the Offenses Clause.[149] She concludes that it is within congressional power, that it has been confirmed by the Supreme Court, and that other exceptions of the FSIA are also used to pull defendants into court.[150]

Additional analysis would note that an expansive reading of the FSIA for the purposes of redressing atrocities committed by the Nazis comports with a sense of fundamental justice, a motivating factor behind the flexibility embodied in the U.S. common law system. An example of just this type of reasoning lies in the comparative characterizations of the Nazi party in *Menzel v. List* and *Cassirer v. Kingdom of Spain*. In *Menzel*, the court determined the Nazi party was not a sovereign in order to keep the plaintiff's suit in court.[151] In *Cassirer*, the court determined the Nazi party *was* a sovereign for the same reason.[152] Overly rigid readings of either the FSIA or the Act of State doctrine would result in denial of judicial hearings of possibly meritorious claims.

Moreover, congressional intent accords with these judicial readings of the FSIA. Congress devoted Title II of the Holocaust Victims Redress Act to "Works of Art."[153] Congress found that "The Nazis' policy of looting art was a critical element and incentive in their campaign of genocide against individuals of Jewish and other religious and cultural heritage."[154] They also found, "the same international legal principles applied among states should be applied to art and other assets stolen from victims of the Holocaust."[155] In explicitly authorizing the application of international legal principles to Holocaust art, Congress must be understood as implicitly authorizing the assertion of jurisdiction over those foreign states reluctant to return such art. Indeed, Congress concluded in § 202:

> It is the sense of the Congress that consistent with the 1907 Hague Convention, all governments should undertake good faith efforts to facilitate the return of private and public property, such as works of art, to the rightful owners in cases where assets were confiscated from the claimant during the period of Nazi rule and there is reasonable proof that the claimant is the rightful owner.[156]

But what about Soviet trophy art? In the same Act, Congress also found that "In the aftermath of the war, art and other assets were transferred from territory previously controlled by the Nazis to the Union of Soviet Socialist Republics, much of which has not been returned to rightful owners."[157] This carefully worded admonition avoids a finding as to the nature of the "transfer" itself, while appealing to Russia in its general conclusion for the return of such art "to rightful owners." Russia, however, is reluctant to do so. This section will discuss the application of the FSIA in *Agudas Chasidei Chabad v. Russian Federation*, the first case involving the return of Russian "twice saved" cultural property.

## "Twice Taken" in *Agudas Chasidei Chabad v. Russian Federation*

### Factual Disposition of *Agudas Chasidei Chabad v. Russian Federation*

Agudas Chasidei Chabad is a Jewish organization incorporated in the United States that oversees the worldwide Chasidic spiritual movement Chabad-Lubavitch.[158] Generally known as Chabad, the movement was formed in 1775 in Russia,[159] and was led by a succession of spiritual Rebbes (Rabbis) who over the course of the movement's history collected a vast number of books, manuscripts, and documents that "comprise the textual basis for the group's core teachings and traditions."[160] Large portions of this collection were lost first during World War I and the Bolshevik Revolution, and second during World War II.[161] These form the core of the dispute in *Agudas Chasidei Chabad v. Russian Federation*.

The lower court recognized two distinct sets of property at issue in the case: the "Library" and the "Archive."[162] The Library, based on a collection beginning in 1772, consists of more than 12,000 books and 381 manuscripts,[163] while the Archive is comprised of "over 25,000 pages of Chabad Rebbes' handwritten teachings, correspondence, and other records."[164] Both the Library and the Archive have deep spiritual, religious, and historical significance for Chabad.[165]

As the German army advanced on the Eastern Front in 1915, the Fifth Rebbe fled Lubavitch and sent the Library to a private warehouse in Moscow.[166] The Soviet government seized the Library during the aftermath of the subsequent Bolshevik Revolution and transferred it to a state facility.[167] In 1921, the Soviet Department of Scientific Libraries approved the return of the Library to the Sixth Rebbe (the Fifth Rebbe having died in 1920), though he lacked the funds to secure their return.[168] By 1925, however, the Soviet government "appear[ed] to have finally rejected pleas for the return of the

Library" and stored it at the Lenin Library, which later became the Russian State Library (RSL).[169] The Sixth Rebbe was arrested in 1927 for "counter revolutionary activities" (establishing Jewish schools) and sentenced to death.[170] Bowing to international pressure, the Soviets allowed him to leave for Latvia, where he resettled—leaving behind the Library, but taking the Archive—and became a citizen.[171]

In 1933 the Sixth Rebbe moved to Poland, bringing the Archive with him.[172] Following the Nazi invasion of Poland in 1939, the Rebbe fled to the United States, leaving the Archive behind.[173] Part of the Archive arrived in the United States under unknown circumstances in 1941.[174] The rest was seized by the Nazis and transferred to a Gestapo-controlled castle at Wölfelsdorf.[175] Soviet military forces seized the Archive from there as "trophy documents" in 1945 and transferred them to what is now known as the Russian State Military Archive (RSMA) in Moscow.[176]

In 1991, Chabad began efforts to retrieve the Library in earnest. According to Chabad, Mikhail Gorbachev instructed the RSL to return the Library on September 6, 1991.[177] Three weeks later, Chabad petitioned an arbitration court in the Soviet Union to order the RSL to return the Library.[178] The State Arbitration Tribunal ruled that the Library had not been nationalized after the Bolshevik Revolution and ordered its return.[179] Upon arrival at the RSL to receive the Library, however, the Chabad delegation was met by an angry mob of RSL staff, who taunted them with "anti-Semitic slurs and threats of violence" while "30 baton-wielding RSL police officers allegedly attacked" them.[180]

The Soviet Union collapsed on December 25, 1991. On January 29, 1992, according to Chabad's account, the Deputy Chairman of the Russian Federation again ordered the Library returned to the Chabad delegation.[181] Once again, the delegation encountered an anti-Semitic mob "incited by an RSL director" when it arrived to take possession of the Library.[182] Shortly thereafter, the Deputy Chief State Arbiter of the Russian Federation purported to overturn the previous court order mandating the Library's return.[183] A few days later, a session of the Supreme Soviet nullified the Deputy Chairman's decree.[184]

### The Lower Court's Ruling

Chabad brought suit against the Russian Federation for the return of both the Archive and the Library under the second clause of FSIA's expropriation exception, which allows jurisdiction when "rights in property taken in violation of international law are in issue and . . . that property . . . is owned or operated by an agency or instrumentality of the foreign state and that agency or instrumentality is engaged in a commercial activity in the United States."[185]

The lower court had no trouble asserting jurisdiction over the Archive under the FSIA's expropriation exception.[186] First, it asserted that "the defendant-state need not be the state that took the property in violation of international law," citing *Altmann*, dispelling any defense Russia may have raised as the successor to the Soviet Union, but not the "taker" of property.[187] Using the factors asserted in *Siderman de Blake v. Republic of Argentina*, the court found both the Nazi "taking" during World War II and the Soviet "taking" in 1945 to be "in violation of international law."[188] Neither taking was for a public purpose, and neither offered the payment of just compensation.[189] The taking by the Nazis, moreover, was also discriminatory, fulfilling all three categories of a "taking in violation of international law.[190] The court also found that the RSMA's commercial publication contracts with Yale University Press and Primary Source Media (both U.S. companies) satisfied the FSIA requirement that the agency owning the Archive was "engaged in a commercial activity in the United States."[191]

Neither did the Act of State doctrine preclude the court from adjudicating the issue with respect to the Archive. Despite an ambiguity at argument whether the Russian Federation was actually attempting to apply the Act of State doctrine to the Archive,[192] the court clarified that the Act of State doctrine applies only to "acts of foreign sovereigns . . . within their own jurisdictions."[193] It determined that "[t]he Nazi taking of Jewish property during the Holocaust was manifestly illegal."[194] Additionally, whether or not the Soviet Army's taking was "an official government act," the Act of State doctrine did not apply because the taking occurred in Poland and not Soviet territory.[195]

The Library was a different story. Though the Library was also not taken for a public purpose, was discriminatory, and was not followed by just compensation, the court determined that because the Fifth and Sixth Rebbes were Russian citizens at the time, principles of international law did not apply.[196] Though Chabad argued that the "taking" at issue was when the Soviet Union nullified the order to release the Library to Chabad in 1992,[197] the court concluded that "the Library's taking took place in or around 1920, when the Soviet government sealed it and moved it to a state facility, or, at the latest, in 1921, when, in unclear circumstances, the Sixth Rebbe had the opportunity to retrieve it but could not afford to."[198]

Moreover, regardless of when the taking of the Library occurred, the court determined that adjudicating the unlawfulness of such an act on the merits would be precluded by the Act of State doctrine.[199] Under Chabad's theory that the taking occurred judicially in 1992 rather than physically in 1920, the court would have to review an official judicial decision, which, "even . . . tainted by allegations of impropriety . . . is an official act of a sovereign nation."[200] The court asserted, "Chabad is in effect asking this Court to sit in review of the Deputy Chief State Arbiter of the Russian Federation. That this Court cannot do."[201] Under the theory the court did adopt, placing the taking in 1920, the Act of State doctrine "would squarely apply," since the Library's taking was pursuant to "official government directives."[202]

## Appellate Clarification of the FSIA's Proof Standard

The appellate court affirmed the district court's ruling with respect to the Archive, but reversed with respect to the Library.[203] More importantly, the court clarified the expropriation exception's burden of proof standard and established a template for a new type of taking in violation of international law, in both cases expanding the FSIA's jurisdictional reach.

First, the court determined that the expropriation exception of the FSIA has two types of jurisdictional questions: 1) factual propositions independent of the merits of the case, and 2) assertions of a particular claim.[204] Each of these carries a different burden of proof. For factual propositions, the plaintiff has the burden of production, and then the foreign sovereign claiming immunity has the burden of persuasion, and "must establish the absence of the factual basis by preponderance of the evidence."[205] Assertions of a particular claim, however, are held to the less demanding "substantial and non-frivolous" standard articulated in *Bell v. Hood*.[206] These do not have to be resolved prior to judgment on the merits; the assertions simply have to be "not wholly insubstantial and frivolous" in order for jurisdiction to be asserted.[207]

The expropriation exception involves both types of questions. The two alternative clauses of the FSIA that allow jurisdiction for property either 1) "present in the United States in connection with a commercial activity carried on in the United States," or 2) "owned or operated by an agency or instrumentality of the foreign state" that "is engaged in commercial activity in the United States," involve purely factual predicates.[208] These must be resolved favorably to the plaintiff before the suit can proceed.[209]

Assertions that rights in property are at issue, or that the property was in fact taken in violation of international law, are of the second type.[210] A plaintiff must assert both claims and produce sufficient evidence, but a threshold jurisdictional inquiry does not have to definitively resolve these questions. The court explained that despite the fact that a foreign sovereign defendant has asserted "various legal and factual inadequacies in the claims" as their defense, "*Bell* requires only that such potential inadequacies do not render the claims 'wholly unsubstantial' or 'frivolous.'"[211] The court pointed to the *West v. Multibanco Comermex* case, where the Ninth Circuit found the plaintiff's claim "substantial and non-frivolous" for the purposes of jurisdiction, though ultimately ruled against him on the merits.[212]

### The "Twice Taken" Template and the FSIA

The court then applied this standard to Chabad's claims to the Library. It identified the two possible "takings," the first in 1917–1925, and the second in 1991–1992.[213] Under the theory of the first taking, which the lower court held as definitive, Russia relied on the fact that the Sixth Rebbe was a Soviet citizen at the time, and therefore the taking did not implicate international law.[214] This depends on the contention, however, that the Library and Archive "were the personal property of the Fifth or Sixth Rebbe . . . [and] not of Chabad."[215] As evidence of this, Russia relied on the ruling of a previous case, *Agudas Chasidei Chabad of United States v. Gourary*, which resolved that a different set of books and manuscripts possessed by the Sixth Rebbe in New York were the property of Chabad, but only on the narrow grounds that the Sixth Rebbe had transferred them to Chabad, not based on a broader theory that the Rebbe had at all times been acting on behalf of the religious community.[216]

The appellate court determined that Russia's reliance on this case was misplaced, since the *Gourary* case involved a different set of materials, and the ultimate resolution in favor of Chabad on the narrow grounds did not require the rejection of the broad theory.[217] For the purposes of jurisdiction, the court determined that Russia's "proposed misapplication of the *Gourary* case" failed to show Chabad's claim of ownership to the Library was "insubstantial or frivolous."[218] The plaintiff's simple contention that "the worldwide Chabad organization, not any Soviet citizen, owned the Library," is sufficient for a substantial and non-frivolous claim that the taking in 1917–1925 was in violation of international law.[219]

Moreover, the "substantial and non-frivolous" standard resuscitated Chabad's claim that the Library had been "retaken" in 1991–1992. The court found a template for such a taking in the facts of *Altmann v. Republic of Austria*.[220] In that case, the heirs to the Bloch-Bauer Klimts "recovered" title to the paintings (presumably when Austria declared takings by the Nazis null in 1946), but then, in exchange for export licenses, "donated" them to the Austrian Gallery.[221] The 1948 "donation" was the taking at issue in the case.[222] The court extended the analogy: "Here, Agudas Chasidei Chabad never recovered *possession* of the Library, but we should think that a final court decree in its favor, subject to no *lawful* appeal, might be considered a recovery, such that governmental frustration of the decree's enforcement could qualify as a renewal of the earlier taking."[223]

In fact, the court presented two possible "retakings" of the Library on *Chabad's* facts, either of which fulfilled the FSIA's "substantial and non-frivolous" requirement. First, there was substantial and non-frivolous basis for believing that the Soviet State Arbitration Tribunal and Chief State Arbiter's decision in late 1991 to order the transfer of the Library to Chabad "represented a legal recovery."[224] Chabad's efforts to actually regain possession of the property was frustrated by anti-Semitic and baton-wielding RSL staff members.[225] Second, in January 1992 after the collapse of the Soviet Union, the Deputy Chairman of the Russian Federation ordered the Library returned to the Chabad delegation.[226] The delegation again encountered an anti-Semitic mob at the RSL, preventing it from retaking possession.[227] Furthermore, the Deputy Chief Arbiter "purported to reverse the prior court orders" on February 14, and a legislative decree was issued on February 19 nullifying the executive order.[228] The *Chabad* court concluded:

> To the extent that Shokhin's decree or the Chief State Arbiter's order effected a recovery of the Library (within the meaning of *Altmann*), the actions of the Deputy Chief State Arbiter and the Supreme Soviet, coupled with the RSL action on the ground, would appear to have effected a retaking.[229]

The court's ruling has broad implications for what can constitute a "taking in violation of international law" for the purposes of the expropriation exception of the FSIA. By its terms, the court's ruling allows judicial or executive decrees of "recovery," and then subsequent frustration of that recovery by both political and practical state action, to constitute a taking. (Presumably, the legislative branch could also effect a "recovery.") But at what level must the decrees of recovery and subsequent frustration come? The court emphasized that in *Chabad*, a judgment from "the highest available judicial authority" that was abruptly "reversed" by a "lower" court would certainly constitute a retaking.[230] Additionally, high executive action "paralleling" those of the "highest court," but then "followed by countermanding legislative action" "enhance[s] the retaking case."[231] At the very least, the ruling opens up jurisdiction under the FSIA to property initially "taken" physically, and then "retaken" politically. This is particularly significant for property that may not otherwise have qualified as "taken in violation of international law" under the expropriation exception due to other circumstances.[232]

Moreover, the court emphasizes that recovery "within the meaning of *Altmann*" is a necessary element of the retaking template. But to what extent did the Bloch-Bauer heirs actually "recover" the Klimt paintings prior to Austria's retaking in 1948? They received no judicial or executive decree effecting an explicit recovery of their paintings; rather, the Gallery claimed title to the paintings under color of Adele's will, and was even preparing a lawsuit for return of the additional Klimt paintings not yet in its possession.[233] In fact, the Ninth Circuit's opinion on whether or not there was a "taking in violation of international law" analyzes the taking by the Nazis, not the taking by the museum.[234] Only in a footnote does it mention the possibility that the Austrian Gallery's actions in 1948 may also be a taking.[235] It was the Supreme Court opinion, which ruled only on the question of the FSIA's retroactivity, that suggested it applied "to petitioners' 1948 actions."[236]

This raises the question to what extent a "recovery" is actually a necessary component of a "twice taken" claim. If the original taking was in fact a violation of international law, as, for example, all Nazi seizures are *per se* considered, then no lawful title is held by the foreign sovereign. It is difficult to see why a later action somehow frustrating an attempt at return to a lawful owner, if that action itself meets the *West* factors for a "taking in violation of international law,"[237] should be dependent on a prior declaratory judgment effecting a "recovery."

### "Twice Taken" Implications for the Act of State Doctrine

The "twice taken" theory also has implications for the Act of State doctrine, one of the strongest defenses for sovereigns facing an expropriation claim under the FSIA. The Act of State doctrine was codified in *Banco Nacional de Cuba v. Sabbatino*, in which the Supreme Court declined to examine the validity of a decree of the Cuban government expropriating sugar from a Cuban company whose stock was held by U.S. residents.[238] The Court decided that the judicial branch:

> will not examine the validity of a taking of property within its own territory by a foreign sovereign government, extant and recognized by this country at the time of suit, in the absence of a treaty or other unambiguous agreement regarding

> controlling legal principles, even if the complaint alleges that the taking violates customary international law.[239]

As previously discussed, the Act of State doctrine was alleged by the defendant in *Menzel v. List*, but the court decided that the Nazi party was not a sovereign for the purposes of the doctrine.[240] It was also asserted in *Malewicz v. City of Amsterdam*, where the court determined that acquisition of artworks by a museum was not pursuant to a state's *jure imperii*.[241] The reach of this holding is unclear; though artwork acquisition may be construed as commercial activity, the "taking of property by a foreign sovereign government" is explicitly what the Act of State concerns.[242]

The Second Hickenlooper Amendment, however, precludes the application of the Act of State doctrine to takings occurring after 1959.[243] The Second Hickenlooper Amendment was enacted by Congress in response to the unsatisfactory outcome of *Sabbatino*. It reads in its relevant part:

> Notwithstanding any other provision of law, no court in the United States shall decline on the ground of the federal act of state doctrine to make a determination on the merits giving effect to the principles of international law in a case in which a claim of title or other right to property is asserted by any party including a foreign state (or a party claiming through such state) based upon (or traced through) a confiscation or other taking after January 1, 1959, by an act of that state in violation of the principles of international law, including the principles of compensation and the other standards set out in this subsection. . . .[244]

Even if a taking of property in violation of international law was an "act of state," if it occurred after January 1, 1959, the Second Hickenlooper Amendment allows courts to adjudicate it on the merits.

As the appellate court in *Chabad* points out, the district court erred in suggesting that the 1991–1992 "taking" claim, even if accepted by the court, would be barred by the Act of State doctrine.[245] Notwithstanding the fact that the Deputy Chief State Arbiter's decision and the Supreme Soviet's decree are acts of state, they occurred after 1959, and therefore, under the Second Hickenlooper Amendment, the Act of State doctrine does not apply.

Having given the district court an easy way to gain jurisdiction over the Library by determining the 1991–1992 acts to be a "second taking" and applying the Second Hickenlooper Amendment, the appellate court then raises several issues questioning the application of the Act of State doctrine to the 1917–1925 seizure.[246] The court examines the quotation establishing the Act of State doctrine in *Sabbatino* and discusses possible factors suggested by *Chabad* that might militate against the application of the doctrine. The strongest is in the case of regime change, relying on the language that the taking be by a "sovereign government, extant and recognized by this country at the time of suit."[247] In this case, however, the court suggested that determining whether the transition from the Soviet Union to the Russian Federation is comparable to other radical regime changes would be a political question.[248]

A second possibility relies on the *Sabbatino* Court's suggestion that "the greater the degree of codification or consensus concerning a particular area of international law, the more appropriate it is for the judiciary to render decisions regarding it."[249] *Chabad* suggested that takings "in a campaign to suppress the practice of Judaism" violate *jus cogens* norms, parallel to racial discrimination.[250] Though the court found this "intuitively appealing," it questioned whether there is "nearly universal consensus against religious prejudice" sufficient to comprise a *jus cogens* norm, and concluded, "a glance around the world exposes glaring examples to the contrary."[251] Nonetheless, the court vacated the lower court's ruling.

The "twice taken" template established by the *Chabad* court thus dramatically expanded the opportunities for disputes over property taken in violation of international law to be brought into court. First, it allows for secondary administrative or governmental frustrations of attempts to recover property to be considered "takings" for the purposes of the expropriation exception. Second, because many of these secondary administrative takings will have occurred after 1959, it dismantles the Act of State doctrine by virtue of the Second Hickenlooper Amendment.[252] Both these expansions will be useful for plaintiffs in recovering wrongfully taken property.

These expansions may have particular consequences for Russia. The confusion of the political structure just after the fall of the Soviet Union worked in the plaintiff's favor in *Chabad*.[253] Additionally, however, the "twice taken" template may implicate Russia's Federal Law on Displaced Cultural Valuables.

## Is Russia's Federal Law on Displaced Cultural Valuables a Taking?

### The Federal Law on Displaced Cultural Valuables

In 1997, the Russian Duma passed a law "On Cultural Valuables Displaced to the U.S.S.R. as a Result of World War II and Located on the Territory of the Russian Federation."[254] President Yeltsin, who believed the law was contrary to international law norms and also contrary to the Russian Constitution, initially refused to sign it.[255] The Duma overrode his veto, which forced his signature in 1998, and he immediately appealed to the Constitutional Court regarding the validity of the law. The basic text of the law was upheld, though the Court suggested a number of legal irregularities. It was amended and signed into law by President Vladimir Putin in 2000.

The law employs the concept of compensatory restitution as justification for its possession of "displaced cultural valuables." The law defines compensatory restitution under Art. 4 as:

> A form of international legal material responsibility of an aggressor state, applied in cases when implementation of said state's responsibility in the form of regular restitution is impossible, consisting of the responsibility to compensate for the material damage inflicted on another state by handing over to the affected state objects of the same kind (or by their removal by the affected state for its own benefit) as those that were plundered and illegally removed by the aggressor state from the territory of the affected state.[256]

Importantly, the definition makes a distinction between the aggressor state's "plunder" and "illegal removal," and the compensatory "handing over" or "removal" of property by the affected state. This distinction is the basis of the Russian position on its ownership of trophy art: Nazi plunder and destruction occurred *during* World War II, and thus violated the Hague Convention (1907) prohibiting plunder and the taking of property from individuals and religious and cultural institutions.[257] The idea of compensatory restitution, however, occurs *outside* the time of war, and is thus not governed by this or similar treaties.[258] Russia's position is therefore that the actions of its "trophy brigades" were not in any way similar to the actions of the Nazis, because it was acting under the "lawful" concept of restitution, rather than unlawful wartime pillage.[259]

Compensatory restitution, however, is not generally accepted as a lawful norm. Though international customary law is not uniform, subsequent treaties, such as the 1954 Hague Convention on the Protection of Cultural Property in the Event of Armed Conflict, the 1977 additional Protocols to the Geneva Human Rights Convention, and the 1970 UNESCO Convention on the Means of Prohibiting and Preventing the Illicit Import, Export and Transfer of Ownership of Cultural Property,[260] have both reinforced the idea of international recognition and protection of cultural property (belonging to the heritage of all mankind) while also recognizing that individual nations have a right to their own determined cultural heritage.[261] Some scholars have "wonder[ed] if, in the decades following the Second World War, an *opinio juris* has been found which by now excludes the retention or handing over of cultural property for reparations in any form, in consideration of a more general principle of territorial connection between cultural property and country of origin."[262] Russia's insistence on the trophy art's legality, moreover, is undermined by the secrecy with which the acquisition of "displaced cultural valuables" was carried out, and its subsequent denial of their existence.[263] Nonetheless, the Russian Constitutional Court took the concept of compensatory restitution for granted when it ruled on the constitutionality of the law.[264]

The Federal Law on Displaced Cultural Valuables essentially automatically nationalizes "displaced cultural property" in Russia originating in the territory of Germany or its former allies. Article 3 of the law regarding its applicability states: "The present Federal law shall be applicable to all displaced cultural valuables, determined by Article 4 of the present Federal law, irrespective of their actual ownership."[265] Article 4 defines "displaced cultural valuables" as:

> Any cultural valuables removed in implementation of compensatory restitution from the territories of Germany and its former military allies—Bulgaria, Hungary, Italy, Romania and Finland—to the territory of the U.S.S.R., pursuant to orders of the Soviet Army military command, the Soviet Military Administration in Germany or instructions of other competent bodies of the U.S.S.R. and that are located at the present time on the territory of the Russian Federation.[266]

This by its terms precludes items originating in countries victimized by the Nazis such as France or Poland (a key 2000 revision), though such items may still require governmental approval for transfer out of the country.[267] Article 6 effects the nationalization of all displaced cultural valuables subject only to certain temporary exceptions:

> All displaced cultural valuables imported to the U.S.S.R. in realization of its right to compensatory restitution and located on the territory of the Russian Federation, with the exception of those specified in Articles 7 and 8 of the present Federal Law, are the property of the Russian Federation and are federally owned.[268]

Article 7 guarantees the rights of ownership of former Soviet territories: Belarus, Latvia, Lithuania, Moldova, Ukraine, and Estonia.[269] At first, this would seem to be a redundant measure, since Article 3 stipulates that the law applies only to cultural property from Germany or German allies. It is in fact a holdover from the 1998 version of the law, which applied to "*all* cultural property . . . irrespective of the actual possessor and the circumstances leading to this actual possession" (emphasis added).[270] It was only with the 2000 Amendment that the law was restricted to so-called "enemy states."

Article 8 provides that Article 6 shall not apply to three categories of exceptions:

> 1) Cultural valuables of an interested state forcefully taken and unlawfully removed by former enemy states . . . ; 2) Cultural valuables which were the property of religious organizations or private charitable organizations and which were used exclusively for religious or charitable purposes and did not serve the interests of militarism and (or) Nazism (Fascism); 3) Cultural valuables which belonged to individuals who were deprived of these valuables because of their active struggle against Nazism (Fascism), including their participation in national resistance against the occupation regimes of former enemy states and collaborationist regimes, and (or) because of their race, religion, or national affiliation.[271]

"Interested states" as defined in Article 4 are those states that were occupied in full or in part by the military forces of enemy states.

Article 9, however, stipulates that these exceptions are only temporary. The original 1997/8 law stipulated that cultural valuables specified in the exceptions in Article 8, "for which interested parties have not filed a claim for return within 18 months of the entry into force of the present Federal Law . . . shall become federal property."[272] The current law has been amended, only specifying that the 18-month time limit begins to toll after a description of the cultural valuable in question has been published in an official catalogue.[273] Currently, that catalogue is published online at http://lostart.ru, which offers descriptions and images of items, but is available only in Russian and has no search function.[274]

The procedures for implementation of the law, moreover, include a number of provisions that highly restrict the actual claim and transfer of cultural property. With the exception of "family heirlooms," for which limited returns are available to individuals,[275] claims may only be made by "the government of the claimant state"; "claims of natural and legal persons, municipal bodies, non-governmental and other organizations and associations are not subject to consideration."[276] Second, all claims are subject to payment of expenses associated with its "identification, expert examination, storage and restoration, as well as for its transfer (transportation costs, etc.)."[277] Indeed, individuals claiming "family heirlooms" are required to pay their full reimbursement value, in addition to the costs listed above.[278] Finally, all claims must be approved by a political body, either by the Inter-Agency Council on Restitution, or, for items considered unique or particularly valuable (even those that by its terms do not fall under the Federal Law), by an act of the Duma.[279] Such procedures severely limit the possibility that this law will ever be satisfactorily used for the return (as opposed to the retention) of cultural property in Russia.

**Is the Federal Law a Taking?**

Could a law that essentially nationalizes all "displaced cultural property," regardless of claims of ownership, be considered a "taking in violation of international law" under the template suggested by the appellate court in *Agudas Chasidei Chabad v. Russian Federation*? Or at least, for the purposes of gaining jurisdiction under the FSIA, could such a claim be considered "not wholly insubstantial and frivolous"?[280]

Yes. First, *Chabad* held that a legislative order that frustrates an earlier recovery effected by either a judicial or executive decree may constitute a "retaking."[281] It is possible that other claimants of displaced cultural property besides Chabad also sought the restitution of their property in the 1990s. If any of them received an order or judgment in their favor, which was then frustrated or reversed either by the Duma's moratorium on restitution in 1995,[282] or the enactment Federal Law in 1998, they ought to be able to plausibly argue that such frustration effected a "retaking" of the property.

Second, as discussed above, under the *Altmann* model it is unclear to what extent a specific political or judicial decree is actually necessary to constitute a "recovery."[283] In *Altmann*, the Austrian Gallery's offer to "exchange" the Klimt paintings for export permits in 1948 was not contingent on a prior recovery; the Gallery *never* had good title to the paintings.[284] A direct parallel can be seen with the Federal Law on Displaced Cultural Valuables.[285] The law affects cultural valuables "irrespective of their actual ownership" (Art. 3). It either nationalizes all the valuables immediately (Art. 4), or, for those items falling within an exception in Article 8, within eighteen months of the publication of a description on a Russian-only website (Art. 9). Those items actually claimed under the law's provisions are subject to the exaction of payment for identification, examination, restoration, and transfer as well as 50 years of storage expenses (Art. 18(4)). Individual claimants of family heirlooms must also pay its reimbursement value (Art. 19(2)); essentially they must buy their property back from Russia.

The key element in this analogy is the question of whether Russia *ever* had good title to the displaced cultural property. In *Altmann,* the Gallery did not have title because the underlying taking by the Nazis violated international law.[286] Under Russia's theory of compensatory restitution, the takings by the Soviet trophy brigades were legal.[287] However, under the definition of a "taking in violation of international law" used by U.S. courts, the Soviet Army's actions are also in violation of international law. The lower court in *Chabad* held that the Archive seized by the Soviet Army as "trophy documents" in Poland "was neither taken nor held for a public purpose, as the Soviet Union did not even make it available for public use and long denied that it even had it," and that "regardless who the legal owner . . . was at the time, the Soviet Union neither provided nor offered compensation for it."[288]

Third, if a "taking in violation of international law" is in fact a taking that is 1) not for a public purpose, 2) discriminatory, or 3) one for which just compensation has not been paid, Russia's Federal Law on Displaced Cultural Valuables begins to look more like a *de facto* taking analogous to other nations' property nationalization laws. A host of factors militate against the contention that the nationalization serves a "public purpose," such as the fact that most of the cultural valuables covered by the law—particularly books and archives—have yet to be found and catalogued, and are certainly not available for public use.[289]

At the very least, the Law's provisions stipulating payment, particularly in the case of family heirlooms, offends the notion of providing "just compensation" for taken property. In fact, this was alluded to by the *Chabad* court in reference to Russia's contention that the FSIA carried with it an exhaustion requirement, obliging the plaintiff "to pursue and exhaust remedies it has in the Russian Federation."[290] Russia pointed to the procedures outlined in its Federal Law on Displaced Cultural Property.[291] The court determined that the FSIA carries with it no such exhaustion requirement, but that assuming it did, Russia's remedy was inadequate. The court, citing the provisions stipulating the "payment of its value as well as reimbursement of the costs of identification, expert examination, storage, restoration, and transfer (transportation, etc.)," resolved: "Whatever the valuation method, and assuming *arguendo* that Russia's *payment* of compensation would satisfy the requirements of international law, obviously Russia's mere willingness to *sell* the plaintiff's property back to it could not remedy the alleged wrong."[292]

### The Federal Law and the Act of State Doctrine

For the purposes of gaining jurisdiction under the FSIA, any one of the above-mentioned theories could support a "substantial and non-frivolous" claim for property "twice taken" in violation of international law. Ordinarily, the Act of State Doctrine precludes a court from examining the validity of a taking of property by 1) a foreign sovereign government, 2) extant and recognized by the United States at the time of suit, 3) when the taking occurred within the territorial limits of that government, and 4) when the taking was not a violation of a treaty obligation.[293]

In the event of a claim that the Federal Law on Displaced Cultural Valuables constituted a taking, however, the Act of State doctrine would not apply. As discussed above, the Second Hickenlooper Amendment bars its application for takings after January 1, 1959.[294] The date of the Federal Law's taking (or "retaking") would be when the law was enacted or amended, either 1998 or 2000.

There is nevertheless a possibility that the Act of State doctrine may be applied by the courts, though not in response to a defense raised by a defendant foreign state. The Second Hickenlooper Amendment makes an exception for "any case with respect to which the President determines that application of the act of state doctrine is required in that particular case by the foreign policy interests of the United States and a suggestion to this effect is filed on his behalf in that case with the court."[295] Should the executive branch determine that foreign policy interests are at stake, it may request that the case not be adjudicated.[296]

## "Twice Taken" Implications and Enforcement Issues

Despite the fact that there is now a strong argument for determining that Russia's Federal Law on Displaced Cultural Valuables is a "taking in violation of international law" for the purposes of FSIA jurisdiction, the question remains: should such an argument be made? Recognizing Russia's Federal Law on Displaced Cultural Valuables as a "second taking" would allow all "trophy art" in Russia to be the subject of suit in the United States. Cultural property falling under the purview of the law would be "taken" in the sense of being nationalized. Cultural property falling outside the purview of the law, thanks to the 2000 amendments limiting its application, is nevertheless still subject to governmental limitations on return.[297] Indeed, the property at issue in *Chabad* would seem to be totally outside the purview of the law, since the Archive was seized by the Soviets in Poland, which is not named in Article 4 as a former military ally of Germany.[298] The Archive is therefore not within the definition of the "displaced cultural valuables" to which the law ostensibly applies.[299] Nevertheless, Russia argued that the Federal Law provided a local remedy that had not been attempted by Chabad.[300]

Does the "twice taken" template introduced in *Chabad* impermissibly expand the FSIA? The mere fact that judicial, political, or administrative "takings" can trigger the expropriation exception does not seem to pose too great a problem. The Supreme Court in *Altmann* assumed that the taking at issue was the 1948 offer by the Austrian Gallery to accept a "donation" of the Klimts in exchange for export licenses.[301] Since at least two of the Klimts were already in the possession of the Gallery, this was in essence an administrative taking. Additionally, the "twice taken" template accords with the intent of Congress in the Holocaust Victims Redress Act, discussed above, which calls for all Holocaust art, including "art and other assets . . . transferred . . . to the Union of Soviet Socialist Republics," to be returned to their rightful owners.[302]

There is, however, a question of how useful this new tool will be against Russia. Generally, Western European countries haled into U.S. court for Holocaust art restitution cases engage in litigation until the motion to dismiss stage, and then (should they lose) agree to settlement or arbitration.[303] This reflects the general attitude of such countries that Nazi art hanging in their museums is a cause for concern. By contrast, Russia's attitude is that such property is legal, compensatory restitution for extreme loss of life and property suffered at the hands of Nazi Germany.[304] Such an attitude can be seen in a quote by the Russian Duma's Chair on the Committee of Culture as the Duma struggled with Yeltsin to pass the Federal Law on Displaced Cultural Valuables. He compared the law to the Battle of Stalingrad, and, "thinking only of the 27 million who perished and the graves on the Volga," he implied that "even symbolic restitution . . . [is] like spitting on those graves."[305] It is therefore not surprising that Russia's general approach is not to consider court decisions from the United States or other Western countries valid.[306]

Indeed, in *Chabad*, Russia argued pursuant to a defense of *forum non conveniens* that a judgment requiring the return of the Collection to Chabad "would have a far greater chance of being enforced in Russia if it were to come from a Russian court rather than a U.S. court."[307] The district court responded icily,

> The defendants appear to be suggesting that this Court should divest itself of jurisdiction because if it rules against the defendants, they may refuse to abide by its judgment. Such an argument is an affront to this Court and does not militate in favor of dismissal on the grounds of *forum non conveniens*.[308]

The appellate court affirmed, and noted that the FSIA allows attachment of certain Russian government property which Chabad argued may "give it significant leverage over the defendants, [and] enhanc[e] the likelihood that Russia or its courts would respect the judgment of a U.S. court. Russia does not reply to the point, and it seems plausible."[309]

But the appellate court's decision may not have had the consequences intended. Russia has refused to communicate with its American lawyers since it lost its appeal, and the law firm has requested to withdraw from the case.[310] Moreover, on January 27, 2009, the district court issued a preliminary injunction against the Russian Federation, Russian Ministry of Culture and Mass Communication, Russian State Library and Russia State Military Archive (all listed as defendants in the case), directing them to produce the full Archive and Library for inspection by a committee.[311] Based on affidavits, the court found that "pages of the 'Archive' appear to have been surreptitiously removed from their repository in the Russian State Military Archive in Moscow and transported to Israel for possible sale to private parties."[312] It ordered them to "take all measures necessary to secure, protect and preserve the property at issue in this litigation."[313]

## Conclusion

The template for "twice taken" cultural property introduced in *Chabad v. Russian Federation* expands the definition of a "taking in violation of international law" under expropriation exception of the FSIA to include governmental takings of property initially taken by either the Nazis or the Soviets. This will allow more individuals to press claims for restitution of Holocaust art by offering multiple opportunities for "substantial and non-frivolous" takings claims for the purposes of gaining jurisdiction, and (because many "second" takings will have occurred after 1959) avoiding implication of the Act of State doctrine. It may also specifically implicate Russia's Federal Law on Cultural Valuables, which, under the FSIA's low jurisdictional standard, qualifies as a "taking."

It remains to be seen, however, whether this approach is at all effective against Russia. The only returns of cultural property from Russia thus far have been effected diplomatically, not judicially.[314] Over the summer, Russia informed the court that it would no longer participate in the action, and on October 29, 2009, the judge entered a default judgment in favor of Chabad.[315] It is unclear how the situation will be resolved. One may hope, however, that this new tool will allow for greater leverage in the efforts toward the return of cultural property.

## Notes

1. Foreign Sovereign Immunities Act, 28 U.S.C. §§ 1602-1611 (2008); *Agudas Chasidei Chabad v. Russian Federation*, 528 F.3d 934, 943-46 (D.C. Cir. 2008).
2. *Chabad*, 528 F.3d at 944.
3. *See* Lynn H. Nicholas, *World War II and the Displacement of Art and Cultural Property*, *in* THE SPOILS OF WAR: WORLD WAR II AND ITS AFTERMATH: THE LOSS, REAPPEARANCE, AND RECOVERY OF CULTURAL PROPERTY 39 (Elizabeth Simpson ed., 1997). *See generally* LYNN H. NICHOLAS, THE RAPE OF EUROPA: THE FATE OF EUROPE'S TREASURES IN THE THIRD REICH AND THE SECOND WORLD WAR (1994) (describing in detail the systematic Nazi appropriation of art).
4. Nicholas, *World War II*, *supra* note 3, at 39.
5. *Id.*; JOHN HENRY MERRYMAN ET AL., LAW, ETHICS AND THE VISUAL ARTS 16 (5th ed. 2007).
6. HEILMUT LEHMANN-HAUPT, ART UNDER A DICTATORSHIP 78-87 (1954), *reprinted in* MERRYMAN, *supra* note 5, at 638-43; NICHOLAS, RAPE OF EUROPA, *supra* note 3, at 3-6 and 21-24.
7. MERRYMAN, *supra* note 3, at 641.
8. *Id.* at 640.
9. Nicholas, *World War II*, *supra* note 3, at 40.
10. *Id.* at 41. *See generally* NICHOLAS, RAPE OF EUROPA, *supra* note 3, at 41-49.
11. Nicholas, *World War II*, *supra* note 3, at 41; MERRYMAN, *supra* note 5, at 16. *See generally* NICHOLAS, RAPE OF EUROPA, *supra* note 3, at 125 et seq. Rosenberg produced a catalogue of seized materials that was 39 volumes long with about 2500 photographs; had all the loot collected been catalogued and photographed, it would have run to about 300 volumes. MERRYMAN, *supra* note 5, at 16.
12. Nicholas, *World War II*, *supra* note 3, at 41.
13. Andrea Gattini, *Restitution by Russia of Works of Art Removed from German Territory at the End of the Second World War*, 7 EUR. J. INT'L L. 67, 74 (1996), *available at* http://ejil.oxfordjournals.org/cgi/reprint/7/1/67.

14. Mikhail Shvidkoi, *Russian Cultural Losses During World War II*, *in* THE SPOILS OF WAR, *supra* note 3, at 68.
15. *Count Three: War Crimes, (E) Plunder of Public and Private Property*, 1 TRIAL OF THE MAJOR WAR CRIMINALS BEFORE THE INTERNATIONAL MILITARY TRIBUNAL: NUREMBERG 14 NOVEMBER 194–1 OCTOBER 1946, at 55-60 (1948) [hereinafter *Nuremberg Indictment*], *available at* http://www.loc.gov/rr/frd/Military_Law/NT_major-war-criminals.html.
16. Shvidkoi, *supra* note 14, at 68.
17. *Id.* at 69-70.
18. *Id.* at 69.
19. KONSTANTIN AKINSHA & GRIGORII KOZLOV, BEAUTIFUL LOOT: THE SOVIET PLUNDER OF EUROPE'S ART TREASURES 12 (1995).
20. MERRYMAN, *supra* note 5, at 21; *see Nuremberg Indictment*, *supra* note 15, at 55-60.
21. Hague Convention (IV) Respecting the Laws and Customs of War on Land, October 18, 1907, 36 *Stat.* 2277, T.S. 539, 3 *Martens Nouveau Recueil* (ser. 3) 461, *reprinted in* 2 AM. J. INT'L L. 90 (1908); *Nuremberg Indictment, supra* note 15, 55-60.
22. *Two Hundred and Eighteenth Day, Tuesday, 1 October 1946, Morning Session (Rosenberg)*, 22 TRIAL OF THE MAJOR WAR CRIMINALS BEFORE THE INTERNATIONAL MILITARY TRIBUNAL: NUREMBERG 14 NOVEMBER 1945–1 OCTOBER 1946, at 540-41 (1948) [hereinafter *Nuremberg Judgment*], *available at* http://www.loc.gov/rr/frd/Military_Law/NT_major-war-criminals.html.
23. *Nuremberg Judgment*, *supra* note 22, at 588.
24. Nicholas, *World War II*, *supra* note 3, at 43. "Monuments officers" had been stationed within each army group, who collectively became known as the Monuments, Fine Arts, and Archives section (MFA&A). *Id.* First-person accounts of these officers at their collecting points are found in *Part 4: Repatriations following World War II*, *in* THE SPOILS OF WAR, *supra* note 3, at 122-141. *See generally* NICHOLAS, RAPE OF EUROPA, *supra* note 3, at 382 *et seq.*
25. Nicholas, *World War II*, *supra* note 3, at 44.
26. *Id.*
27. *Id.*
28. *Id.*; Walter I. Farmer, *Custody and Controversy at the Weisbaden Collecting Point*, *in* THE SPOILS OF WAR, *supra* note 3, at 133. The MFA&A officers issued the "Wiesbaden Manifesto," which directly compared the U.S. orders with Nazi "sequestering, under pretext of 'protective custody,' the cultural treasures of German-occupied countries." *Id.*
29. Farmer, *supra* note 28, at 134; NICHOLAS, RAPE OF EUROPA, *supra* note 3, at 402-405. The show was the first "blockbuster" art exhibit, opening to nearly 10,000 on the first day, and eventually surpassing 250,000 visitors. *Id.* This does not include some pieces that were looted by individuals.

30. Nicholas, *World War II*, *supra* note 3, at 42.
31. AKINSHA & KOZLOV, *supra* note 19, at 19.
32. AKINSHA & KOZLOV, *supra* note 19, at 20; Konstantin Akinsha & Grigorii Kozlov, *The Discovery of the Secret Repositories*, *in* THE SPOILS OF WAR, *supra* note 3, at 163. The full name of the Commission was the Extraordinary State Commission on the Registration and Investigation of the Crimes of the German-Fascist Occupiers and Their Accomplices and the Damage Done by Them to the Citizens, Collective Farms, Public Organizations, and Institutions of the USSR. *Id.*
33. Akinsha & Kozlov, *Discovery*, *supra* note 32, at 163.
34. *Id.*
35. *Id.*
36. *Id.* at 163.
37. Letter of Khrapchenko and Merkurov, *quoted in* Akinsha & Kozlov, *Discovery*, *supra* note 32, at 164.
38. AKINSHA & KOZLOV, *supra* note 19, at 45.
39. *Id.*
40. *Id.* at 45-46. Ironically, many of them consulted their Baedeker guidebooks for information about landmarks and collections in Germany that they were about to loot. *Id.* at 47.
41. *Id.* at 157.
42. *Id.* at 78, 81-83, 112. Additionally, for descriptions of these treasures and their fates, see Part II of Lina M. Montén, Comment, *Soviet World War II Trophy Art in Present Day Russia: The Events, the Law, and the Current Controversies*, 15 DEPAUL-LCA J. ART & ENT. L. 37 (2004-2005).
43. AKINSHA & KOZLOV, *supra* note 19, at 79 (Berlin) and 121 (Dresden).
44. Akinsha & Kozlov, *Discovery*, *supra* note 32, at 164. The Pushkin Museum prepared an exhibition of the trophy art in 1946 but it was unexpectedly called off due to the worsening political situation leading up to the Cold War. AKINSHA & KOZLOV, *supra* note 19, at 184-85. The Pushkin itself was then denuded of its permanent collection as a proletariat-oriented exhibition, Gifts for Stalin, was launched; its collection was only restored after Stalin's death in 1953. *Id.* at 187-91.
45. AKINSHA & KOZLOV, *supra* note 19, at 192; Montén, *supra* note 42, at 51.
46. *Id.* at 196.
47. *Id.* at 198.
48. *Id.* at 216.
49. AKINSHA & KOZLOV, *supra* note 19, at 206 and 212-18. In all, an estimated 2.5 million works of art had been transferred from Germany to the USSR. This number does not include losses sustained by other countries, such as Poland, or counts of books and archives. *See* Wilfried Fielder, *Legal Issues Bearing on the Restitution of German Cultural Property in Russia*, in THE SPOILS OF WAR, *supra* note 3, at 176.

50. Montén, *supra* note 42, at 54.
51. Konstantin Akinsha & Grigorii Kozlov, *The Spoils of War: The Soviet Union's Hidden Art Treasures*, 90 ARTNEWS 130-141 (1991).
52. AKINSHA & KOZLOV, *supra* note 19.
53. *Id.* at 256-59; *see* MERRYMAN, *supra* note 5, at 63.
54. Alan Riding, *Are Finders Keepers?*, N.Y. TIMES, Mar. 12, 1995, *available at* http://www.nytimes.com/1995/03/12/weekinreview/the-world-are-finders-keepers.html.
55. AKINSHA & KOZLOV, *supra* note 19, at 258.
56. Riding, *supra* note 54; AKINSHA & KOZLOV, *supra* note 19, at 257.
57. RETURNED FROM RUSSIA: NAZI ARCHIVAL PLUNDER IN EASTERN EUROPE AND RECENT RESTITUTION ISSUES 6-8, 106 (Patricia Kennedy Grimsted et al. eds., 2007).
58. Riding, *supra* note 54.
59. Treaty on Good-Neighborliness, Partnership and Cooperation, Nov. 9, 1990, F.R.G. – U.S.S.R. 30 I.L.M. 504. *See* S. Shawn Stephens, *The Hermitage and Pushkin Exhibits: An Analysis of the Ownership Rights to Cultural Properties Removed from Occupied Germany*, 18 HOUS. J. INT'L L. 59 (1995); Silvia L. Depta, Comment, *Twice Saved or Twice Stolen?: The Trophy Art Tug-of-War Between Russia and Germany*, 10 TEMP. INT'L & COMP. L.J. 371 (1996); Andrea Gattini, *Restitution by Russia of Works of Art Removed from German Territory at the End of the Second World War*, 7 EUR. J. INT'L L. 67 (1996), *available at* http://ejil.oxfordjournals.org/cgi/reprint/7/1/67.
60. Charles A. Goldstein, The Russian Position: Trophy Art Belongs to Russia As Compensation for World War II Cultural Losses, Paper for "Spoils of War v. Cultural Heritage" Symposium, Harvard University, Feb. 8-9, 2008, www.commartrecovery.org/docs/THE_RUSSIAN_POSITION_2008II.DOC; Stephens, *supra* note 59.
61. MERRYMAN, *supra* note 5, at 63, Riding, supra note 54.
62. *See* AKINSHA & KOZLOV, *supra* note 19, at 258-59 ("A group of paintings from the collections of the great Hungarian Jewish families rounded out the ["Twice Saved"] show. The works by Corot, Manet, and Degas from the Hatvany collection, and canvases that had belonged to the Herzogs. . .")
63. *See generally, Losses During and as a Consequence of World War II*, in THE SPOILS OF WAR, *supra* note 3.
64. Helen Fawkes, *Netherlands Hails the Return of Stolen Art*, BBC News, Apr. 20, 2004, *available at* http://news.bbc.co.uk/2/hi/entertainment/3640951.stm. Ukraine, unlike Russia, has been very open to returning looted art. For the story of the Koenigs collection, which was first sold to the Rotterdam museum under duress by a fleeing Franz Koenigs, and then "sold" again to the Dresden Gallery after Nazi occupation, see Christine F. Koenigs, *Under Duress: The Sale of the Franz Koenigs Collection*, in THE SPOILS OF WAR, *supra* note 3, at 237-40.
65. *See* RETURNED FROM RUSSIA, *supra* note 57, at 3, and passim.

66. *See generally* WAYNE SANDHOLTZ, PROHIBITING PLUNDER: HOW NORMS CHANGE (2007), particularly Chapter 9.
67. A theme generally repeated in article titles: Depta, *supra* note 59 ("Twice Saved or Twice Stolen"); Patricia Kennedy Grimsted, *Twice Plundered or "Twice Saved"?: Identifying Russia's "Trophy" Archives and the Loot of the Reichssicherheitshauptamt*, 15.2 HOLOCAUST AND GENOCIDE STUDIES 191 (2001), *available at* http://hgs.oxfordjournals.org/cgi/reprint/15/2/191. Newspaper articles often refer to the art simply as "stolen." See Fawkes, *supra* note 64.
68. Montén, *supra* note 42, at 67.
69. O moratorii na vozvrashchenie kul'turnykh tsennostei, peremeshchennykh v gody Velikoi Otechestvennoi voiny (On a moratorium on the return of cultural valuables displaced in the years of the Great Fatherland War): Postanovlenie Gosudarstvennoi Dumy Federal'nogo sobraniia Rossiiskoi Federatsii (Decree of the State Duma of the Federal Assembly of the Russian Federation), 21 April 1995, no. 725-IGD, Sobranie Zakonadatel'stva Rossiiskoi Federatsii [SZ RF] [Russian Federation Collection of Legislation], 1995, No. 19, Item 1721. Reported in RETURNED FROM RUSSIA, *supra* note 57, at 300.
70. O kul'turnykh tsennostiakh, peremeshchennykh v Soiuz SSR v rezul'tate Vtoroi mirovoi voiny i nakhodiashchikhsia na territorii Rossiiskoi Federatsii' (On cultural valuables displaced to the USSR as a result of the Second World War and located on the territory of the Russian Federation): Federal'nyi zakon (Federal Law), 15 April 1998, no. 64-FZ, Sobranie Zakonadatel'stva Rossiiskoi Federatsii [SZ RF] [Russian Federation Collection of Legislation], 1998, No. 16, Item 1879. Reported in RETURNED FROM RUSSIA, *supra* note 57, at 301. An English translation is available at http://docproj.loyola.edu/rlaw/r2.html.
71. Montén, *supra* note 42, at 72. *See also* her analysis generally of the law, and also "Is Russia's Federal Law on Displaced Cultural Property a Taking?"
72. "Holocaust art" is a term used to refer generally to art displaced during World War II. MERRYMAN, *supra* note 5, at 23.
73. Tate Letter, 24 Dep't of State Bull. 984 (1952). *See generally* GARY BORN, INTERNATIONAL CIVIL LITIGATION IN U.S. COURTS (1996), particularly Chapter 3, "Foreign Sovereign Immunity and Jurisdiction of U.S. Courts Over Foreign States."
74. Tate Letter, *supra* note 73.
75. MERRYMAN, *supra* note 5, at 51-55. *See generally* BORN, *supra* note 72, particularly Chapter 9, "Act of State and Foreign Sovereign Compulsion Doctrines." A fuller discussion appears later in the article.
76. MERRYMAN, *supra* note 5, at 51-55.
77. *Menzel v. List*, 267 N.Y.S.2d 804 (N.Y. Sup. Ct. 1966); MERRYMAN, *supra* note 5, at 23, 24-29, and 51-55.
78. *Menzel*, 267 N.Y.S.2d at 806.

79. *Id.* at 812, passim.
80. *Id.* Nazi actions *do* count as sovereign acts for the purposes of gaining jurisdiction under FSIA, as will be discussed below.
81. *Kunstsammlungen zu Weimar v. Elicofon* 478 F.2d 231 (2d Cir. 1973) and 678 F.2d 1150 (2d Cir. 1982) (returning two Dürer paintings bought by a good faith purchaser to a museum in East Germany); *United States v. One Tintoretto Painting*, 691 F.2d 603 (2d Cir. 1982) (fining a former Soviet soldier for misrepresenting looted artwork on a U.S. Customs form; U.S. unsuccessfully urged East Germany to sue for possession); *Price v. United States*, 707 F. Supp. 1465 (S.D.Tex. 1989) (ordering return of Hitler watercolors and photographs that had been confiscated by U.S. military to heirs of the owner, who had received them as a personal gift from Hitler).
82. MERRYMAN, *supra* note 5, at 22.
83. These were Nicholas's *The Rape of Europa* (*supra* note 3) from 1994, and Hector Feliciano's *Le musée disparu*, which appeared in English as *The Lost Museum* in 1997.
84. See *supra*, "Twice Saved" or Twice Stolen?" (text associated with footnotes 51-57).
85. The symposium was held in January 1995, and the proceedings were published as *The Spoils of War*, *supra* note 3, in 1997. MERRYMAN, *supra* note 5, at 22.
86. In 1998, the Presidential Advisory Commission on Holocaust Assets was created. The American Association of Museums established a Task Force on the Spoliation of art during the Nazi Era, and the American Association of Museum Directors released a report instructing its members to resolve claims in "an equitable, appropriate, and mutually agreeable manner." MERRYMAN, *supra* note 5, at 23.
87. H.R. Rep. No. 94-1487, 94th Cong., 2d Sess. (1976).
88. FSIA, 28 U.S.C. § 1602.
89. *Id.* at § 1604.
90. *Id.*
91. 28 U.S.C. §1330. § 1330(b) reads "Personal jurisdiction over a foreign state shall exist as to every claim for relief over which the district courts have jurisdiction under subsection (a) [under any exception to the FSIA] where service has been made under section 1608 [proper service under the FSIA] of this title."
92. *See, e.g., Malewicz v. City of Amsterdam*, 517 F. Supp. 2d 322, 337 (D.D.C. 2007); ("It is important to note that the act of state doctrine is not a jurisdictional limit on the courts. Thus, a motion to dismiss based on the act of state doctrine is properly considered under Rule 12(b)(6), not Rule 12(b)(1)" (internal citations omitted).)
93. 28 U.S.C. § 1605(a)(3).
94. *West v. Multibanco Comermex*, S.A., 807 F.2d 820, 831 (9th Cir. 1987); *Siderman de Blake v. Republic of Argentina*, 965 F.2d 699, 711 (9th Cir. 1992). The factors were applied by the D.C. District Court in *Agudas Chasidei Chabad v. Russian Federation*, 466 F. Supp. 2d 6, 15-16 (D.C. Cir. 2006).
95. *West*, 807 F.2d at 832.

96. *Id.*
97. *See, e.g., Cassirer v. Kingdom of Spain*, 461 F. Supp. 2d 1157, 1164-65 (C.D.Cal. 2006) (holding jurisdiction over Spain for property taken by a Nazi agent). This case discussed more at length, *infra* note 135. Note that at the time of publication of this article, *Cassirer* is pending appellate rehearing *en banc.*
98. *Siderman de Blake*, 965 F.2d at 711.
99. Some previous courts had held the FSIA applied prior to 1976, but only to actions that postdated the Tate Letter in 1952, after the United States adopted a restrictive theory of sovereign immunity. See the discussion in the appellate level decision of *Altmann. Altmann v. Republic of Austria*, 317 F.3d 954 (9th Cir. 2002).
100. *Republic of Austria v. Altmann*, 541 U.S. 677 (2004).
101. *Altmann*, 317 F.3d at 959.
102. *Id.*
103. *Id.* at 960.
104. *Id.* at 959.
105. *Id.*
106. *Id.* at 960.
107. *Id.*
108. *Id.*
109. *Altmann*, 541 U.S. at 684 (2004) (internal quotations omitted).
110. *Altmann*, 317 F.3d at 961 (finding the Austrian Gallery, an agency or instrumentality of the foreign state, engaged in commercial activity in the United States).
111. *Altmann*, 541 U.S. at 692.
112. *Id.* at 696-97.
113. 28 U.S.C. § 1602; *Altmann*, 541 U.S. at 697 (emphasis in Court decision).
114. *Altmann*, 541 U.S. at 697.
115. *Id.*
116. Sharon Waxman, *A Homecoming, in Los Angeles, for Five Klimts Looted by Nazis*, N.Y. TIMES, Apr. 6, 2006, at E1, *available at* http://www.nytimes.com/2006/04/06/arts/design/06klim.html.
117. *Id.*
118. Lauren Fielder Redman, *The Foreign Sovereign Immunities Act: Using a "Shield" Statute as a "Sword" for Obtaining Federal Jurisdiction in Art and Antiquities Cases*, 31 FORDHAM INT'L L. J. 781 (2008). Her discussion also covers the four cases discussed here (*Altmann*, *Malewicz*, *Cassirer*, and *Chabad*), though she does not cover the appellate opinions of either *Malewicz* or *Chabad*.
119. *Malewicz v. City of Amsterdam*, 362 F. Supp. 2d 298 (D.D.C. 2005).
120. See discussion *supra*, "Introduction."
121. MERRYMAN, *supra* note 5, at 50.
122. *Id.*

123. *Malewicz*, 362 F. Supp. 2d at 303.
124. 28 U.S.C. § 1605(a)(3).
125. *Malewicz*, 362 F. Supp. 2d at 303.
126. *Id.* at 310; *see* Redman, *supra* note 118, at 795.
127. *Malewicz*, 362 F. Supp. 2d at 315-16.
128. *Malewicz v. City of Amsterdam*, 517 F. Supp. 2d 322 (D.D.C. 2007).
129. *Id.* at 332.
130. *Id.* at 337.
131. *Id.* at 339.
132. *Id.* at 340. In 2008, the court granted a joint motion to dismiss, probably implying a settlement or removal to arbitration. *Malewicz v. City of Amsterdam*, No. 07-5247, 2008 WL 2223219, at *1 (D.C. Cir. May 14, 2008).
133. 28 U.S.C. § 1603(a) reads: "A 'foreign state', except as used in section 1608 of this title, includes a political subdivision of a foreign state or an agency or instrumentality of a foreign state as defined in subsection (b)." Subsection (b) reads: "An 'agency or instrumentality of a foreign state' means any entity—(1) which is a separate legal person, corporate or otherwise."
134. *United States v. Portrait of Wally*, 105 F. Supp. 2d 288 (S.D.N.Y. 2000). The painting had been exacted from a Jewish gallery owner by a Nazi party member in 1939.
135. *Cassirer v. Kingdom of Spain*, 461 F. Supp. 2d 1157, 1161 (C.D.Cal. 2006), *aff'd in part and rev'd in part*, 580 F.3d 1048 (9th Cir. 2009), *rehearing granted en banc*, 590 F.3d 981 (9th Cir. 2009).
136. *Id.*
137. 28 U.S.C. § 1605(a)(3).
138. In *Altmann* the "taking" was considered Austria's 1948 bargain to exchange the Klimts for an export permit for additional paintings. *Republic of Austria v. Altmann*, 541 U.S. 677, 697 (2004). In *Malewicz*, the City of Amsterdam had purchased the paintings under "suspect circumstances," Redman, *supra* note 118, at 794.
139. *Cassirer*, 461 F. Supp. 2d at 1164-66.
140. *Id.* at 1164.
141. *Id.*
142. *Menzel v. List*, 267 N.Y.S.2d 804 (N.Y. Sup. Ct.1966), see *supra* text associated with footnotes 71-75. The *Menzel* court found that applying the Act of State doctrine failed on all four prongs, any one of which can bar its application. Importantly, one of those prongs is that the foreign sovereign must be extant at the time of suit, certainly not the case of the Third Reich in 1966.
143. *Cassirer*, 461 F. Supp. 2d at 1165.
144. *Id.* (quoting *Altmann*, 317 F.3d at 968).
145. *Id.* (quoting plaintiff's evidence).
146. 28 U.S.C. § 1603(a). See text of the statute at note 133.

147. Factors from *West v. Multibanco Comermex, S.A.*, *supra* note 94.
148. Redman, *supra* note 118, at 802-05.
149. U.S. CONST. art. III; U.S. CONST. art. I, § 8, cl. 3; U.S. CONST. art. I, § 8, cl. 10; *Verlinden v. Central Bank of Nigeria*, 461 U.S. 480 (1983); Redman, *supra* note 118, at 802-03.
150. *Id.* This final claim of Redman's would seem to in fact be the *very purpose* of the exceptions.
151. *Menzel v. List*, 267 N.Y.S.2d 804, 812 (N.Y. Sup. Ct. 1966).
152. *Cassirer v. Kingdom of Spain*, 461 F. Supp. 2d 1157, 1164 (C.D.Cal. 2006).
153. Holocaust Victims Redress Act (HVRA), Pub.L. 105-158, § 201-02, 112 Stat. 15 (1998).
154. HVRA, *supra* note 141, § 201(4).
155. *Id.* § 201(5).
156. *Id.* § 202.
157. *Id.* § 201(6).
158. *Agudas Chasidei Chabad v. Russian Federation*, 528 F.3d 934, 938 (D.C. Cir. 2008) (hereinafter *Chabad II*).
159. *Agudas Chasidei Chabad v. Russian Federation*, 466 F. Supp. 2d 6, 11 (D.D.C. 2006) (hereinafter *Chabad I*).
160. *Chabad II*, 528 F.3d at 938.
161. *Chabad I*, 466 F. Supp. 2d at 11-12.
162. *Id.* at 11.
163. *Id.* at 11-12.
164. *Id.* at 12.
165. *See id.* at 10-14; *see also* Plaintiff's Supplemental Brief in Opposition to Defendant's Motion to Dismiss on Grounds of Lack of Subject Matter Jurisdiction, Foreign Sovereign Immunity, Failure to State a Claim (Act of State Doctrine) and *forum non conveniens*; and Request for Oral Argument, at 9, *Agudas Chasidei Chabad v. Russian Federation*, 528 F.3d 934 (D.C. Cir 2008) (No. 1:05-CV-01548 (RCL)) ("This is not a routine property case. . . . It cannot be compared to a suit over an Old Master painting or an antique silver tea set . . . ").
166. *Chabad I*, 466 F. Supp. 2d at 12.
167. *Id.*; *Chabad II*, 528 F.3d at 938.
168. *Chabad I*, 466 F. Supp. 2d at 12.
169. *Chabad II*, 528 F.3d at 938.
170. *Id.*
171. *Chabad I*, 466 F. Supp. 2d at 12.
172. *Id.*
173. *Id.*
174. *Id.*

175. *Id.*; *Chabad II*, 528 F.3d at 938.
176. *Chabad I*, 266 F. Supp. 2d at 13. See the discussion of Soviet "trophy" seizures *supra*, "Russia's 'Twice Saved' Trophy Art."
177. *Id.*
178. *Id.*
179. *Id.*
180. *Chabad II*, 528 F.3d at 945.
181. *Chabad I*, 266 F. Supp. 2d at 13.
182. *Id.*
183. *Id.*
184. *Chabad II*, 528 F.3d at 944.
185. 28 U.S.C. § 1605(a)(3).
186. *Chabad I*, 266 F. Supp. 2d at 19-20. See also the discussion in Redman, *supra* note 118, at 800-802.
187. *Chabad I*, 266 F. Supp. 2d at 19. And subsequently affirmed in *Cassirer*, *supra* note 135.
188. *Id.* at 19-20. See *supra* note 94.
189. *Id.* at 19-20.
190. *Id.* at 19. The court refrained from determining whether the Soviet taking was also discriminatory because its appropriation of the Archive satisfied the two other criteria. *Id.* fn. 15, at 20.
191. *Id.* at 24-25.
192. *Id.* at 26.
193. *Id* at 25.
194. *Id.* at 26.
195. *Id.*
196. *Id.* at 16.
197. *Id.*
198. *Id.* at 19.
199. *Id.* at 26-27.
200. *Id.* at 26.
201. *Id.* In fact, it can. See discussion associated with notes 292-295, "The Federal Law and the Act of State Doctrine."
202. *Id.* at 27.
203. *Chabad II*, 528 F.3d at 939.
204. *Id.* at 940.
205. *Id.*
206. *Id.* (quoting *Bell v. Hood*, 327 U.S. 678, 682-83 (1946)).
207. *Id.*
208. *Id.*

209. *Id.* at 941.
210. 28 U.S.C. § 1605(a)(3); *Chabad II*, 528 F.3d at 941.
211. *Chabad II*, 528 F.3d at 941.
212. *Id.*
213. *Id.* at 943.
214. *Id.*; *Chabad I*, 466 F. Supp. 2d at 16.
215. *Chabad II*, 528 F.3d at 943.
216. *Id.*; *Agudas Chasidei Chabad v. Gourary*, 650 F. Supp. 1463 (E.D.N.Y. 1987), *aff'd*, 833 F.2d 431 (2d Cir. 1987).
217. *Chabad II*, 528 F.3d at 943.
218. *Id.*
219. *Id.*
220. *Id.* at 944; *Altmann v. Republic of Austria,* 317 F.3d 954 (2002). *See supra* text associated with notes 99-117.
221. *Id.*
222. *Id. See Republic of Austria v. Altmann*, 541 U.S. 677, 697 (2004) ("This leaves only the question whether anything in the FSIA . . . suggests that we should not apply it to petitioners' 1948 actions.").
223. *Chabad II*, 528 F.3d at 944.
224. *Id.*
225. *See id.*
226. *Id.*
227. *Id.*
228. *Id.*
229. *Id.*
230. *Id.*
231. *Id.*
232. For example, under the theory that the Library was the personal property of the Sixth Rebbe, the first taking would not be eligible because the Rebbe was a Soviet citizen. By the time of the "retaking" in 1991, however, the property belonged to Chabad.
233. *Altmann*, 317 F.3d at 960.
234. *Id.* at 968.
235. *Id.* at n. 4.
236. *Altmann*, 541 U.S. at 697.
237. *I.e.* Not for a public purpose, discriminatory, or without just compensation. See *supra* note 94 and associated text.
238. *Banco Nacional de Cuba v. Sabbatino*, 376 U.S. 398, 427-28 (1964).
239. *Id.*

240. *Menzel v. List*, 267 N.Y.S.2d 804, 812 (N.Y. Sup. Ct. 1966). See *supra* notes 77-80 and associated text.
241. *Malewicz v. City of Amsterdam*, 517 F. Supp. 2d 322, 340 (D.D.C. 2007). See *supra* notes 130-32 and accompanying text.
242. *See Sabbatino*, 376 U.S. at 427-28.
243. 28 U.S.C. § 2370(e)(2).
244. *Id.*
245. *Agudas Chasidei Chabad v. Russian Federation*, 528 F.3d 934, 953 (2008); *Agudas Chasidei Chabad v. Russian Federation*, 466 F. Supp. 2d 6, 27 (2006).
246. *Chabad II*, 538 F.3d at 953.
247. *Id.* at 954.
248. *Id.*
249. *Sabbatino*, 376 U.S. at 428.
250. *Chabad II*, 538 F.3d at 954.
251. *Id.*
252. The D.C. Circuit's decision not to apply the Act of State Doctrine was criticized in a case note in the *Harvard Law Review* for failing to adequately consider the constitutional justifications for the doctrine. It remains the case, however, that the Second Hickenlooper Amendment was appropriately applied according to its facial meaning, despite certain circuits' more narrow interpretations. *See* Recent Case, *International Law—Act of State Doctrine—D.C. Circuit Declines to Apply Act of State Doctrine to Claim of Russian Seizure of Religious Property—Agudas Chasidei Chabad of United States v. Russian Federation* 528 F.3d 934 (D.C. Cir. 2008). 122 Harv. L. Rev. 1985 (2009).
253. *Chabad II*, 528 F.3d at 946.
254. Federal Law on Displaced Cultural Valuables (Russia), *supra* note 70.
255. Montén, *supra* note 42, at 72. See her analysis generally of the law; and an excellent analysis in RETURNED FROM RUSSIA, *supra* note 57, at 120-27.
256. Federal Law on Displaced Cultural Valuables, *supra* note 70, art. 4. English translation from http://docproj.loyola.edu/rlaw/r2.html. Note that this is the 1998 (unamended) version of the law.
257. Hague Convention (IV), *supra* note 21, art. 47 ("Pillage is formally forbidden.") and art. 56 ("The property of municipalities, that of institutions dedicated to religion, charity and education, the arts and sciences, even when State property, shall be treated as private property. All seizure of, destruction or wilful damage done to institutions of this character, historic monuments, works of art and science, is forbidden, and should be made the subject of legal proceedings.").
258. *See* Gattini, *supra* note 13, at 70. Though it is difficult to see how the actions of the trophy brigades, whose lists had been drawn up in 1943 and who were fol-

lowing closely behind the footsteps of the Soviet army, were "outside" the theater of war. *See* AKINSHA & KOSLOV, *supra* note 19.

259. *See* Goldstein, *supra* note 60.

260. Hague Convention (IV), *supra* note 21; Hague Convention for the Protection of Cultural Property in the Event of Armed Conflict, May 14, 1954, 249 U.N.T.S. 215; Additional Protocol II to the Geneva Conventions, 8 June 1977, 1125 U.N.T.S. 609; Convention on the Means of Prohibiting and Preventing the Illicit Import, Export and Transfer of Ownership of Cultural Property, Nov. 14, 1970, 823 U.N.T.S. 231.

261. *See* John Henry Merryman, *Two Ways of Thinking About Cultural Property*, 80 AM. J. INT'L L. 831 (1986).

262. Gattini, *supra* note 13, at 84.

263. *See id.* at 86.

264. Tim Schröder, *The Russian Constitutional Court's Decisions on the Restitution of Cultural Valuables*, 7 SPOILS OF WAR, INT'L NEWSLETTER 6, 7 (2000).

265. Federal Law on Displaced Cultural Valuables (Russia), *supra* note 70, art. 3. Note that the 2000 Amendment is different from the 1998 version, which is the version of the English translation. *See* also Montén, *supra* note 42, at 80 n. 240. The 1997 version read that the law was applicable to all displaced cultural property "irrespective of the actual possessor and the circumstances leading to this actual possession." Translations not provided by the English version or Montén are done by the author.

266. Federal Law on Displaced Cultural Valuables (Russia), *supra* note 70, art. 4.

267. *See* RETURNED FROM RUSSIA, *supra* note 57, at 122, 125-27, and the discussion of the Rothschild Archive, at 287-95.

268. Federal Law on Displaced Cultural Valuables (Russia), *supra* note 70, art. 6.

269. *Id.* art. 7.

270. *See* Federal Law on Displaced Cultural Valuables, *supra* note 70, art. 3, English translation version (1998 version).

271. *Id.* art 8. Exception (1) was amended in 2000 and was thus translated by the author. The text of the law used for purposes of translation was downloaded from the UNESCO Cultural Heritage Law Database.

272. *See id.* art. 9, English translation version (1998 version).

273. *Id.* art. 9; *see* RETURNED FROM RUSSIA, *supra* note 57, at 123-24.

274. Kul'turniye tsennosti—Zhertvii Voini (Cultural Valuables—Victims of War), http://lostart.ru/.

275. Federal Law on Displaced Cultural Valuables, *supra* note 70, art. 12.

276. *Id.* art. 18(1).

277. *Id.* art. 18(4).

278. *Id.* art. 19(2).

279. RETURNED FROM RUSSIA, *supra* note 57, at 123-25.
280. The distinction is important, because simply defeating a motion to dismiss often compels nations to settle or submit to arbitration, as occurred in *Altmann*, and possibly in *Malewicz*. Though not in *Chabad*; see "Conclusion."
281. *Agudas Chasidei Chabad v. Russian Federation*, 528 F.3d 934, 946 (2008). See *supra* notes 213-232 and accompanying text.
282. For the moratorium see *supra* note 69.
283. *Altmann v. Republic of Austria*, 317 F.3d at 960. *Supra* notes 233-236 and accompanying text.
284. *Id.* Unless the 1946 nullification of Nazi transactions was a "recovery," but the Gallery asserted its claims of ownership based on Adele's will and an alleged transfer in 1936.
285. *See* text of the Federal Law, *supra* notes 265-79, with accompanying text.
286. *Altmann*, 317 F.3d at 960.
287. *See supra* notes 255-58 and associated text.
288. *Agudas Chasidei Chabad v. Russian Federation*, 466 F. Supp. 2d 6, 20 (2006). They do not address whether the taking was also discriminatory, since any one of the factors satisfies the issue. *Id.* fn. 15.
289. *See* RETURNED FROM RUSSIA, *supra* note 57, at 125-27.
290. *Chabad II*, 598 F.3d at 948.
291. *Id.* at 949.
292. *Id.* at 949-50.
293. *Banco Nacional de Cuba v. Sabbatino*, 376 U.S. 398, 428 (1964). Text accompanying *supra* note 239.
294. 28 U.S.C. § 2370(e)(2). See *supra* note 243-44.
295. *Id.*
296. An interesting question remains: notwithstanding the Second Hickenlooper Amendment, to what extent would the Act of State doctrine apply at all if Russia's Federal Law on Displaced Cultural Valuables is considered in violation of a treaty obligation? *Sabbatino* specifies that the Act of State doctrine applies "even if the complaint alleges that the taking violates customary international law," but makes an exception for the presence of "a treaty or other unambiguous agreement regarding controlling legal principles." The Federal Law on Displaced Cultural Valuables seems on its face to contradict an earlier bilateral treaty with Germany (the so-called Good-Neighborliness Treaty), which provides: "The Federal Republic of Germany and the Union of Soviet Socialist Republics will seek to ensure the preservation of cultural treasures of the other side in their territory. They agree that missing or unlawfully removed art treasures which are located in their territory will be returned to the owners or their legal successors." Needless to say, Russia and Germany have widely divergent interpretations of the phrase

"missing or unlawfully removed art treasures." It is therefore unlikely that the resolution of such a political question would come from American courts. Treaty on Good-Neighborliness, *supra* note 59; *see* Depta, *supra* note 59.

297. *See* RETURNED FROM RUSSIA, *supra* note 57, at 123-25 and *supra* note 279.

298. *Chabad II*, 528 F.3d at 939; Federal Law on Displaced Cultural Valuables (Russia), *supra* note 70, art. 4.

299. *See* Federal Law on Displaced Cultural Valuables (Russia), *supra* note 70, art. 3.

300. *Chabad II*, 528 F.3d at 949-50.

301. *Altmann*, 541 U.S. at 697.

302. Holocaust Victims Redress Act, *supra* note 153, § 201(6) and § 202.

303. As occurred in *Altmann* and probably *Malewicz*.

304. *See supra* discussion of history and later analysis.

305. Quoted in RETURNED FROM RUSSIA, *supra* note 57, at 121.

306. Mark Boguslavsky, *Legal Aspects of the Russian Position in Regard to the Return of Cultural Property*, *in* THE SPOILS OF WAR, *supra* note 3, at 190.

307. Defendant's Supplemental Brief, *quoted in Chabad I*, 466 F. Supp. 2d at 29.

308. *Chabad I*, 466 F. Supp. 2d at 29.

309. *Chabad II*, 528 F.3d at 951.

310. Edwin Black, *Charismatic Jewish Group Wages International Legal Fight for Its Spiritual Soul*, THE CUTTING EDGE NEWS, Feb. 10, 2009, http://www.thecuttingedgenews.com/index.php?article=1089.

311. Preliminary Injunction Order, *Agudas Chasidei Chabad v. Russian Federation*, No. 1:05-CV-01548-RCL (D.D.C. Jan. 27, 2009), *available at* http://www.commartrecovery.org/docs/Chabad-OrderGrantingMotionfor012709.pdf.

312. *Id.*

313. *Id.*

314. *See* RETURNED FROM RUSSIA, *supra* note 57, particularly concerning the Rothschild Archives. *See also* Montén, *supra* note 42, at 85-96, though her analysis of the Rothschild Archives and Ukrainian frescoes does not accord with either the Returned from Russia account or the exception for Ukraine under the Federal Law. Chabad, incidentally, has already exhausted the diplomatic route, presenting letters addressed to Presidents Yeltsin and Putin signed by all one hundred senators and over three hundred members of the House of Representatives to the district court. *Chabad I*, 466 F. Supp. 2d at 30.

315. Nedra Pickler, *Russia Won't Participate in Jewish Documents Suit*, ABC NEWS, June 26, 2009, *available at* http://abcnews.go.com/US/wireStory?id=7941280; Associated Press, *U.S. Judge: Russia Defaults on Jewish Document Suit*, ABC NEWS, Oct. 29, 2009, *available at* http://abcnews.go.com/Politics/wireStory?id=8947373.

# Deaccessioning: A Necessary Evil?

## *A Tax Code Perspective Regarding Museum Deaccessioning Practices*

• • •

*Melanie Greer*

*2nd Place Winner 2009 LCCHP/Andrews Kurth LLP Law School Writing Competition*

### Introduction

On January 26, 2009, the Board of Trustees of Brandeis University shocked the art and museum communities when it announced that it would close the university's Rose Art Museum in the summer of 2009, publicly auction the museum's collection, and convert the museum space to other purposes.[1] It declared its intention to invest all proceeds from the art sales in other academic functions of the university, as was necessary to combat the university's funding problems in the current economic crisis.[2]

The Brandeis announcement came on the heels of another controversial museum deaccessioning.[3] In late 2008, the National Academy of Design sold Frederic Church's *Scene on the Magdalene* and Sanford Gifford's *Mount Mansfield, Vermont* from its collection.[4] According to Academy interim director, Carmine Branagan, the almost 15 million dollars were desperately needed to cover operating costs and to display more of the Academy's 7,000-work collection.[5] As in many museums, only a fraction of the extensive collection is displayed, with most works held in storage.[6]

The approximately 8,000 objects in the Brandeis collection were donated to the museum or were purchased with donated funds.[7] The entire collection of the National Academy is donated art.[8] Under the Internal Revenue Code, since 1917, donors of appreciated cultural property to either of these institutions have received significant tax deductions.[9] These tax incentives encourage donations of art to charitable organizations, and in so doing raise questions about the latitudes recipient organizations can exercise over their collections. For example, certain observers in the art community have decried these announcements of deaccessioning.[10] A specific source of criticism is the museums' intent to use the raised funds for general educational purposes or operating costs. The two major professional associations in the museum industry, the American Association of Museums (AAM) and the Association of Art Museum Directors (AAMD), allow deaccessioning only in specific situations; they forbid member museums from deaccessioning cultural property to support operating costs.[11] Both organizations limit how such funds can be used—either only to purchase replacement art (AAMD), or to purchase new art or maintain the current collection (AAM).[12] Such a policy is intended to foster wise stewardship of collections and promote donations and other forms of public support.

Although important and beneficial, AAM and AAMD membership is only voluntary. Consequently, deaccessioning to raise operating funds is not forbidden by law. There is, however, a line of reasoning that argues that because donors of appreciated personal property receive highly favorable tax treatment when donating the artwork to the public sphere, the property should not be sold back into the private market.

This article discusses the relationship between the tax code, museum association standards, and museum deaccessioning. It first outlines the rules that the AAM and AAMD impose on member museums. It then explains the tax code governing charitable donations of tangible personal property. It next analyzes the interaction between the tax code and the AAM and AAMD standards. The analysis focuses on a key question: Does the tax code support the associations' proscriptions of deaccessioning or encourage museums' resort to deaccessioning?

Finally, the article proposes possible private or legislative solutions to the deaccessioning problem, such as limiting the future transferability of donated artwork and changing tax code provisions.

## Background of Museum Standards and Tax Law

Museums, galleries, and other charitable organizations benefit significantly from tax code provisions that allow large tax deductible donations of appreciated property. These deductions are subject to certain restrictions, which are generally found in Section 170 of the Internal Revenue Code, as well as the Treasury Regulations and legislative history that pertain to this statute. Additionally, the majority of museums in the United States are members of the two major museum associations. These associations impose strict guidelines on member museum behavior with respect to deaccessioning. This paper outlines the AAM and AAMD standards, as they relate to deaccessioning and introduces the general tax laws surrounding charitable deductions. It then explains how these rules apply to appreciated personal property that is donated to qualified institutions, and it illustrates how different forms of the same donation result in different tax deductions. Finally, this paper details the limitations on deductibility in policy and law.

## AAM and AAMD Standards

As museums consider deaccessioning as a means to remedy budget issues in the current downcast economy, it is vital that the boards of these charitable organizations are aware of and, whenever possible, conform to the expected professional and industry standards. In the field of museum management, the two most prominent associations are the AAM and the AAMD. These groups have issued Codes of Ethics, as well as other publications, directed at informing member museums of their responsibilities. Those standards are:

**AAM Standards** The AAM is the only organization that represents the entire spectrum of museums and museum employees, including both professional and volunteer staff.[13] The AAM's mission is "to enhance the value of museums to their communities through leadership, advocacy, and service."[14] Member museums are required to abide by the Code of Ethics or lose AAM accreditation. The Code of Ethics states that a member museum should ensure that "disposal of collections through sale, trade, or research activities is solely for the advancement of the museum's mission."[15] In other words, artwork in a museum's collection should only be disposed of if it fails to advance the museum's mission. The AAM further requires that "[p]roceeds from the sale of nonliving collections are to be used consistent with the established standards of the museum's discipline, but in no event shall be used for anything other than acquisition or direct care of collections."[16] Thus, the AAM is flexible in that it allows for proceeds from art sales to be used to expand or care for collections; however, it strictly prohibits any use of funds to cover operating expenses or capital developments to the museum itself.

**AAMD Standards** The AAMD represents directors of major art museums in North America.[17] The Association's stated purpose is to "support its members in increasing the contribution of art museums to society."[18] It attempts to accomplish this purpose by:

> establishing and maintaining the highest standards of professional practice; serving as a forum for the exchange of information and ideas; acting as an advocate for its member art museums; and being leaders in shaping public discourse about the arts community and the role of art in society.[19]

The AAMD establishes professional practice standards, by which its members are required to abide. In 2007, the AAMD issued a position paper regarding the practice of deaccessioning amongst its member museums, clarifying and solidifying the standards that already existed in AAMD's *Professional Practices in Art Museums*.[20] The AAMD explained that deaccessioning from a member museum's collection is only permitted when:

1. [D]eaccession is made solely to improve the quality, scope, and appropriateness of the collection and to support the mission and long term goals of the museum; and
2. Proceeds from a deaccessioned work are used only to acquire other works of art—the proceeds are never used as operating funds, to build a general endowment, or for any other expenses.[21]

The suitability of these standards is currently under debate in a variety of forums, resulting in proposed state legislation, numerous media articles, and heated online blog forums.[22] Critics of the restrictions on deaccessioning focus on the dangers and impracticabilities that arise when struggling museums that hold valuable objects cannot afford to display or maintain the work.[23] A lack of operating expenses can lead to a myriad of problems that directly affect the value of art. Items in a cash-poor museum's collection are less likely to be displayed or maintained. Further, security and insurance are both expensive—yet necessary—measures that may be neglected because of their cost. Finally, critics of the deaccessioning standards also question whether museums should be forced into a "catch twenty-two," where they must choose between loss of AAM/AAMD accreditation or bankruptcy.[24]

Proponents of deaccessioning regulations instead argue that museums facing dire economic situations will always be able to solve operating expense shortfalls by engaging in a third option: aggressive fundraising.[25] They also maintain that museums hold the objects in the public trust, and therefore have no right to sell the items.[26] Although the policy arguments on both sides of the debate are interesting, they ignore a significant piece of legislation that has largely affected the donations of cash and art over the past century: Section 170 of the tax code.

**Charitable Deductions in the Tax Code**

While it is important that museums understand the professional and industry standards that they must follow, it is also imperative that art donors and recipient donees are aware of the tax laws that govern an exchange of cash or personal property. Since 1917, the United States tax code has allowed a taxpayer to deduct charitable donations against his or her adjusted gross income.[27] The code allows deductions of both cash and personal property charitable contributions, provided the donations meet all code requirements.[28] Charitable contributions are defined in section 170(c) of the code, as follows:

[T]he term 'charitable contribution' means a contribution or gift to or for the use of —

(1) A State, a possession of the United States . . . , or the United States or the District of Columbia, but only if the contribution or gift is made for exclusively public purposes.

(2) A corporation, trust, or community chest, fund or foundation—

 (A) created or organized in the United States . . . ;

 (B) organized and operated exclusively for religious, charitable, scientific, literary or educational purposes . . . ;

 (C) no part of the net earnings which inures to the benefit of any private shareholder or individual; and

 (D) which is not disqualified for tax exemption under section 501(c)(3) by reason of attempting to influence legislation and which does not participate in . . . any political campaign on behalf of . . . any candidate for public office.[29]

These statutory requirements are almost identical to those that determine whether an organization qualifies as a section 501(c)(3) tax exempt organization. In both definitions, donations are classified as tax-deductible charitable contributions only if the donees are organized domestically and operated exclusively for one of the statutorily listed exempt purposes. Additionally, a charitable contribution is only deductible under section 170 if the donee organization ensures that no part of its earnings privately benefit a shareholder or individual, and the organization cannot be involved in political lobbying or campaigning that would disqualify it from section 501(c)(3) tax exempt status. Common suitable recipient organizations include public educational institutions (such as colleges and universities), hospitals, churches, libraries, and museums.

The code not only limits which entities can *receive* deductible charitable contributions—as explained above—but also restricts the *amount* of contributions a single taxpayer may deduct.[30] Section 170(b)(1)(A) states that a taxpayer can deduct a maximum of 50% of his contribution base[31] in charitable contributions given to statutorily defined organizations, including publicly supported museums.[32] The statute also limits the amount of charitable deductions that can be taken for contributions of capital gain property[33] to 30% of the donor's contribution base.[34]

In summary, donors contributing cash to qualified recipients, such as public museums or charitable educational institutions may deduct up to 50% of their contribution base. However, if a donor gives appreciated artwork, the donor's deduction is limited to 30% of his contribution base, and any excess may be carried over to future years, for up to five years.[35]

### Charitable Contribution of Capital Gain Personal Property

As explained above, the tax code allows a deduction for donors who have paid taxes on cash they later give to a charitable institution. From a policy perspective, the deduction allows the taxpayer to recover the taxes already paid on the amount he or she later chose to generously give to a charitable organization. When art is donated to a museum or university, the changing value of the art complicates the deduction determination. Should artwork that was purchased three years ago for $50,000, but now donated to a museum with a present market value of $100,000, entitle the donor to a $100,000 deduction? Should the deduction be restricted to $50,000?

Generally, a taxpayer is entitled to deduct the fair market value of contributed property on the date of the contribution. However, for certain contributions of property, the deductible amount is reduced, and a donor may only deduct an amount equal to his basis.[36] This rule applies to contributions of: (1) ordinary income property; (2) tangible personal property that is used by the donee in a manner unrelated to the donee's exempt (or governmental) purpose; and (3) property given to or for the use of a private foundation (other than a foundation defined in section 170(b)(1)(E)).[37] Donated artwork falls into the second category, *tangible personal property*; thus, a donor may only deduct the fair market value if the art is used by the donee organization in a use "related" to its 501(c)(3) exemption, that is, its organizational purpose.[38] If it is not put to a "related use," the donor may only deduct his or her basis. Thus, changes in use can complicate matters for the donor.

This provision, allowing deductions of property at fair market value, results in a significant tax benefit for a donor who contributes highly appreciated personal property to a qualified institution. The tax benefit is best illustrated by studying the differing outcomes of the following hypothetical.

In December of 2004, Alf, Bev, and Charlie each agreed to invest $50,000 for a period of three years. Additionally, each pledged to donate to Big Town Museum a charitable contribution of the $50,000 principal, as well as any subsequent gain or interest that the $50,000 earned in the five years it was invested. Alf chose to invest his $50,000 in high-yield CDs which returned $50,000 in interest by December of 2009. Alf then donated the entire $100,000 to Big Town Museum, as pledged. Alf had first paid ordinary income tax on the initial $50,000 when he earned it. Throughout the five years of investment, Alf also paid ordinary income tax on the interest payments that he realized. When he donated the $100,000 of cash to Big Town, Alf was able to claim an ordinary income deduction on the entire amount, recouping the tax that he had paid on the $100,000. In summary, Alf deducted the same amount of income in 2009 on which he had already paid tax in previous years.

Bev instead chose to spend her $50,000 on a sculpture, which she proudly displayed in her foyer for five years. In December 2009, Bev sold the sculpture for $100,000 and donated the funds to Big Town Museum. Bev had already paid ordinary income tax on the $50,000 of principal she used to purchase the sculpture when she first earned this money. Upon sale of the sculpture, Bev was assessed capital gain tax upon the $50,000 of gain that she realized because of the sculpture's increase in value.[39] After donating the $100,000, Bev was able to take a deduction against her ordinary income for the full amount of $100,000. Bev benefited from a full $100,000 deduction against ordinary income, even though she had only paid ordinary income tax rates on $50,000 of income, and capital gain rate on the $50,000 gain.

Finally, in December 2004, Charlie purchased a $50,000 painting from a promising local artist. By December 2009, the painting was valued at $100,000. Unlike Bev, instead of selling the painting and donating the funds,

Charlie chose to contribute the painting to Big Town Museum. Provided that all of the Section 170(e) requirements are met, Charlie can claim a $100,000 tax deduction against his 2009 ordinary income, even though he only invested $50,000 in the painting. Charlie never realized the $50,000 gain so he did not pay tax on it; however, the tax code allowed him to claim a deduction for the market value of the painting.

In the first scenario, Alf did not gain any significant tax benefit by donating cash. He simply claimed a deduction equal to the amount that he had already paid tax on. Bev, the taxpayer who sold appreciated art and then donated the funds, may gain a small tax benefit. Even though she paid capital gain tax on the $50,000 she realized upon sale of the sculpture, capital gain is taxed at a rate of 28%, whereas Bev could claim a $50,000 deduction against her ordinary income that could be subject to 35% tax, if in the highest tax bracket.[40] Charlie—the taxpayer who contributed a painting directly to Big Town—received the largest tax benefit. Charlie invested $50,000 of principal, on which he had already paid ordinary income tax. Upon donation of the painting, Charlie can correctly claim a $100,000 deduction, reducing his tax liability by $35,000 if he is in the highest tax bracket.[41]

As evidenced by the choices of Alf, Bev, and Charlie, donating appreciated personal property to organizations is much more lucrative—from a tax deduction perspective—than simply donating the equivalent amount in cash. A taxpayer donating cash has already paid tax on the full amount of the deduction. However, a taxpayer donating property has only paid tax on the basis he invested in the property when he purchased it. Usually, when a taxpayer sells personal property he pays capital gain tax on the difference between his basis and the fair market value. However, when a contribution meets the requirements of section 170(e) of the tax code, the taxpayer receives a double benefit: He avoids realizing a profit *and* still deducts the total value of donated appreciated personal property. The next section discusses these section 170(e) requirements.

**Section 170(e) and Pension Protection Act Limitations**

Section 170(e)(1) governs the deductibility of appreciated personal property. The statute requires that any deduction for a charitable contribution of property be reduced by the amount of short-term gain[42] that would have been realized if the contributed property had been sold by the taxpayer at fair market value.[43] Additionally, a donor may not deduct long-term gain[44] that would be realized if the property were sold at fair market value unless the property is (1) held by the donee organization beyond the year in which the contribution was made, and (2) used by the donee organization in a manner related to the basis for its exemption. As illustrated in the above hypothetical, a significant tax benefit is gained when donor taxpayers are able to deduct the entire fair market value of a donated property. For this reason, taxpayers are careful to meet the section 170(e) requirements so that their gifts are not reduced by the amount of long-term gain.

There are two major issues with regard to section 170(e) requirements—the donee's holding period of the contribution, and the donee's use of the contribution. This creates an interesting situation because the donor's fair market value deduction is completely dependent on the recipient organization's handling of the donated objects. These requirements are discussed in more detail below.

**Time During Which the Property Is Held by the Organization** Section 170(e) prevents a donor from deducting an amount beyond his or her basis in donated personal property unless the property is held by the recipient organization beyond the year in which the contribution was made.[45] Donors can easily meet this requirement by attaching a condition to the gift which requires that the donee organization hold the donated property for a set time. Adding such a condition ensures the possibility that a gift will be "disposed of by the donee before the last day of the taxable year in which the contribution was made" is rather low. Given that this rule is based simply on the timing of disposition, there are few (if any) complications with determining whether it is met in specific situations.

Additionally, the Pension Protection Act, passed in 2006, added another timing condition by enacting a recapture provision that limits a donor's deduction to his or her basis in the property if a donee charity sells the property within three years of the day the property was contributed.[46] If a donor has already taken a deduction, he or she is subject to recapture.[47] The donor must report, as ordinary income in the year of the donee's disposition of the property, the amount by which the claimed fair market value exceeded the donor's basis.[48]

**Related Use Rule** In contrast to the easily managed timing restriction on disposition, the "related use" requirement is somewhat ambiguous. The "related use" rule limits the donor's deduction if "the use by the donee is unrelated to the purpose or function constituting the basis for its exemption under section 501."[49] If the recipient organization uses donated appreciated property in a manner inconsistent with its charitable purpose tax exemption, a donor is only permitted to deduct his or her basis in the property—not the fair market value.

Given the broad wording of this statute, a creative donor may assume that an appreciated gift would still be used in a 'related way' if, after the timing restriction, the property is sold and the funds are used for the exempt purpose. However, both legislative history and the Treasury Regulations explain that the actual gifted property must be used in a manner related to the purpose of the donee organization's exempt status.

The House Congressional Record from December 22, 1969, reveals how Congress, when enacting section 170(e), expected the related use requirement to be interpreted narrowly, as seen in the following exchange between New Jersey congressman Peter Frelinghuysen and Arkansas Representative Wilbur Mills, Chairman of the House Ways and Means Committee:

> *Mr. Frelinghuysen:* Supposing an art object were to be given to a university. Would that require a tax on the appreciation?
>
> *Mr. Mills:* Not if the university used it in accordance with some educational program of the university, in an art appreciation course or something of that type.
>
> *Mr. Frelinghuysen:* Suppose it were to be sold by the university if an object of art were given to a hospital, for example, in order to have that object sold for the use of the hospital or the money to be used for that purpose?
>
> *Mr. Mills:* It is the use of the property that is the determining factor. If it was contemplated that the property would be sold rather than used for the organization's exempt purposes, then the appreciation must be taken into account for tax purposes by the donor.
>
> * * *
>
> *Mr. Frelinghuysen:* If, for instance, an object were given to a hospital and the intention on the part of the donor and hospital was to sell the object, would that require a tax on the appreciation of that?
>
> *Mr. Mills:* The appreciation would be taken into account for tax purposes in that case, because of the requirement that the property be given where it is really used for the exempt purpose of the organization.[50]

Subsequently, the Treasury issued regulations echoing the interpretation discussed on the House floor. In Treasury Regulation § 1.170A-4(b)(3), "unrelated use" is defined as a "use unrelated to the purpose or function constituting the basis of the charitable organization's exemption under section 501."[51] The regulations then illustrate an unrelated use, explaining that "if a painting contributed to an educational institution is used by that organization for educational purposes by being placed in its library for display and study by art students, the use is not an unrelated use; but if the painting is sold and the proceeds used by the organization for general educational purposes, the use of the property is an unrelated use."[52]

The congressional history and regulations clearly interpret "related use" narrowly. It is not enough to use funds derived from sale of an item in a "related use." The donee must use the *actual item* given in a related manner. The statutory requirement to determine whether an item is used in a related manner is vague. Once again, one must look to the regulations for guidance. In this instance, the Treasury Regulations explain how the "related use" requirement can be proven. There are two approaches a donor may use to prove a "related use."[53]

A donor may prove that the property is not being put to an unrelated use by meeting the "wait and see" approach.[54] In this approach, the donor simply establishes that the donee organization did, in fact, use the donated property in a manner consistent with its exempt purpose. The second approach, considered the "Reasonable Anticipation" approach, allows the donor to take a full deduction of the appreciated property, provided that "at the time of the contribution . . . , it is reasonable to anticipate that the property will not be put to an unrelated use by the donee."[55] This standard also includes a presumption specifically related to art donations to museums. The regulation states that "in the case of a contribution of personal property to or for the use of a museum, if the object donated is of a general type normally retained by such a museum or other museum for museum purposes, it will be reasonable for the donor to anticipate, unless he has actual knowledge to the contrary, that the object will not be put to an unrelated use by the donee, whether or not the object is later sold or exchanged by the donee."[56]

The tax code provisions allow those who donate appreciated art to charitable organizations in such a way that they meet the section 170(e) requirements to favorably minimize their tax liability. The following section will analyze how these benefits influence donor behavior and industry standards.

## Discussion of Tax Code–Influenced Donor Actions

Legislation is rarely, if ever, enacted without regard to policy. This is seldom more evident than in the area of tax legislation, where laws are often enacted to encourage or discourage certain actions by offering financial reward or punishment. One of the largest financial "rewards" the tax code gives taxpayers is the ability to deduct the fair market value of artwork donated to charitable organizations, irrespective of the cost basis of the property. This policy decision has benefitted the art world significantly by encouraging donations of stunning, high-value gifts that may have never otherwise entered the public arena. However, this article argues that the tax laws have likely contributed to the imbalance between cash and appreciated property donations, resulting in many art-rich but cash-poor museums. Even so, the two main professional museum associations—the AAM and AAMD—still forbid museums from selling art in order to cover operating expenses. The following analysis will focus on those two key issues: (A) whether the AAM and AAMD standards limiting deaccessioning are supported by the tax code, and (B) whether the tax code policies that strongly support appreciated personal property donations have created an environment that fosters deaccessioning.

### The Tax Code and Possible Limits on Deaccessioning

This section will first examine whether there is any legislative support for the AAM and AAMD limitations on deaccessioning. As explained in the background, the AAM and AAMD only permit member museums to deaccession artwork that falls outside of the scope of the mission of the museum. More importantly, both associations limit how museums may use the funds obtained through a sale of deaccessioned art. The AAM and AAMD require that funds be used to purchase replacement art, and the AAM also allows a deaccessioning museum to use the finances to maintain its collection. There is some legitimacy to the argument that the treasury regulations, legislative history, tax code, and recent amendments all seem to support some degree of limitation on deaccessioning. However, as the following discussion will conclude, the code does not forbid deaccessioning, even of cultural property that is heavily subsidized by the federal tax deductions.

**Arguments Against Deaccessioning Based in the Tax Code** Recall that section 170 of the Code mandates that appreciated property is deductible at its fair market value only if it is given to a public organization that will put it to a "Related

Use." The "Related Use" requirement in the statute is stated in broad terms, and begs the question as to whether an organization could receive appreciated property, hold it for the required holding period, sell it, and use the funds for the "Related Use." Although there is no case law clarifying the correct breadth of interpretation, the congressional intent and Treasury Regulations make it quite clear that the actual donated property must be put to a "Related Use." It is insufficient for a donee organization to sell the property and use the funds derived from the sale in a related manner. This narrow interpretation seems to indicate, from a policy perspective, that Congress intended to encourage donors to give appreciated property to organizations that need such property to fulfill their missions. Additionally, Congress expected the recipient organizations to maintain possession of the property, at least for some time, to meet the related use requirement.

The AAM and AAMD standards restricting deaccessioning do gain some support from these tax laws and policies. First, if—as it seems—the congressional intent was to facilitate donations of expensive appreciated art to charitable organizations, it makes sense that donated objects should then stay in the public forum indefinitely. From a tax perspective, at the point that an art object enters the public arena through a donation that lowers the donor's tax liability, the public subsidizes the museum's acquisition of the artwork.[57] Under current tax law, if a museum later chooses to deaccession art it received from a donor who took a deduction on the appreciated value of the property, there are no restrictions preventing this work from being sold back into the private marketplace. This result seemingly contradicts the congressional intent to assist public museums to acquire high-cost art. Additionally, it means that art could circulate in and out of private and public arenas, being sold to private owners and then "re-donated," with the result that the public "re-subsidizes" acquisition of the same piece of art limitless times.

Second, tax laws surrounding charitable contributions of appreciated art also favor museum and educational facilities above other charitable organizations. Congress encouraged donors to contribute high-cost property donations by allowing excess deductions equal to the unrealized gain. By treating art gifts more favorably than simple cash donations, museums and educational facilities that can put the art to a "Related Use" are able to take advantage of these tax laws, while many other organizations cannot. It would be unfair to allow the museums and educational facilities to take advantage of the tax laws, accept high-income donations, and then sell these to meet operating costs.

This would put these organizations at a significant fundraising advantage over and above other charitable organizations, and would abuse the privilege the tax law created to encourage the donation of high-worth gifts.

Finally, Congress also recently extended a recapture provision in the tax code to prevent favorable tax treatment if the work of art is sold by the donee within three years of the contribution. Under the provision, if the donee organization disposes of the applicable property within the three-year time period, the donor is subject to an adjustment of his or her tax benefit.[58] The recapture requires the donor to include, as ordinary income for its taxable year in which the disposition occurs, an amount equal to the excess (if any) of (i) the amount of the deduction previously claimed by the donor as a charitable contribution with respect to such property, over (ii) the donor's basis in such property at the time of the contribution.[59] By extending the required holding period, the 2006 Congress obviously intended to ensure that personal property given to a museum by an individual—yet compensated by the taxes of society—spend sufficient time in the public arena.

**Arguments in Support of Deaccessioning Based in the Tax Code** The Congressional intent seems to support the AAM and AAMD limitations on deaccessioning; however, the tax code does not absolutely prohibit the sale of donated artwork. Furthermore, as the following discussion indicates, numerous references in the tax code seem to acknowledge the possibility of deaccessioning once-donated works.

First, by extending time limits on the recapture provision, Congress has simply extended the time period before deaccessioning can take place.[60] It has not legislated against deaccessioning. By creating such a small recapture time period, Congress actually acknowledged that after those short three years, museums are free to do what they like with the contributed art. Any action they take no longer risks the deduction taken by the donor. Congress could have further limited the transferability of items given to museums through the tax code deductions, but chose not to.

Second, Congress also acknowledged that deaccessioning may, at times, be necessary—even within the first three years of ownership. Even in the most recent recapture provision, which extends the required holding period of the donee, Congress included an exception which does not require recapture even if the contributed property is sold within the three year recapture period. There is no adjustment of the tax benefit if the donee organization makes a certification to the Secretary, by written statement signed under penalties of perjury by an officer of the organization.[61] The statement must either (1) certify that the use of the property by the donee was related to the purpose or function constituting the basis for the donee's exemption, and describe how the property was used and how such use furthered such purpose or function; or (2) state the intended use of the property by the donee at the time of the contribution and certify that such use became impossible or infeasible to implement.[62]

Thus, even in provisions requiring possession for a length of time, Congress has allowed for deaccessioning in special instances. An organization could, conceivably, issue a statement certifying that because of financial troubles the intended use became impossible to implement, requiring sale of the donated art. In this instance, even though financial causes may lead to deaccessioning soon after receipt of the contribution, the donor would still successfully claim a deduction at fair market value.

Finally, it could be argued that future donors will struggle to meet the "reasonable anticipation" approach of the "proof of use" requirement if a museum habitually deaccessions donated works of art. While it is true that it may be difficult to show a "reasonable anticipation of related use" when previous donated property has been deaccessioned soon after it was obtained, this reasoning does not carry weight when one considers the presumption allowed in the Treasury Regulations. Section 1.170A-4(b)(3)(ii)(b) creates a presumption of related use in instances where tangible personal property is donated to or for the use of a museum, provided that the property given is of a type that would generally be given to a museum. This presumption exists, regardless of whether the museum will later put the property to an unrelated use, or will sell or exchange it, provided the donor lacks actual knowledge of these future plans.

The presumption weighs against the argument that the Tax Code forbids deaccessioning. In actuality, the Regulations explicitly provide for maximum deductibility of all tangible personal property given to museums, irrespective of the museum's past history of deaccessioning.

Although tax policy encourages the contribution of tangible personal property for the use of the donee, the tax code also acknowledges that there are instances where the donated property will be sold or disposed of. Congress has taken a balanced approach, allowing for early sales of donated property—when necessary—yet still incentivizing contributions of appreciated property. This incentive extends even to museums that may choose to sell large amounts of donated property (within the framework set up by section 170(e)). The presumption set up by the regulations also allows for future donors to deduct fair market value of personal property under the "reasonable anticipation" rule, even in cases where a museum has previously deaccessioned.

In conclusion, although some aspects of the tax code exist to protect the taxpayer-subsidized investment in donated art, many more provisions that exist acknowledge deaccessioning, and even protect donor tax deductions if the donee is no longer able to maintain possession of the donated work. Thus, the AAM and AAMD standards that oppose deaccessioning art to raise operating expenses are not completely supported by the tax code. The code does, however, contain recent legislation enacted to prevent abuse of the deduction and to encourage longevity of possession of the art given to museums and other educational facilities. The tax code reaches a compromise which acknowledges that although it would prefer that the work remain in museums and the public forum, it will not control the long-term transferability of artwork.

**The Tax Code Disadvantages Museums**

Favorable tax treatment of personal property donation may have contributed to many of the operating expense problems that exist in the museum world. While the tax code does not explicitly encourage deaccessioning, there are elements of the code that may, unintentionally, promote deaccessioning. Recall Alf, Bev, and Charlie. Each of these individuals invested the same amount of money, over the same period of time, and gave the same resultant amount to a charitable foundation—Big Town Museum. Their tax liability, however, differed vastly because of the form in which each gave his or her contribution to Big Town.

The donation of appreciated personal property is one of the most lucrative ways to lower one's tax liability. Given a choice based solely on tax reduction, an owner of appreciated art will always choose to give art, rather than cash. This favorable treatment of personal property donations likely results in the benefit of an abundance of contributed art.[63] More problematic, however, is the likelihood that because donors are giving art, they are less inclined to also give cash donations.

This policy, and the resultant imbalance in donations, puts museums in an awkward position. While no museum director would (or should) complain about incentivizing personal property contributions, museums need funds to continue operations. If a large number of highly wealthy donors are seeking to reduce their tax liability, these donors will generally choose to give the museum art objects, not cash.

For some museums, deaccessioning may be the only way to repay creditors and continue to show some of the many pieces of work that often sit in a storeroom. Furthermore, deaccessioning may simply be the necessary evil that is coupled to the "good" of favorable tax treatment with regard to property donations.

## Impact of the Tax Code: Intended or Unintended Consequences

While the tax code does not forbid deaccessioning, it does seem to foster an environment where highly wealthy donors would be more inclined to give art rather than funds. Low cash donations and a crippled economy are wreaking havoc on museum operating funds and endowments, and more museums are considering deaccessioning as a means to stabilize their financial situation. In this section, I will discuss the possible options a museum has under current law if a museum truly is insolvent, and propose legislation that will protect art once it has entered the public arena.

### Current Options for Insolvent Museums

By forbidding member museums from deaccessioning to replenish meager operating funds, the AAM and AAMD may be backing some of their member museums into bankruptcy court. National Academy director Carmine Branagan acknowledged that the sale of the two paintings from the National Academy collection meant that the museum could now pay bills that had been languishing unpaid.[64] Undoubtedly, in the current economic climate other museums are struggling to make ends meet. If these museums are unable to raise the necessary funds to survive, bankruptcy may be the only option.

Bankruptcy may provide a means by which to "weed out" the badly managed museums; however, it also puts the bankrupt museum's collection at great risk. It is unlikely that artwork in a bankrupt estate will be protected from sale to private collectors. Thus, rather than allowing one or two works to enter the private arena through deaccessioning, a museum forced into bankruptcy may see many, many more of its works lost from public viewing. Although some works may be sold to other, better-managed museums, there is no guarantee that this will occur. Therefore, bankruptcy is not the ideal solution to operating expense problems.

Rather, deaccessioning of excess pieces of stored art may be a means by which to keep the lights on and the remainder of the collection safe, insured, and on display. For years, museums have benefited from the tax laws that encouraged donations of appreciated property. In fact, many of the pieces in museum collections today are likely there because of the tax deduction that encouraged donors—like our fictional Charlie—to invest in and then give appreciated property, rather than cash. Museums are now art rich but cash poor. Minimal deaccessioning may be necessary because of the tax policy that has encouraged property donations but also likely hindered cash gifts from highly wealthy donors.

### Proposed Legislation that will Protect Donated Art in the Public Arena

The preferential treatment of art donations warrants responsible ownership and handling of art by the museum. Society subsidizes charities through (1) giving and (2) preferential tax treatment of donations. As has been shown throughout this article, tax treatment makes art donations to museums much more favorable. Cash donations to museums likely suffer because of this. Additionally, charities that cannot put highly appreciated personal property to a "related use," such as a homeless shelter, may be neglected in place of organizations that can meet the tax requirements for deductions at fair market value.

This preferential treatment has led some states to consider enacting legislation to protect society's investment in the donated art. New York assemblyman Richard Brodsky has also submitted legislation limiting deaccessioning, and other states could soon follow suit. Although this would encourage leaving art in the museum, it does not consider the worst-case scenario when bankruptcy is the only option. For this reason, it is important to enact legislation that will prevent all donated art from entering the private market.

## Conclusion

The policy preferences that encourage donation of personal property have resulted in art-rich, cash-poor museums. In the current economy, with endowments losing significant amounts of savings and donors less likely to part with their dwindling savings, deaccessioning some of the art that has been given in place of money may be the only viable solution for some museums to survive.

Deaccessioning is not inherently wrong, and for now, it may be a necessary evil that will assist museums to survive hard times. Eventually, works that are donated through § 170 should be protected from being deaccessioned back into the private sphere because they now belong to every taxpayer who subsidized their donation. This could be done by preventing donated property from being sold back into the private sphere, even in cases of bankruptcy. Legislation and a larger "public trust" could protect property and maintain public access to art already subsidized by the public.

## Notes

1. Letter from Jehuda Reinharz, President of Brandeis University, to the University community, *available at* http://www.theasa.net/caucus_visual/item/brandeis_to_close_rose_art_museum/. On July 27, 2009, three overseers of the Rose Art Museum filed a suit against Brandeis University to prevent it from closing the museum. Randy Kennedy, *Lawsuit Filed to Halt Closure of Brandeis Art Museum*, N.Y. TIMES, July 27, 2009, *available at* http://artsbeat.blogs.nytimes.com/2009/07/27/lawsuit-filed-to-halt-closure-of-brandeis-art-museum/.
2. *Id.* After the press release and the attendant public backlash, Brandeis revised its initial decision, and now states that "the school plans to sell 'a limited number' of pieces, if any, and has formed a special committee to review its actions." John Hechinger, *New Unrest on Campus as Donors Rebel*, WALL STREET JOURNAL, April 23, 2009 *available at* http://online.wsj.com/article/SB124043394794145007.html.
3. Deaccessioning is defined by the AAMD as "the practice by which an art museum formally transfers its ownership of an object to another institution or individual by sale, exchange, or grant, or disposes of an object if its physical condition is so poor that it has no aesthetic or academic value." AAMD, *Art Museums and the Practice of Deaccessioning*, November 2007 *available at* http://www.aamd.org/papers/, [hereinafter AAMD *Position Paper*].
4. Randy Kennedy, *National Academy Sells Two Hudson River School Paintings to Bolster Its Finances*, N.Y. TIMES, December 6, 2008, *available at* http://www.nytimes.com/2008/12/06/arts/design/06acad.html.
5. *Id.*
6. *Id.*
7. The Rose Endowment has been used to purchase 259 artworks. Many other works have been donated. Hechinger, *supra* note 2.
8. "Most works of art owned by the Organization have been given to it by its artist members in order to fulfill the membership requirements while a smaller group of works have been donated by others. The collections are maintained for the promotion of American art, rather than for financial gain." National Academy of Design Notes to Financial Statements June 30, 2005 and 2004, Note 1(i), *available at* http://www.nationalacademy.org/doc/financial_statements.pdf.

9. Donors of appreciated artworks are generally able to deduct the fair market value of the donated art. After the 1969 legislative changes, an artist-donor could no longer reduce his ordinary income by the fair market value of the gift. Rather, artist-donors can only deduct the cost of art materials used in the creation of the piece of donated artwork. 26 U.S.C. § 170(e)(1)(A).
10. Lee Rosenbaum's many posts opposing deaccessioning are available at http://www.artsjournal.com/culturegrrl/. Ford W. Bell, *Letter: Museum Art, Held in Trust*, N.Y. TIMES, March 23, 2009, *available at* http://www.nytimes.com/2009/03/31/opinion/lweb31museums.html?_r=2.
11. *See infra* notes 25-35 and accompanying text (sections on AAM and AAMD).
12. AAMD *Position Paper supra* note 3. AMERICAN ASSOCIATION OF MUSEUMS, AAM CODE OF ETHICS, *available at* http://www.aam-us.org/museumresources/ethics/coe.cfm [hereinafter AAM CODE OF ETHICS].
13. American Association of Museums, About AAM, http://www.aam-us.org/aboutaam/ (last visited Dec. 1, 2009).
14. *Id.*
15. AAM CODE OF ETHICS, *supra* note 12.
16. *Id.*
17. Association of Art Museum Directors, About AAMD, http://www.aamd.org/about/ (last visited Dec. 1, 2009).
18. *Id.*
19. *Id.*
20. AAMD Position Paper, *supra* note 3.
21. *Id.*
22. New York state assemblyman Richard Brodsky introduced a bill attempting to legislate specific standards as to when and how museums can deaccession. Assemb. B. No. A06959, (N.Y. 2009) *available at* http://graphics8.nytimes.com/packages/pdf/arts/03182009-bill.pdf. Bloggers Lee Rosenbaum and Donn Zaretsky take opposing sides in the argument as to the appropriateness of deaccessioning. Lee Rosenbaum, www.artsjournal.com/culturegrrl/ (last visited Dec. 1, 2009); Donn Zaretsky, http://theartlawblog.blogspot.com/ (last visited Dec. 1, 2009).
23. *See* Zaretsky, *supra* note 22.
24. *Id.* Even though the NAD withdrew its AAMD membership after news surfaced that it had deaccessioned the Church and Gifford paintings, the Association responded by requiring all other AAMD member museums to suspend loans of artwork to the museum and end any ongoing collaborations, essentially blackballing the NAD from the museum community. ARTINFO, *AAMD Censures National Academy Museum*, Dec. 5, 2008, *available at* http://www.artinfo.com/news/story/29702/aamd-censures-national-academy-museum/ (last visited Dec. 1, 2009).
25. Rosenbaum includes two examples of last-ditch fundraising efforts that successfully raised necessary funds to prevent deaccessioning at-risk art, and she

uses these examples to argue that all museums will survive by fundraising if they have no other option. Lee Rosenbaum, *National Academy Lessons: The Fallacy of Deaccession-or-Die UPDATED*, Dec. 30, 2008 *available at* http://www.artsjournal.com/culturegrrl/2008/12/national_academy_lesson_the_fa.html (last visited Dec. 1, 2009).

26. Bell, *supra* note 10. These commentators argue that because the art is held in the public trust it cannot be deaccessioned *to raise operating expenses*; however, it can be deaccessioned if the money is used to buy new art. Notably, they do not argue that deaccessioning is inherently evil, but only that the public trust is violated if the funds are used in a manner inconsistent with current industry standards. This logical inconsistency weakens the "public trust" argument.
27. 26 U.S.C. § 170(a)(1). Adjusted gross income is income (including wages, interest, capital gains, income from retirement accounts, and alimony received) adjusted downward by specific "above-the-line" deductions (such as contributions to deductible retirement accounts and alimony paid; but not including standard or itemized deductions).
28. 26 U.S.C. §§ 170(a)(3), (e)(1). These requirements are discussed in greater detail in the remainder of this section.
29. 26 U.S.C. § 170(c).
30. 26 U.S.C. § 170(b).
31. According to § 170(b)(1)(G) "For purpose of this section, the term 'contribution base' means adjusted gross income (computed without regard to any net operating loss carryback to the taxable year under section 172)."
32. Permitted § 170(b)(1)(A) organizations include religious organizations, educational institutions, medical facilities, government funded organizations, and other smaller categories, as defined in the code. Specifically, § 170(b)(1)(A)(vi) classifies publicly supported museums as permitted organizations. Charitable contributions that cannot be categorized under § 170(b)(1)(A) are subject to further limitations, located at § 170(b)(1)(B).
33. Capital gain property means any capital asset held for personal or investment purposes (such as stocks, bonds, jewelry, and collectibles), or property used in the taxpayer's trade or business, if its sale at fair market value would have resulted in long-term capital gain. Artwork is considered capital gain property.
34. 26 U.S.C. § 170(b)(1)(C).
35. 26 U.S.C. § 170(b)(1)(C). The code also contains a carry-over provision so that contributions of capital gain property that exceed 30% of the donor's contribution base may be carried forward for up to five years. Also, this 30% limit is reduced to 20% if the contribution is not given to a § 170(b)(1)(A) permitted organization.
36. The basis of property is "the cost of property" when it was first purchased by its current owner, as distinct from its current fair market value, which is the cost an uninterested party would pay for the property. 26 U.S.C. § 1012.

37. Joint Committee on Taxation, *Technical Explanation of H.R. 4, the "Pension Protection Act of 2006," as Passed by the House on July 28, 2006, and as Considered by the Senate on August 3, 2006*. August 2, 2006 at 297–300 *available at* http://www.house.gov/jct/x-38-06.pdf.
38. U.S.C § 170(e).
39. The sale of a collectible is assessed at a 28% capital gain rate. 26 U.S.C. § 1(h)(4)-(5). Bev had a $14,000 tax liability when she sold the painting (28% of the $50,000 gain).
40. Here, Bev benefits by taking a deduction against her income that was to be taxed at a rate 7% higher than the capital gain tax she paid.
41. Charlie would have paid $17,500 in tax on the first $50,000 he used to purchase the painting. When he reduces his tax liability by $35,000, he not only saves that initial $17,500, but also gets a savings of a further $17,500, simply for giving appreciated property rather than first selling it and then donating the profit.
42. Short-term gain is gain realized when a property held for less than one year is sold for a profit.
43. "(e) Certain contributions of ordinary income and capital gain property

    (1) General rule The amount of any charitable contribution of property otherwise taken into account under this section shall be reduced by the sum of—

    (A) the amount of gain which would not have been long-term capital gain (determined without regard to section 1221 (b)(3)) if the property contributed had been sold by the taxpayer at its fair market value (determined at the time of such contribution), and

    (B) in the case of a charitable contribution—

    (i) of tangible personal property—

    (I) if the use by the donee is unrelated to the purpose or function constituting the basis for its exemption under section 501 (or, in the case of a governmental unit, to any purpose or function described in subsection (c)), or

    (II) which is applicable property (as defined in paragraph (7)(C)) which is sold, exchanged, or otherwise disposed of by the donee before the last day of the taxable year in which the contribution was made and with respect to which the donee has not made a certification in accordance with paragraph (7)(D),

    * * *

    the amount of gain which would have been long-term capital gain if the property contributed had been sold by the taxpayer at its fair market value (determined at the time of such contribution). 28 U.S.C. § 170(e).

44. Long-term gain is gain realized when a property is disposed of after being held for at least one year.
45. 28 U.S.C. § 170(e)(1)(B)(II).
46. 28 U.S.C. 170(e)(7). Recapture occurs when a donor-taxpayer's gift fails to meet the statutory requirements and he is taxed in a later year on the amount he deducted in an earlier year.
47. *Id.*
48. 28 U.S.C. 170(e)(7)(A).
49. 28 U.S.C. 170(e)(1)(B)(i)(I).
50. 91 CONG. REC. H40869 (Dec. 22, 1969) (statements of Rep. Frelinghuysen and Rep. Mills).
51. Treas. Reg. § 1.170A-4(b)(3) (1972).
52. Treas. Reg. § 1.170A-4(b)(3)(i) (1972).
53. Treas. Reg § 1.170A-4(b)(3)(ii) (1972).
54. Treas. Reg § 1.170A-4(b)(3)(ii)(a) (1972).
55. Treas. Reg § 1.170A-4(b)(3)(ii)(b) (1972).
56. *Id.*
57. This figurative "subsidy" exists because when a taxpayer takes a large tax deduction on donated appreciated property, the rest of the taxpaying community must contribute more to meet the required federal tax burden.
58. 28 U.S.C. § 170(e)(7).
59. If the donee fails to meet the holding period requirement, the donor must "pay back" the tax deduction he took against his ordinary income when he first gave the gift. He does so by adding the excess deduction he took to his income. He can find the excess deduction by subtracting his cost basis in the property from the amount of the deduction he took for the charitable contribution. The resulting number is the excess deduction, and should be added to his ordinary income in the year in which the donee prematurely disposes of the property.
60. Section 170(e) of the code initially prevented the donee from disposing of the art in the year in which it was received. In 2006, the Pension Protection Act extended this provision, allowing for recapture of the deduction attributed to capital gain if the property was disposed of within three years. *See* 28 U.S.C. § 170(e)(7).
61. 26 U.S.C. § 170(e)(7)(B).
62. 26 U.S.C. § 170(e)(7)(D).
63. "Most big museums can't show 90 percent of the objects they own—it's all in storage. . . . What's wrong with selling these objects to smaller museums or even private collectors who are more likely to put them on display?" Jori Finkel, *Whose Rules Are These, Anyway?* N.Y. TIMES, Dec. 24, 2008 *available at* http://www.nytimes.com/2008/12/28/arts/design/28fink.html?_r=3&ref=arts&pagewanted=all (quoting Mr. Michael O'Hare, cultural policy professor at the University of California, Berkeley).

64. Carmine Branagan claimed that prior to the sale of the Church and Gifford works, there was no money to pay the guards or even buy ink cartridges. She states that she even worked a few months for free. Jim Zarroli, *Museums Exhibit Signs of Economic Distress*, NPR, Jan. 5, 2009, *available at* http://www.npr.org/templates/story/story.php?storyId=99017732.

ARTICLE

# The Duty Under NAGPRA to Inform Repatriation Recipients of Potentially Hazardous Substances

## *A Best-Practice Guide*

• • •

*Lydia Grunstra*

*Finalist 2009 LCCHP/Andrews Kurth LLP Law School Writing Competition*

### Introduction

David Hostler's arrival at Harvard University's Peabody Museum of Archaeology and Ethnology in 1997 marked the culmination of a long struggle.[1] For almost a century, his tribe's sacred regalia—religious items believed to embody the spirit of the creator[2]—had lain locked away in the museum.[3] Now a federal law, the Native American Graves Protection and Repatriation Act (NAGPRA), required museums and federal agencies to return Native American human remains and cultural items under their control to lineal descendants, culturally affiliated Indian tribes, and Native Hawaiian organizations.[4] A curator for the Hupa Valley Indian Tribe, Hostler had come to collect seventeen artifacts on behalf of his reservation. "As we started going through the collections," he said of the Peabody staff, "I was forewarned to wear gloves and a breathing apparatus. . . . They said, 'We don't know what's on this stuff, but to be safe, you should wear gloves.' I didn't get no clear understanding of the problem until I got back, but that's when I first learned about the poison."[5]

As Hostler soon discovered, the items were saturated with mercury, naphthalene, and DDT,[6] chemicals applied by museum curators to ward off pests and forestall decay.[7] The practice was a common one, dating back to the 18th century[8] and continuing well into the 1970s and '80s,[9] when the chemicals' harmful effects on human health first became apparent.[10] But until NAGPRA's enactment in 1990, no one foresaw that native people would once again control these cultural items and, importantly, that they would use them for their intended purposes.[11]

Under NAGPRA,

> the museum official or Federal agency official must inform the recipients of repatriations of any presently known treatment of the human remains, funerary objects, sacred objects, or objects of cultural patrimony with pesticides, preservatives, or other substances that represent a potential hazard to the objects or to persons handling the objects.[12]

A museum that has failed to comply with this requirement is liable for civil penalties.[13]

To date, none of the counts alleged under 43 C.F.R. § 10.12(b)(1)(viii), for failure to inform, have yet been investigated, let alone substantiated. Nonetheless, publications have documented the dissatisfaction[14] of tribal members who waited years for sacred objects to be repatriated, only to find that the items were toxic and unusable for the purposes for which they were made.[15] Native American activists have been vocal about museums' moral obligation to the tribes, with some arguing that the institutions should take responsibility for the objects' testing and decontamination.[16] Conservators have convened symposia to highlight the problem and discuss potential solutions,[17] and articles on the topic have appeared in medical and environmental journals.[18] Several museums have been sued for exposing their own employees to pesticides, in violation of OSHA standards.[19] As one of NAGPRA's savings provisions, at 43 C.F.R. § 10.15(d)(4), states that nothing in the regulations can be construed to "limit any procedural or substantive right which may otherwise be secured to individuals or Indian tribes or Native Hawaiian organizations," Native Americans might, similarly, seek redress through tort litigation for injuries caused by exposure to contaminated cultural items.

No legal analysis of a museum or federal agency's duty to inform repatriation recipients of any presently known treatment of repatriated items with hazardous substances, under NAGPRA or any other law, has yet been done. This paper attempts to fill that void by providing guidance to museums and federal agencies on this duty. The paper first describes NAGPRA and the process it provides for repatriating certain cultural items from museums and federal agencies to lineal descendants, Indian tribes, and Native Hawaiian organizations, and the unintended consequences of this transfer of control. Next described are the historic treatment of cultural items with toxic materials and the risk this poses to recipients of repatriated items. The paper then lays out the duty to inform and the potential legal action that might be initiated against a museum or federal agency for breach of that duty. It next examines how "presently known treatment" might be proved. Finally, it suggests a best practice for satisfying the duty to inform recipients of repatriations of any presently known treatment of cultural items with potentially hazardous substances.

## Background: Repatriation under NAGPRA

NAGPRA is a federal law that requires federal agencies and museums receiving federal funds as of November 16, 1990, to return Native American human remains, funerary objects, sacred objects, and objects of cultural patrimony, under their control, to lineal descendants, culturally affiliated Indian tribes, and Native Hawaiian organizations, as appropriate.[20]

The repatriation process begins with museums and federal agencies completing, as required, either descriptive summaries of cultural items or itemized inventories of Native American human remains and funerary items over which they have control. In consultation with tribal government or Native Hawaiian organization officials, traditional religious leaders, and lineal descendants, a determination is first made as to whether an item fits a NAGPRA category and, if so, determining to which party or parties with standing to request the repatriation the item is culturally affiliated. Museums and federal agencies must prepare item-by-item inventories of all human remains and associated funerary objects under their control, also in consultation with tribes, and, if cultural affiliation is determined, notify the appropriate tribe or tribes through a Notice of Inventory Completion. For unassociated funerary objects, sacred objects, and objects of cultural patrimony, museums and agencies must provide summaries (rather than object-by-object inventories) describing "the scope of the collection, kinds of objects included, reference to geographical location, means and period of acquisition and cultural affiliation, where readily ascertainable." Finally, the museum or agency must "expeditiously" repatriate these human remains, funerary objects, and objects of cultural patrimony to a culturally affiliated tribe or a lineal descendant upon request following publication of a Notice of Intent to Repatriate Cultural Items, or upon a claim for cultural items and publication of a Notice of Intent to Repatriate. As a result of this process, objects that, for decades, might have lain untouched in display cases and storage facilities are once again being put to the uses for which they were made, or subject to handling in the process of reburial.

## Historic Treatment of Cultural Items with Toxic Materials

While repatriation returns control of cultural items to lineal descendants and Native people, the result also poses risks. For many years, curatorial procedures included applying pesticides to individual artifacts, as well as to the areas where artifacts were stored, in order to protect museum collections from biodeterioration. Standard treatments in the late 19th and early 20th centuries included arsenic, boric acid, and mercuric chloride. Later, when museums began using closed cabinets to store their collections, volatile fumes—including naphthalene, tar camphor, paradichlorobenzene, carbon disulfide, cydrocyanic acid, and fluorosilicate compounds—became popular. In the 1950s, pesticides that had been developed for agricultural use—sprays, dusts, fogs, and resin strips containing chlorinated hydrocarbons and organic phosphates—found their way into curatorial usage, as did crack-and-crevice pesticides containing carbamates and boric acid. Even in the latter part of the 20th century, pressurized fumigation chambers employing ethylene oxide, methyl bromide, and sulfuryl fluoride were considered a safe and effective means of eradicating pests.[21]

Eventually, with tighter restrictions on the manufacture and sale of pesticides at the end of the 20th century and growing awareness of the effects of pesticides on human health and the environment, museums began to limit their use of these chemicals. Today, integrated pest management programs, which establish guidelines for pest prevention and removal, include nonchemical insect-killing methods such as freezing, high heat, and oxygen deprivation.[22] While these programs bode well for future museum acquisitions, many of the older items now being reintegrated into tribal communities have already been contaminated with toxins.

Were repatriated items merely stored in tribal museums in the same manner and for the same uses as in the repatriating institutions, the risk of injury to recipients caused by exposure to toxins likely would be equivalent to the risk assumed by collections staffs at federal agencies and museums. Instead, sacred objects and objects of cultural patrimony often are worn against the skin during religious ceremonies,[23] placed in food storage structures to ensure a bountiful harvest,[24] or ritually destroyed via burial or burning,[25] while human remains and funerary objects are reburied, thus allowing chemical residues to seep into the earth.[26] Each of these activities creates an opportunity for potentially hazardous substances to enter the body through absorption,[27] inhalation,[28] or consumption.[29]

## Duty to Inform and Potential Legal Consequences for Breach of That Duty

In some situations, transferring toxic items to another might carry a risk of legal liability for the transferor. Through regulation, NAGPRA explicitly imposes a duty on museums and federal agencies to "inform the recipients of repatriations of any presently known treatment of the human remains, funerary objects, sacred objects, or objects of cultural patrimony with pesticides, preservatives, or other substances that represent a potential hazard to the objects or to persons handling the objects."[30] Failure to comply with this requirement can subject a museum to a NAGPRA civil penalty or a federal agency to injunctive or other relief under the Administrative Procedure Act. In addition, breach of this duty might subject a museum or federal agency to tort liability under, respectively, the common law and the Federal Tort Claims Act.

### Failure to Comply with the Requirement of NAGPRA at 43 C.F.R. § 10.10(e)

In NAGPRA, Congress tasked the Secretary of the Interior with promulgating regulations for the imposition of civil penalties against museums that have failed to comply with the requirements of the law.[31] The civil penalty regulations are codified at 43 C.F.R. § 10.12. The Secretary of the Interior is responsible for assessing civil penalties and has delegated this authority to the Assistant Secretary for Fish and Wildlife and Parks.[32] Anyone may bring an allegation of museum failure to comply but must do so in writing.

There are eight ways in which a museum might fail to comply with the requirements of NAGPRA.[33] "Whether a museum has failed to comply is determined under a strict liability standard."[34] In other words, intent is not an element of the violation. Violations are civil in nature, with recourse for violations assessed as penalty amounts paid to the government.

A museum has failed to comply with the requirements of NAGPRA if it breaches the duty to inform set forth at 43 C.F.R. § 10.10(e).[35] According to the plain meaning of the words in 43 C.F.R. § 10.10(e), the duty extends only to "recipients of repatriations" and not, for example, to all the individuals who consulted with the museum during the NAGPRA process and, in the course of NAGPRA consultation, came into contact with an item. Also, the duty is restricted to NAGPRA items actually repatriated. The breach of duty need not cause an actual injury in order for a violation to exist under NAGPRA. If a museum breaches the duty to inform and does cause an injury in fact, the Assistant Secretary may assess the museum a penalty amount based on economic and noneconomic damages suffered by the aggrieved party, in addition to the base penalty amount of $5,000 or .25% of the museum's budget, whichever amount is less.

Unlike museums, federal agencies are not subject to the civil penalty provisions of NAGPRA, but they nevertheless are subject to the law's requirements, including the duty to inform in 43 C.F.R. § 10.10(e). Consequently, a federal agency that breaches that duty could be subject to an action under the Administrative Procedure Act (APA).[36] Under the APA, "a person suffering legal wrong because of agency action, or adversely affected or aggrieved by agency action within the meaning of the relevant statute" is entitled to judicial review of that action.[37] The APA allows the aggrieved party to bring an action for injunctive relief (not money damages) in federal court and to name the U.S. as a defendant, provided that one or more federal officers are identified as being responsible for compliance with any injunctive decree issued.

A court hearing a claim under the APA can either compel an agency to act when action has been "unlawfully withheld or unreasonably delayed," or set aside an agency action found to be arbitrary, capricious, or otherwise unlawful.[38] In the case of an individual who has been harmed by an agency's failure to warn that an artifact had been treated with pesticides prior to repatriation, neither compelling the agency to warn nor halting repatriation would be effective, since repatriation has already occurred and the harm has been done. However, the employee responsible for returning the artifact without a proper warning still faces disciplinary action. If the Office of Special Counsel determines that the employee has "violated the provisions of any law, rule, or regulation" within the Special Counsel's purview, it may prepare a written complaint against the employee and present it to the Merit Systems Protection Board, which may in turn suspend or reprimand the employee, impose a fine of up to $1,000, demotion, or debarment from federal employment for a period of up to five years.[39]

## Private Tort Actions for Injury Caused by a Breach of the Duty to Inform

While museums face NAGPRA civil penalties and federal agencies face disciplinary action if they fail to comply with the duty to inform in 43 C.F.R. § 10.10(e), they both face being sued in private tort actions if their breach of that duty causes an injury.

NAGPRA states that "any museum which repatriates any item in good faith pursuant to this Act shall not be liable for claims by an aggrieved party or for claims of breach of fiduciary duty, public trust, or violations of state law that are inconsistent with the provisions of this Act."[40] At the same time, the law has a savings provision stating that "nothing in this Act shall be construed to . . . deny or otherwise affect access to any court or limit any procedural or substantive right which may otherwise be secured to individuals or Indian tribes or Native Hawaiian organizations."[41] Thus, should a museum or federal agency fail to repatriate in good faith, NAGPRA would not preclude an injured party from suing the museum or agency. A museum that repatriates a NAGPRA item and fails to inform the recipient of any presently known treatment of the cultural item with a substance that is potentially hazardous to either people or the object itself is not repatriating the item in compliance with NAGPRA. A noncompliant repatriation might reasonably be deemed bad faith repatriation. Thus, NAGPRA would not preclude a plaintiff who had been injured as the proximate result of the museum or agency's breach of the duty to inform from bringing an action in tort against the museum or federal agency.

Federal agencies may only be sued under the Federal Tort Claims Act (FTCA), which waives the government's sovereign immunity. The FTCA serves as "the legal mechanism for compensating persons injured by negligent or wrongful acts of Federal employees committed within the scope of their employment."[42] When a federal employee is sued pursuant to the FTCA, the government stands in as the defendant. The head of the agency is authorized to settle claims in any amount, although compensation over $25,000 must be approved by the Attorney General. Claims of less than $2,500 must be paid out of the agency's appropriations. Museums and museum employees, having no sovereign immunity to waive, may be sued at common law.

If a museum or federal agency fails to inform a tribe that a repatriated mask is known to have been treated with arsenic and an individual becomes sick after wearing the mask, the tribe or individual could sue the United States under the FTCA for the federal agency official's negligence or bring a private tort action for negligence against the museum or museum employee. To establish a case for negligence, a plaintiff must show that (1) the defendant museum or agency owed the plaintiff a duty (such as the statutory duty to warn of known pesticide treatment), (2) the museum or agency breached its duty, (3) injury occurred to the plaintiff or plaintiff's property, and (4) a direct causal relationship existed between the injury and the defendant's breach. Plaintiffs in negligence actions for improper application of pesticides can recover for damage to the artifact and personal bodily injury—including pain and suffering, medical expenses, future disability or subsequent disease, aggravation of a previously existing condition, or impairment of earning capacity—as well as punitive damages; that is, additional amounts where there is egregious behavior on the part of the defendant.[43]

**Determining "Presently Known Treatment"**

In any of the three actions outlined above—NAGPRA civil penalty, APA action, or private tort suit—an aggrieved party must show that the museum or federal agency failed to inform the recipient about the repatriated artifact's "presently known treatment" with a potentially hazardous substance. As the term "presently known treatment" is a constituent element of the duty to inform—and the breach of that duty—it is important to determine the facts that might satisfy this element.

At first glance, 43 C.F.R. § 10.10(e) seems fairly straightforward. Indeed, the proposal that museums and federal agencies be required to inform recipients about a repatriated artifact's known treatment with potentially hazardous substances merits only one sentence in the statute's legislative history,[44] indicating its seemingly uncontroversial nature. Nevertheless, museums and federal agencies cannot always account for the history or the treatment of an object, even during the period when the item was in their control. Thus, determining what museums and agencies "know" about their collections is necessarily a task to be performed on a case-by-case, totality-of-the-circumstances basis.

If asked about how an object has been preserved, a museum official would probably turn to conservation records first.[45] In theory, each object in a collection would have its own documentation detailing if, when, and how it was treated with preservatives.[46] In practice, however, these records are often incomplete or missing.[47] While museum records can help identify potential toxins,[48] they are not always accurate or comprehensive,[49] and often they cover only certain time periods.[50] Even if a museum has documented an object's treatment in painstaking detail, there is no guarantee that the archaeologist or collector who acquired the piece did not treat it prior to its acquisition by the museum.[51]

When written records are lacking, some museums interview prior employees about chemicals used on collection items during their tenure at the museum.[52] However, given that many items were acquired several generations ago,[53] the person who might originally have treated the item is not always available for comment. Historical practices are relevant here.

An artifact's physical appearance can provide clues to its treatment, as when arsenic crystals are clearly visible on the object's surface.[54] However, most pesticides and preservatives are not visible to the naked eye and, as a result, a battle of the experts could ensue concerning whether the pristine condition of a cultural item that otherwise should have deteriorated due to age or infestation shows, more likely than not, that the item has been preserved.[55]

Chemical analysis is the only surefire method of determining what preservatives have been applied to an artifact.[56] Testing each object for the presence or absence of a myriad of potentially hazardous substances, though, would be a guessing game, since a lab must first have some sense of what chemicals to look for before it can choose the appropriate method of analysis.[57] Testing equipment is available, but each can detect some, not all, toxins.

A museum might not have *actual* knowledge that a particular object in its collection was treated with a potentially hazardous substance. Nonetheless, knowledge that hazardous chemicals were routinely used throughout most of the 20th century to preserve collections is widespread in the curatorial community.[58] So, if museum or federal agency professionals, to whom specialized knowledge is imputed, know that, at some time in the past, the industry standard was to treat certain materials or categories of materials with potentially hazardous substances, and if the repatriated cultural items contain those materials, then that knowledge might satisfy the meaning of "presently known treatment," which, in turn, would trigger the duty to inform imposed by 43 C.F.R. § 10.10(e). On the other hand, if "presently known treatment" applies only to a museum or federal agency's *actual* knowledge that potentially hazardous substances were applied to a particular repatriated item, then the museum's duty, at least under NAGPRA, is more circumscribed. Thus, the meaning of the term "presently known treatment" is key to understanding the duty to inform.

Legal analysis suggests that a court would interpret the phrase "presently known treatment" to encompass both actual *and* constructive knowledge of an artifact's treatment, thus imposing on museums and federal agencies a broad duty to inform. When the language of a statute is ambiguous, common-law principles provide courts with a valuable guide in interpreting the statute's meaning. In fact, "where there is a limitation by statute which is capable of more than one construction, the statute must be given that construction which is consistent with common law."[59] Therefore, a court interpreting a museum's duty to warn under NAGPRA would look to prior common law actions in which defendants had supplied third parties with dangerous items without warning them of the danger in advance.

According to the Second Restatement of Torts:

> One who supplies directly or through a third person a chattel for another to use is subject to liability to those whom the supplier should expect to use the chattel with the consent of the other or to be endangered by its probable use, for physical harm caused by the use of the chattel in the manner for which and by a person for whose use it is supplied, if the supplier (a) *knows or has reason to know* that the chattel is or is likely to be dangerous for the use for which it is supplied, and (b) has no reason to believe that those for whose use the chattel is supplied will realize its dangerous condition, and (c) fails to exercise reasonable care to inform them of its dangerous condition or of the facts which make it likely to be dangerous.[60]

Under this doctrine, the duty to inform recipients of a repatriated cultural item's treatment with a potentially hazardous substance is imposed when the supplier knew—or even when he or she merely "had reason to know"—that the object was dangerous for its intended use and when the recipients would not have realized its dangerous condition. A party "has reason to know" something when he "has information from which a person of reasonable intelligence, or of the superior intelligence of the actor, would infer that the fact in question exists, or would govern his or her conduct upon the assumption that it does exist."[61]

Like the "supplier"[62] referenced above, museums and federal agencies know that chemically treated, repatriated cultural items are dangerous for the use for which they are supplied. Collection staffs themselves take precautions when handling items that have been treated[63] and, therefore, would realize that, even if a toxic object never left a tribal museum or repository, it would pose a risk to tribal curators unaware of its toxic properties. The risk increases for items not consigned to display cases, such as sacred objects; that is, "specific ceremonial objects which are needed by traditional Native American religious leaders for the practice of traditional Native American religions by their present day adherents."[64] Because museums and federal agencies know that such objects will be handled or worn during religious ceremonies, they know that any toxic residues on the objects would make them "dangerous for their intended use."

Collection staffs, to whom specialized knowledge is imputed, also know that the recipients will not suspect the potentially hazardous condition of the cultural items being repatriated to them, as (1) laymen are unlikely to be familiar with conservation procedures, (2) presentations aimed at alerting recipients of repatriations to the hazards of exposure to potentially toxic substances are a recent phenomenon,[65] and (3) even when informed that an object is coated with potentially hazardous substances, the recipients are often unaware of the health risks these substances pose.[66]

As long as a plaintiff can prove that museum or federal agency personnel "knew or had reason to know" that cultural items had been treated with potentially hazardous substances prior to repatriation, the museum or agency can be held liable in tort for an injury proximately caused by the failure to inform the recipient(s).

There are several ways a plaintiff might prove a museum or federal agency's knowledge that a repatriated cultural item had been treated with a potentially hazardous substance. First, they could show that the repatriating museum or federal agency had applied the injurious substance. Second, they could offer facts contained in the museum or agency's records to show that, more likely than not, a collection professional would know that the injurious cultural item had been treated with a potentially hazardous substance. Third, demonstrative evidence for the physical presence of a potentially hazardous substance on the repatriated cultural item—including the presence of arsenic crystals or other residues,[67] a distinctive smell,[68] evidence of prior infestation and repair,[69] or signs that an organic object was unusually well-preserved for its age[70]—might be proffered to prove that the museum or federal agency knew or should have known that the item had been treated. Fourth, evidence showing that the museum or federal agency knew or should have known both that, at some point in time, the repatriated cultural item formed part of a collection and that one or more of the other items in that collection had been treated with a potentially hazardous substance might be dispositive of knowledge that the injurious cultural item itself had been treated.[71] Similarly, evidence showing both that the museum or federal agency acquired other, individual items from the transferor of the repatriated, injurious cultural item, and knew or should have known that one or more of those other acquired items had been treated with a potentially hazardous substance, might satisfy the "presently known treatment" element of the case. Even if, in fact, the injurious cultural item was known not to have been treated with a potentially hazardous substance, perhaps evidence showing that the museum or federal agency knew or should have known that the injurious cultural item came into physical contact with another item that *had* been treated with a potentially hazardous substance might be sufficient to establish the duty to inform and the "presently known treatment" element of the tort.

Finally, the widespread use of pesticides and other poisonous chemicals on items in collections as recently as the 1980s, and the massive attention that such poisonous preservatives have received in recent industry literature, raises the question in a legal sphere of whether there is a preliminary presumption that can easily be made that repatriated cultural items collected prior to the 1980s were treated with potentially hazardous substances. If the answer is yes, then the duty to inform would attach to almost all cultural items repatriated from collections. Such presumption would have an obvious chilling effect on claims and the return of repatriated sacred objects or objects of cultural patrimony to the uses for which they were created, as an unknown health risk to the potential user likely could outweigh the benefits of use.

Although the NAGPRA statute does not explicitly require museums and federal agencies to inform recipients of repatriations about treatments of which they "knew or had reason to know," courts might nevertheless choose to hold them to the same constructive knowledge standard they have applied to suppliers of dangerous chattel, especially when doing so promotes the law's purpose.[72] NAGPRA's legislative history indicates that, in addition to providing a practical framework for repatriating human remains and certain cultural items, the statute was enacted "to reverse several hundred years of abuses of a people, their lands and their very roots,"[73] and "was meant to redress past wrongs against tribes, and to level the playing field, so it's no longer tilted in the favor of scientists."[74]

According to one canon of construction, "statutes benefiting Native Americans should be construed liberally in their favor."[75] NAGPRA benefits Native Americans by effecting the repatriation and disposition of human remains, funerary objects, sacred objects, and objects of cultural patrimony. Because liberally construing the duty of a museum or federal agency to inform the recipient of repatriation that a cultural item has been treated with a potentially hazardous substance would provide greater protection for the recipients, a court might very well interpret "presently known treatment" to include both the actual and constructive knowledge of treatment.

Another legal canon holds that public health and safety statutes should be liberally construed in favor of the public.[76] The requirement of 43 C.F.R. § 10.10(e) serves as a public health safeguard, since it minimizes the chance that repatriation recipients will suffer illness or death as a result of handling toxic cultural items. As a broader construction of "known" advances this interest, a court might hold a museum or federal agency liable for failure to inform if it had reason to know of an artifact's treatment with a potentially hazardous substance.

The duty to inform aside, a museum or federal agency cannot be held liable for failure to test artifacts in order to determine *how* they were treated.[77] The Second Restatement of Torts makes a clear distinction between manufacturers and retailers who supply chattel for business purposes and other types of suppliers: the former are required to test for defects, while the latter are merely required to disclose what they have reason to know based on existing evidence.[78] Because museums and federal agencies gain no financial benefit from repatriation, they are under no duty to routinely test their entire collections for the presence of potentially hazardous substances. The language of 43 C.F.R. § 10.10(e) supports this argument: by restricting the duty to "presently" known treatment, the regulation obviates a museum's duty to acquire additional knowledge through testing, unless and until repatriation becomes a factor.

## Best Practice Model

This paper has focused mainly on the legal duty to inform a recipient of repatriation of the treatment of cultural items with potentially hazardous substances and the possible consequences for the breach of that duty, but it was written against a backdrop of human health and safety. For this reason, a museum or federal agency that reasonably can test cultural items absent and prior to repatriation should do so. Thus, for example, in Washington State, The Burke Museum, which pioneered a testing program for lead, arsenic, and mercury on tribal cultural objects using portable x-ray fluorescence spectrometers,[79] has affirmatively responded to every request to test Native American collections located in the Pacific Northwest.[80] Others have followed suit,[81] including the National Museum of Natural History, which uses x-ray fluorescence to test all of its ethnological items made of wood, feathers, hair, and hide for heavy metals.[82]

Those museums that cannot afford the XFR spectrometer's $40,000–50,000 price tag should follow the advice of Nancy Odegaard and Alyce Sadongei of the Arizona State Museum and determine an artifact's treatment history by conducting "a thorough review of many museum documents, archives, conservation correspondence and reports, and letters to earlier staff members that may be on file."[83] In addition, repatriation officials should look beyond written records and ask themselves whether other types of evidence provide constructive knowledge that a cultural item was treated with a potentially hazardous substance. Odegaard and Sadongei suggest the following checklist:

1. Is there evidence of prior infestation?
2. Are residual pesticides indicated?
3. Is there evidence of museum repairs, restorations, and alterations?
4. Are there any written records that would suggest the use of pesticides?
5. Based on past storage locations, what pesticides might typically have been used on or near this object?[84]

It is advisable for museums and federal agencies to research and answer these questions before they are involved in litigation or a court tells them that they breached their duty to inform. Only after examining all the available evidence can a museum or federal agency satisfy the duty to inform the recipients of a repatriated cultural item's presently known treatment with potentially hazardous substances.

Museums might take a cue from the National Museum of Natural History and supplement the information about *specific* pesticides they provide to repatriation recipients with a more general caution: because there is no way to know with absolute certainty exactly how each artifact was treated, all artifacts should be presumed to be hazardous and handled and stored with care,[85] and recipients should speak to a health professional about the risks of pesticide exposure.[86]

Hopefully, as conservators, tribal representatives, and cultural organizations continue to work together to determine how cultural items were treated, these items may one day be decontaminated and reintegrated into the daily lives of their recipients. In the meantime, compliance with NAGPRA's duty to inform should be construed liberally, in order to minimize the risk of physical harm to recipients during the repatriation process.

## Notes

1. See Claudine Zap, *Trail of Toxins*, EAST BAY EXPRESS, May 11, 2001 (describing the bureaucratic hurdles Hostler had to overcome to convince the Peabody to repatriate Hupa artifacts in their collection, including enlisting an academic to submit a 600-page anthropological analysis of the artifacts); *see also Native American Artifacts Pose Pesticide Exposure Risk*, SCIENCE DAILY, Mar. 20, 2003 (stating that Hostler negotiated with the museum for three years before repatriation of seventeen artifacts was granted).
2. *See* Matt Palmquist, *Poisoned Gods: As Museums Return Stolen Religious Artifacts, Native Americans Are Learning That Their Most Sacred Objects May Kill Them*, SF WEEKLY, Sept. 4, 2002 (describing the Hupa belief that "the spirit of the creator is . . . embodied in the regalia"); *see* also David Hostler, Shawn Kane & Lee Davis, *The Hoopa Tribal Museum's Experience with Chemical Contamination of Repatriated Materials,* in 16 Soc'y for the Pres. of Natural History Collections, Collection Forum 54, 54 (Summer 2001) hereinafter Collection Forum (claiming that "the artifacts are living spirits who cry to come to the ceremonies back home and dance with 'their people'"); cf. Richard Fausset, *Indians Face Dilemma of Toxic Relics*, LOS ANGELES TIMES, Sept. 1, 2002 (conveying the Elem Indians' belief that the headdresses and ceremonial outfits lying on shelves in California state park storage facilities are "tortured souls."); cf. Lynda V. Mapes, *Museum First in Country to Offer Safety Check for Tribal Artifacts*, SEATTLE TIMES, Oct. 6, 2005 (stating that the Tlingit elder responsible for returning a repatriated tunic to his tribe will address the item as "him" rather than "it" "because of the living spirits the clan believes the treasure carries).
3. *Id.* (noting that the objects had remained at the Peabody Museum since being taken from the Hoopa in 1904).
4. 25 U.S.C. § 3001 et. seq.
5. *See* Palmquist, *supra* note 2, at 2.
6. *See* Zap, *supra* note 1 (citing the results of lab tests conducted by Niccolo Caldararo, a conservator and professor at San Francisco State University, which later became the source of a conference on pesticide contamination of repatriated objects).
7. *See* generally Marilen Pool et al., *Identifying the Pesticides: Pesticide Names, Classification, and History of Use,* in Old Poisons New Problems: A Museum Resource for Managing Contaminated Cultural Materials 5, 5 (AltaMira, 2005) hereinafter Old Poisons, New Problems (listing the various insects that pose biodeterioration hazards to museum collections and the 87 different pesticides that museums have applied over the years to "discourage insect activity" and "restrain insect maturation").

8. *See* Zap, *supra* note 1 (stating that the practice dates to as early as 1785, when Charles Wilson Peale, upon opening a natural history museum in Philadelphia, became the first American to use arsenic as a preservative).
9. *See* Nancy Odegaard et al., *Assessing Contamination: Analytical Testing of Cultural Materials for Pesticides,* in Old Poisons, New Problems 54-55 (stating that museums stopped using arsenic and DDT in 1972 and mercury in 1976, when they were banned by the federal government, and that use of carbamate and thiocarbamate pesticides petered out in the 1980s).
10. *See* P. Jane Sirois, *Analysis of Objects for Arsenic and Mercury: Non-Destructive Analysis and Sample Analysis,* in Collection Forum 65, 67 (citing Muir, Lovell, and Peace's 1981 analysis of objects at the Bristol Museum as "one of the first published studies investigating potential health hazards in natural history collections").
11. See Fausset, *supra* note 2 (stating that "some tribes are confronting unforeseen health and religious issues because of the substances used by generations of collectors who never imagined that the Indians would get the items back").
12. 43 C.F.R. § 10.10(e).
13. 43 C.F.R. § 10.12(b)(viii).
14. *See* Zap, *supra* note 1 (stating that repatriation of contaminated objects has "fueled anger and mistrust," with one woman likening the practice to white settlers giving smallpox-contaminated blankets to their Indian neighbors).
15. *See* Fausset, *supra* note 2 (stating that the Onondaga Nation of New York received fifty-seven medicine masks that were contaminated with arsenic in 1998, and that Hopi kachina dolls repatriated in 1999 were covered in pesticides, one so toxic that the Arizona Poison Control Center advised the tribe to not even keep it on the reservation); *see* also Mapes, *supra* note 2 (reporting that the Hearst Museum warned the Tlingit tribe that a tunic repatriated in 2005 might contain DDT).
16. *See* Fausset, *supra* note 2, at 2 (stating that Leigh Kuwanwisiwma, cultural preservation coordinator for the Hopi tribe, wants museums to pay for the removal of toxic chemicals); *see* also Palmquist, *supra* note 2, at 4 (quoting Larry Myers, executive secretary of the California Native American Heritage Commission, as saying, "The tribes feel that the state or the institutions should be paying for chemical testing, and that's perfectly reasonable and logical. . . . They took the damn stuff. And now that they've given it back, it's in this condition"); *see* also Zap, *supra* note 1, at 7 ("Monona Rossol frets that tribes are giving up their rights by too hastily accepting items back from museums. She says tribes should demand at least two tests, one screening for pesticides and one for heavy metals").
17. *See*, e.g., Symposium, *Mitigation of Pesticides on Museum Collections*, hosted by the Smithsonian Institution, April 23, 2007.
18. *See*, e.g., Peter T. Palmer et al., *Analysis of Pesticide Residues on Museum Objects Repatriated to the Hupa Tribe of California*, 37(6) ENVTL. SCI. & TECH. 1083-1088

(2003)(reporting the results of tests for arsenic, mercury, and organic pesticides conducted on seventeen objects repatriated to the Hupa tribe, which "indicate that Hupa tribal members should not wear these objects in religious ceremonies, proper precautions should be followed when dealing with potentially contaminated objects, and that more serious consideration should be given to this issue at a national level"); *see* also S.A. Seifert et al., *Arsenic Contamination of Museum Artifacts Repatriated to a Native American Tribe*, 283(20) J. OF THE AM. MED. ASS'N 2658-2659 (2000)(evaluating three ceremonial objects made of leather, grasses, cornhusks, feathers, horsehair, yarn, and paint that had been repatriated under NAGPRA, and finding that, although none showed visible signs of contamination, two tested positive for arsenic and one for naphthalene).

19. Monona Rossol, *Open Discussion 1*, in Collection Forum 23, 23.
20. 25 U.S.C. § 3001 et seq.
21. *See* Pool, *supra* note 7, at 11-12.
22. *Id.* at 13.
23. *See* Palmquist, *supra* note 2 (describing the White Deerskin Dance and the Jump Dance, two of the Hupa's "most sacred rituals of world renewal," in which "shamanistic figures drape themselves in sacred regalia," including deer hide or cat kilts, dentalia-shell necklaces, wolf-fur headbands, and woodpecker-scalp headdresses); *see also id.* (noting that sacred dances usually take place inside an enclosed structure and that, "when someone is dancing with the item, they're shaking their head, moving around vigorously" and "you're shaking arsenic off your headdress, it's floating around, and it could contaminate the entire roundhouse").
24. *See* Jennifer Knight, *Law Requires UNLV to Give Artifacts Back to Tribe*, LAS VEGAS SUN, Jan. 13, 2003 (describing the Hopi belief that kachina masks "represent the power to bring rain, plentiful crops, or prosperity to the village"); *see also Fausset, supra* note 2 (stating that pesticides were discovered on repatriated kachina dolls only after the dolls had been placed in structures used to store grain and vegetables).
25. *See* Mapes, *supra* note 2, at 1 (stating that sacred objects are sometimes "burned in sacred ceremonies, or re-buried, potentially posing a health risk in some instances if residues are released into the air, groundwater, or transmitted to people").
26. See *id.*
27. *See* Leslie Boyer et al., *Understanding the Hazards: Toxicity and Safety*, in Old Poisons, New Problems 73-77(stating that cumulative exposure to ingested arsenic can lead to neuropathy, anemia, and cancer of the lung, liver, kidney, or bladder; prolonged exposure to mercury can produce tremors, gastrointestinal effects, kidney damage, and hallucinations; and exposure to organophosphates, which "tend to cross the skin barrier easily," can produce heart rhythm disturbance, coma, seizures, and death).

28. *See* Palmquist, *supra* note 2, at 2 (noting that, when Native Americans ritually burn contaminated objects, "they risk scarring their lungs by inhaling the pollutants"); *see also* Boyer, *supra* note 27, at 76 (noting that inhalation of mercury fumes when objects are heated or burned can result in death or central nervous system damage).
29. *See* Palmquist, *supra* note 2, at 2 (noting that, when Native Americans "put down," or ritually bury, an item that has reached the end of its life-span, "they risk contaminating the soil and poisoning their groundwater").
30. 43 C.F.R. § 10.10(e).
31. 25 U.S.C. § 3007.
32. 43 C.F.R. § 10.12(a).
33. 43 C.F.R. § 10.12(b)(1)(i)—(viii).
34. NAGPRA Regulations—Civil Penalties (preamble), 68 Fed. Reg. 16,354 (2003) (to be codified at 43 C.F.R. pt. 10).
35. 43 C.F.R. § 10.12(b)(1)(viii).
36. *See* the 1947 Attorney General's Manual on the APA, available at http://www.law.fsu.edu/library/admin/1947i.html.
37. 5 U.S.C. § 702.
38. 5 U.S.C. § 706.
39. 5 U.S.C. § 1215(a)(3).
40. 25 U.S.C. § 3005(7)(f).
41. 25 U.S.C. § 3009.
42. 28 U.S.C. § 2671.
43. Anne M. Payne, *Cause of Action for Damage from Pesticides*, 39 Causes of Action 2d 579 (2009).
44. Native American Graves Protection and Repatriation Act Regulations, 60 Fed. Reg. 62,134 (Dec. 4, 1995)(to be codified at 43 C.F.R. pt. 10).
45. *See* Nancy Odegaard et al., *Addressing the Problem: The Team Approach,* in Old Poisons, New Problems, 33, 33 ("The first step was to compile and review the documentation already known to exist from the museum's internal records regarding pesticide use," including catalog cards, specimen treatment cards, loan records, and purchase orders for pesticides).
46. *See* Nathan Stolow, *Procedures and Conservation Standards for Museum Collections in Transit and on Exhibition* 22 (UNESCO 1981) ("The condition report is one of the most important documents in the museum. It records historical and acquisition data, describes the technical and compositional nature of the work, and is the time record of its conservation state").
47. *See id.* ("The writing of condition reports is a very imperfect art. In some instances the record is too brief, in others overly detailed"); *see also* Mapes, *supra* note 2 (quoting Jim Nason, director of the NAGPRA program at Seattle's Burke Museum, as saying, "very few museums even know how the objects in their collections

have been treated because they lack records"); *see also* Fausset, *supra* note 2 (stating that, because museum records are incomplete, "suspicion is all they have to go on" when determining whether pesticides or other poisons have been applied to cultural items).

48. *See* Zap, *supra* note 1 (stating that it was museum records that first tipped off tribes that pesticide contamination was an issue).
49. *See* Nancy Odegaard et al., *The Issue of Pesticides on Native American Cultural Objects: A Report on Conservation and Education Activities at University of Arizona*, in Collection Forum 12, 16 (reporting that, during a chemical analysis of Hopi kachina "friends," two tested positive for arsenic even though only one was identified as such in museum documentation).
50. *See*, e.g., Zap, *supra* note 1, at 6 (noting that records at the Phoebe Apperson Hearst Museum of Anthropology at UC Berkeley date back only to the 1960s).
51. *See* Lee Davis et al., *Recommended Actions Regarding the Pesticide Contamination of Museum Materials* (2000), http://bss.sfsu.edu/calstudies/arttest/rec.htm (noting that "pesticides were . . . known to have been applied to artifacts by field collectors, dealers, etc. before they arrived at the museum").
52. *See* Catharine Hawks, *Historical Survey of the Sources of Contamination of Ethnographic Materials in Museum Collections*, in Collection Forum 2, 7 (stating that "interviewing former staff is a growing practice as museums recognize the potential impact of past contamination on all types of collection use, from loans for exhibition and research, to public programs, and object repatriation").
53. *See*, e.g., Knight, *supra* note 24 (stating that many items were acquired during the Dust Bowl era, when starving Hopi Indians traded handcrafted regalia for food).
54. *See* Palmquist, *supra* note 2 ("People would open up books of botanical specimens collected in the 17th century, and they'd find arsenic crystals on the pages."); *see also* Odegaard, *supra* note 45, at 37 (featuring a photograph of a headdress on which white powder—arsenic—is clearly visible amongst the feathers).
55. Compare Zap, *supra* note 1 ("Ironically, one clue of a preservative's presence is that an artifact is in good condition—nothing eaten away, the feathers whole, the colors bright. When an object appears to have not degraded at all, it's a good sign that a permanent—and deadly—substance has been used"), with National Museum of the American Indian: Pesticides FAQ, http://www.nmai.si.edu/subpage.cfm?subpage=collections&second=conserv&third=pest (last visited Oct. 20, 2008) ("It is not advisable to make assumptions on appearances alone about whether or not an artifact is likely to be contaminated with hazardous residues. If an artifact has evidence of prior infestation, this does not mean it is free of pesticide residues—it may have been treated with pesticides as a result of that infestation. Likewise, it is possible that an object in excellent condition has not been treated with pesticides").

56. *Id.*
57. *See* Peter T. Palmer, *A Review of Analytical Methods for the Determination of Mercury, Arsenic, and Pesticide Residues On Museum Objects,* in Collection Forum 25, 39.
58. *See* Claudine Zap, *Poisoned Legacy*, MotherJones, Oct. 24, 2000 (describing pesticide contamination as "no secret in museum circles"); *see also* Odegaard, *supra* note 49, at 13 ("Many museum employees, based on experience or information reported in the literature, have been aware that many institutionally held objects were treated with chemical poisons to aid in their preservation").
59. 2B Sutherland Statutory Construction § 50:1 (7th ed. 2009).
60. Restatement (First) of Torts § 388 (2009).
61. Restatement (Second) of Torts § 12 (2009).
62. The "supplier" referenced here refers not only to manufacturers and retailers, but to "any person, who for any purpose or in any manner gives possession of a chattel for another's use." This category would certainly include museums or agencies that repatriate contaminated cultural items.
63. *See* generally, *Guidelines for Handling Contaminated Museum Collections and Personal Protection Equipment Guidelines*, in Old Poisons, New Problems, 87-90.
64. 25 U.S.C. § 3001(3)(C).
65. *See* Odegaard et al., *Introduction*, in Old Poisons New Problems (describing a symposium convened by the Arizona State Museum as "one of the first forums designed to disseminate information on this issue" to Native American tribes).
66. *See* Palmquist, *supra* note 2 (noting that "some tribes have stubbornly insisted that their gods are powerful enough to overcome the pesticides"); *see also* Zap, *supra* note 1 (citing archaeologist Yolanda Chavez's increased concerns about pesticide contamination after tribe members told her, "Maybe our songs or dances can take care of it").
67. *See* Odegaard, *supra* note 45, at 35 ("Some pesticides, such as mothballs, can be absorbed by artifact materials and later crystallize on the surfaces. In other instances, powders, such as arsenic or DDT, were applied directly to artifacts and remain intact and visible on interior surfaces").
68. *See id.* (citing "odors on or around museum artifacts and in storage and exhibit areas" as one means of assessing whether pesticides were applied).
69. *See* Odegaard, *supra* note 49, at 14.
70. *See* Odegaard, *supra* note 45, at 35 (noting that "old artifacts made of materials known to be susceptible to insect attack" like fur, skin, feathers, and wool "may be considered suspect for having some form of pesticide treatment").
71. *See* Restatement (First) of Torts § 388 cmt. h (2009) ("It is not necessary in order that a supplier of a chattel for another's use shall be liable under the rule stated in this Section that he should know that the particular chattel is dangerous for the use for which it is supplied. It is enough that he knows of facts which make it likely

that the particular chattel may be dangerous, as where he knows that it is part of a lot, some of which he has discovered to be so imperfect as to be dangerous").

72. *See* 2B Sutherland Statutory Construction 46:1 (7th ed. 2009) ("even if the words of a statute are plain and unambiguous on their face the court may still look to the legislative history in construing the statute if the plain meaning of the words of the statute is at variance with the policy of the statute or if there is a clearly expressed legislative intention contrary to the language of the statute").
73. Zap, *supra* note 1, at 2 (quoting Keith Kintigh).
74. 136 Cong. Rec. H10989-90 (statement of Rep. Collins) (daily ed., Oct. 22, 1990).
75. *See Tyonek Native Corp. v. Sec'y of the Interior*, 836 F.2d 1239 (9th Cir. 1988) (citing *Three Affiliated Tribes of the Fort Berthold Reservation v. Wold Eng'g*, 467 U.S. 138, 149).
76. *See* 2B Sutherland Statutory Construction 73:2, 73:4 (7th ed. 2009).
77. *See* Restatement (First) of Torts § 388 cmt. k (2009) ("The fact that a chattel is supplied for the use of others does not of itself impose upon the supplier a duty to make an inspection of the chattel, no matter how cursory, in order to discover whether it is fit for the use for which it is supplied").
78. *See* Restatement (Second) of Torts § 392 cmt. a (2009).
79. *See* Mapes, *supra* note 2.
80. *See* the Burke Museum website at www.washington.edu/burkemuseum/collections/ethnology/index.php.
81. *E.g.*, the Field Museum in Chicago and the Southwest Museum of the American Indian at Autry National Center, http://sarweb.org/index/php?symposium_native_collections_and_pesticides-p:symposiums.
82. NMNH does not test human bones or stone funerary objects because these materials are inert and would not have been treated with preservatives. However, if bone or stone items were stored alongside treated artifacts or housed in containers or rooms where pesticides had been applied, museums and agencies governed by NAGPRA should warn tribal recipients of this fact.
83. Odegaard, *supra* note 49, at 14. This search should include catalog cards, specimen treatment cards, loan records, purchase orders for pesticides, contracts with exterminators, archaeological field notes, routine reports by staff members, and interoffice staff correspondence regarding pesticide application. Odegaard, *supra* note 45, at 33-34.
84. Odegaard, *supra* note 49, at 14.
85. The NMNH's Statement on Pesticides, available at http://anthropology.si.edu/repatriation/pdf/pesticidestatement.pdf, instructs anyone handling ethnographic objects during the consultation or repatriation stage to wear disposable latex gloves while handling the objects, wash exposed skin with soap and water after

contact, and store the objects in a secure container away from food supplies, utensils, clothing, and other items that may be worn or ingested. It also discourages children, pregnant women, the elderly, and people with weakened immune systems from handling the objects and anyone at all from wearing the objects.

86. Phone conversation with Bill Billeck, director of the National Museum of Natural History Repatriation Office, November 20, 2009.

# Review of Books, Articles, and Other Resources

• • •

*Compiled by Gary Nurkin*

*The* Yearbook *seeks to keep readers informed on the growing body of scholarship in the diverse field of cultural property law. The items listed below are not intended to be an exhaustive list. Articles may reflect a diversity of viewpoints. The editors invite information on new items as they are published, past items of ongoing value to readers, as well as information on new websites and in film.*

## Selected Bibliography of Recent Books and Articles

### Books

Paul Barford and Nigel Swift, *Britain Portable Antiquity Heritage: Artefact Collecting and the Archaeological Record* (Boydell Press, 2009).

Catherine Bell and Robert K. Paterson (eds.), *Protection of First Nations Cultural Heritage: Laws, Policy and Reform* (University of British Columbia, 2009).

Ilaria Degini Brey, *The Venus Fixers* (Farrar, Straus & Giroux, 2009).

Noah Charney, *Art and Crime: Exploring the Dark Side of the Art World* (Praeger, 2009).

Stephen Conn, *Do Museums Still Need Objects* (University of Pennsylvania, 2010).

Council of Europe, *Guidance on Inventory and Documentation of the Cultural Heritage : Document Prepared by the Ad Hoc Group for Inventory and Documentation Within the Technical Co-Operation and Consultancy Programme Related to the Integrated Conservation of the Cultural Heritage* (Council of Europe Publishing, 2009).

James Cuno (Ed.), *Whose Culture?: The Promise of Museums and the Debate Over Antiquities* (Princeton University Press, 2009).

Colin Dickey, *Cranioklepty; Grave Robbing and the Search for Genius* (Unbridled Books, 2009).

Craig Forest, *International Law and the Protection of Cultural Heritage* (Routledge, 2009).

Derek Gilman, *Idea of Cultural Heritage* (Cambridge University Press, 2010).

Michael Gross, *Rogues Gallery: The Secret History of the Moguls and the Money That Made the Metropolitan Museum* (Broadway Books, 2009).

Sherry Hutt and David Tarler (Eds.,) *Yearbook of Cultural Property Law* (Left Coast Press, 2009).

Thomas F. King, *Our Unprotected Heritage: Whitewashing the Destruction of Our Culture and National Heritage* (Left Coast Press, 2009).

Katherine Kirkpatrick, *Kennewick Man* (Holiday House, 2010).

Sidney D. Kirpatrick, *Hitler's Holy Relics: A True Story of Nazi Plunder and the Race to Recover the Crown Jewels of the Holy Roman Empire* (Simon & Schuster, 2010).

Simon Mackenzie and Penny Green, *Criminology and Archaeology: Studies in the Looting of Antiquities* (Hart Publishing, Oxford, 2009).

Phyllis Mauch and George S. Smith, *Cultural Heritage Management: A Global Perspective* (University of Florida, 2010).

James A.R. Nafziger and Ann M. Nicgorski, *Cultural Heritage Issues: The Legacy of Conquest, Colonization and Commerce* (Martinus Nijhoff, 2009).

James A. Nafziger, Robert Paterson and Allison Dundes Rentein, *Cultural Law: International, Comparative and Indigenous* (Cambridge University Press 2010).

Webber Ndoro, Albert Mumma, and George Abunga (Eds.), *Cultural Heritage and the Law, Protecting Immovable Heritage in English Speaking Countries of Sub-Sahara Africa* (Iccrom Conservation Studies 8, 2008).

Thomas W. Neumann and Robert M. Sanford, *Practicing Archaeology: An Introduction to Cultural Resources Archaeology*, 2nd Ed. (Altamira Press, 2010).

Lawrence Rothfield, *The Rape of Mesopotamia: Behind the Looting of the Iraq Museum* (University of Chicago, 2009).

Vernon Silver, *The Lost Chalice: The Epic Hunt for a Lost Masterpiece* (Harper Collins, 2009).

Marie Louise Stig Sørensen and John Carman, *Heritage Studies: Methods and Approaches* (Routledge, 2009).

Suzie Thomas and Peter Stone (Eds.), *Metal Detecting and Archaeology* (Boydell Press, 2009).

Jiri Toman, *Cultural Property in War: Improvement in Protection: Commentary on the 199 Second Protocol to the Hague Convention of 1954 for the Protection of Cultural Property in the Event of Armed Conflict* (Unesco Publishing, 2009).

Norman Tyler, Ted J. Ligibel, and Ilene R. Tyler, *Historic Preservation: An Introduction to Its History, Principles and Practice* (W.W. Norton, 2009).

Robert K. Wittman and John Shiffman, *Priceless: How I Went Undercover to Rescue the World's Stolen Treasures* (Crown, 2010).

James O. Young and Conrad G. Brunk, *Ethics of Cultural Appropriation* (Wiley-Blackwell, 2009).

## Articles

Michelle Kay Albert, *Obligations and Opportunities to Protect Native American Sacred Sites Located on Public Lands*, 40 COLUM. HUM RTS. L. REV. 479 (2009).

Kimberly Alderman, *Ethical Issues in Cultural Property Law Pertaining to Indigenous Peoples* 45 IDAHO L. REV. 515 (2009).

Bernard Isaac Weinstein Baskin, *Historical Heist: An Economic Argument Against Embargoing Chinese Cultural Property*, 8 Wash. U. GLOBAL STUD. L. REV. 107 (2009).

J. Peter Byrne, *Hallowed Ground: The Gettysburg Battlefield in Historic Preservation Law*, 22 TUL. ENVTL. L. J. 203 (2009).

Courtney Campbell, Art and Arms: *An Examination of the Looting of the National Museum of Iraq*, 32 B.C. INT'L & COM. L. REV. 423 (2009).

Kristen A. Carpenter, Sonia K. Katyal, and Angela R. Riley, *In Defense of Property*, 118 YALE L. J. 1022 (2009).

Kevin Chamberlain, *Holocaust Art Claims and Public International Law*, 13 ART, ANTIQUITIES AND LAW 351 (2008).

Hyojung Cho, *Conservation of Indigenous Heritage in the United States: Issues and Policy Development,* 38 J. ARTS MGMT. L. SOC 187 (2008).

Jorge A. Sánchez Cordero, *Final Document from the Regional Workshop: "The Protection and Safeguard of Cultural Heritage Property of the Church of Latin America and the Caribbean,"* 16 INT. J. CULT. PROP. 393 (2009).

Edward M. Cotrell, *Keeping the Barbarians Outside the Gate: Towards a Comprehensive International Agreement Protecting Cultural Property*, 9 CHI. J. INT'L L. 627 (2009).

Christopher D. Cutting, *Protecting Cultural Property Through Provenance*, 32 SEATTLE U. L. REV. 943 (2009).

Piers Davis and Paul Myburgh, *The Protected Objects Act in New Zealand: too little, too late?*, 15 INT'L. J. CULTURAL PROPERTY 321 (2008).

Asif Efrat, *A Theory of Internationally Regulated Goods*, 32 FORDHAM INT'L L. J. 1466 (2009).

Derek Fincham, *Towards a Rigorous Standard for the Good Faith Acquisition of Antiquities*, found at: http://papers.ssrn.com/sol3/papers.cfm?abstract_id=1350649.

Derek Fincham, *Navigating the Deaccessioning Crisis*, found at: http://papers.ssrn.com/sol3/papers.cfm?abstract_id=1470211.

Derek Fincham, *Fraud on Our Heritage: Towards a Rigorous Standard for the Good Faith Acquisition of Antiquities*, found at: hpttp://ssm.com/abstract=135069.

Derek Fincham, *How Adopting the Lex Originis Rule Can Impede the flow of Illicit Cultural Property*, 32 COL. L. J.& ARTS 111 (2008).

Craig Forrest: *Historic Wreck Salvage: An International Perspective*, 33 TUL. MAR. L. J. 347 (2009).

Manlio Frigo, *Ethical Rules and Codes of Honor Related to Museum Activities: A Complementary Support to the Private International Law Approach Concerning the Circulation of Cultural Property*, 16 INT'L, J. CULT. PROP. 49 (2009).

Manlio Frigo, *Protection of Cultural Property on Loan—Anti-Seizure and State Immunity Laws: An Italian Perspective*, 14 ART, ANTIQUITIES AND LAW 49 (2009).

Patty Gerstenblith, Laina Lopez, and Lucille Roussin, *Public International law, International Art and Cultural Heritage*, 43 INT'L LAW 814 (2009).

Patty Gerstenblith, *Protecting Archaeological Heritage in Armed Conflict, Looking Back, Looking Forward*, 7 CARDOZO PUB. L. POL'Y & ETHICS J. 677 (2009).

Patty Gerstenblith, *Schultz and Barakat: Universal Recognition of National Ownership of Antiquities*, 14 ART, ANTIQUITIES AND LAW 21 (2009).

Kate Fitz Gibbon, *Dangerous Objects: Museums and Antiquities in 2008*, found at: http://papers.ssrn.com/sol3/papers.cfm?abstract_id=1479424.

Charles A. Goldstein, *Protection of cultural objects on loan: the Israeli perspective*, 13 ART, ANTIQUITY AND LAW, 361 (2008).

Edward J. Goodwin, *The World Heritage Convention, the Environment, and Compliance*, 20 COLO. J. INT'L ENVTL. L. & POL'Y 157 (2009).

Paige S. Goodwin, *Mapping the Limits of Repatriable Cultural Heritage: A Case Study of Stolen Flemish Art in French Museums*, 157 U PA L. R. 673 (2008).

Maria Granovsky, *A Permanent Resolution Mechanisms of Cultural Property Disputes*, 8 PEPP. DISP. RESOL. L. J. 23 (2007).

Nathaniel C. Guest, *Putting History on a Stone Foundation: Towards legal rights for Historic Properties*, 18 TEMP. POL & CIVIL RTS. L REV. 699 (2009).

Sarah Harding, *Perpetual Property*, 61 FL. L. REV. 285 (2009).

Alicia M. Hilton, *Terror Victims at the Museum Gates: Testing the Commercial Activities Exception Under the Foreign Sovereign Immunities Act*, 53 VILL. L. REV. 479 (2008).

Salah H. al-Houdalieh and Robert R. Sauders, *Building Destruction: The Consequences of Rising Urbanization on Cultural Heritage in the Ramallah Province*, 16 INT. J. CULT PROP. 1 (2009).

Edythe E. Huang, *Looting in Iraq, Five Years Later: An Evaluation of the International Protection, Recovery and Repatriation of Looted Cultural Artifacts*, 10 RUTGERS RACE & L. REV. 183 (2009).

Sherry Hutt, *The Evolution of Federal Agency Authority to Manage Native American Cultural Sites*, in TRADITIONAL CULTURAL PROPERTIES, Charles W. Smythe and Frederick York, eds., 26 George Wright Forum, 45 (2009).

Ling Ji, *The Two Zodiacs: Possible Methods for Returning Lost Relics to China*, 14 ART, ANTIQUITIES AND LAW 167 (2009).

Derek R. Kelly, *Illegal Tender: Antiquities Protection and U.S. Import Restrictions on Cypriot Coinage*, 34 BROOK. J. OF INT'L. L. 491 (2009).

Jennifer Anglim Kreder, *The Revolution in U.S. Museums Concerning the Ethics of Acquiring Antiquities*, found at: http://papers.ssrn.com/sol3/papers.cfm?abstract_id=1503430&download=yes.

Jennifer Anglim Kreder, *Cultural Property, Laws and Ethics*, found at: http://papers.ssrn.com/sol3/paers.cfm? abstract_id=1526757.

Jennifer Anglim Kreder, *Essay Upon Reading War and Cultural Heritage: An Analysis of the 1954 Convention for the Protection of Cultural Property in the Event of Armed Conflict and Its Two Protocols, by Kevin Chamberlain*, 14 MEDIA AND ARTS LAW 1 (2009).

Jennifer Anglim Kreder, *The New Battleground of Museum Ethics and Holocaust Era Claims: Technicalities Trumping Justice or Responsible Stewardship for the Public Trust?*, 88 OR. L. REV. 37 (2009).

Jennifer Anglim Kreder, *The Holocaust, Museum Ethics and Legalism*, 18 S. CAL. REV. L & SOCIAL JUSTICE 1 (2008).

Monique Lee, *A Choice of Law Dilemma: The Conflict and Reconciliation of Laws Governing Cross-Border Transfers of Stolen Art*, 7 CARDOZO PUB. L POL'Y & ETHICS 719 (2009).

Jane A. Levine, *The Importance of Provenance Documentation in the Market for Ancient Art and Artifacts: The Future of the Market May Depend on Documenting the Art*, 19 DEPAUL J. ART. TECH. & INTELL. PROP. L. 219 (2009).

Amanda K. Maus, *Safeguarding China's Cultural History: Proposed Amendments to the 2002 Law on the Protection of Cultural Relics*, 18 PAC. RIM L POL'Y J. 405 (2009).

Brian K. McGarry, *Great Lakes Exploration Group v. Unidentified Wreck: Navigating Federalism and Arrest Procedure in Post-Deep Sea Shipwreck Controversies*, 33 TUL. MAR. L. J. 539 (2009).

Toon van Meiil, *Pacific Discourses About Cultural Heritage and Its Protection: An Introduction*, 16 INT. J. CULT PROPERTY, Special Issue 3, 221 (2009).

Saruhan Mosler, *Aspects of Archaeological Heritage in the Cultural Landscapes of Western Anatolia*, 15 INT'L. J. HERITAGE STUDIES 24 (2009).

Phillip Newell, *The PRCs for the Protection of Cultural Relics*, 13 ART, ANTIQUITIES AND LAW 1 (2008).

Anna O'Connell, *The United Kingdom's Immunity from Seizure Legislation*, LSE LAW, SOCIETY AND ECONOMY WORKING PAPERS 20/2008, found at http://papers.ssrn.com/sol3/papers.cfm?abstract_id=1304910 (2008).

Michelle Orloski, *Preventing Gross Injury to Local Cultural Patrimony: A Proposal for State Regulation of Deaccessioning*, 81 TEMP. L. REV. 605 (2008).

Raisa E. Patron, *The Looting of Iraqi Archaeological Sites: Global Implications and Support for an International Approach to Regulating the Antiquities Market*, 40 GEO. WASH. INT'L. L. REV. 465 (2008).

Eric Posner, *The International Protection of Cultural Property: Some Skeptical Observations*, 8 CHI. J. INT'L. L. 213 (2007).

John W. Ragsdale, Jr., *Possession: An Essay on Values Necessary for the Preservation of Wild Lands & Traditional Tribal Cultures*, 40 URB. LAW. 903 (2008).

Alexander MacKintosh Ritchie, *Victorious Youth in Peril: Analyzing Arguments Used in Cultural Property Disputes to Resolve the Case of the Getty Bronze*, 9 PEPP. DISP. RESOL. L. J. 325 (2009).

Lucille Roussin, *The Protection of Cultural Heritage in a Globalized World:The Trade in Antiquities: Heritage for Sale?*, 15 ILSA J. INT'L & COMP L 549 (2009).

Ryan M. Seidemann, *Altered Meanings: The Department of Interior's Rewriting of the Native American Grave and Repatriation Act to identify Culturally Identifiable Human Remains*, 28 TEMP. J. SCI. TECH. & ENVTL. L. 1 (2009).

Gao Sheng, *Recovering Illegally Removed Cultural Property and Improving Cultural Property Protection: A Chinese Perspective*, 14 ART, ANTIQUITIES AND LAW 1 (2009).

Kurt Siehr and Alexander Bauer (eds), *ICOMOS Charter on cultural routes: prepared by the international and scientific commitee on cultural routes (CIIC) ratified by the 16th General Assembly of ICOMOS, Quebec (Candada), on 4 October 2008*, 15 INT'L. J. CULTURAL PROPERTY 385 (2008).

Alex Steel, *Problematic and Unnecessary? Issues with the Use of the Theft Offence to Protect Intangible Property*, 32 SYDNEY L. REV. 575 (2008).

Stephanie Swanson, *Repatriating Cultural Property: The Dispute Between Yale and Peru Over the Treasures of Machu Picchu*, 10 SAN DIEGO INT'L L. J. 469 (2009).

Deborah L. Threedy, *Claiming the Shields: Anthropology, and the Role of Storytelling, in a NAGPRA Repatriation Case Study*, 29 J. LAND RESOURCES & ENVTL L 91 (2009).

Hannibal Travis, *The Cultural and Intellectual Property Interests of the Indigenous People of Turkey and Iraq*, 15 TEX. WESLEYAN L. REV. 415 (2009).

Robert Van Horn, *The Native American Graves Repatriation and Protection Act at the Margin: Does NAGPRA Govern the Disposition of Ancient, Culturally Unidentifiable Human Remains?*, 15 WASH. & LEE J. CIVIL RTS. & SOC. JUST. 227 (2008).

Valentina Sara Vardi, *Investing in Our Culture: Underwater Cultural Heritage and International Investment Law*, 42 VAND. J. TRANSNAT'L. L. 853 (2009).

Katherine D. Vitale, *The War on Antiquities: United States Law and Foreign Cultural Property*, 84 NOTRE DAME LAWYER 1835 (2009).

Ana Filipa Vrdoljak, *Unravelling the cradle of civilization "layer by layer": Iraq, its Peoples and Cultural Heritage*, found at: http://works.bepress.com/ana_filipa_vrdoljak/7.

Ana Filipa Vrdoljak, *History and Evolution of International Cultural Heritage Law: Through the Question of the Removal and Return of Cultural Objects*, found at: http://papers.ssrn.com/sol3/papers.cfm?abstract_id=1336359.

Ana Filipa Vrdoljak, *Cultural Heritage in Human Rights and Humanitarian Law*, found at: http://papers.ssrn.com/sol3/papers.cfm?abstract_id=1401231.

Ana Filipia Vrdoljak, *Cultural Rights: The Possible Impact of Private Military and Security Companies*, found at: http://papers.ssrn.com/sol3/papers.cfm?abstract_id=1401182.

Tony Ward, *Antiquities, Forests and Simmel's Sociology of Value*, found at: http://papers.ssrn.com/sol3/papers.cfm?abstract_id=1412328.

Lea J. Weiss, *The Role of Museums in Sustaining the Illicit trade in Cultural Property*, 25 CARDOZO ARTS & ENT. L. J. 837 (2007).

Matthias Weller, *The Safeguarding of Foreign Cultural Objects on Loan in Germany*, 14 ART, ANTIQUITIES AND LAW 63 (2009).

Helen White, *Protecting the Past to Preserve the Future: A Case for International Protection of the National Palace Museum of Taipei, Taiwan*, 19 KANSAS J. LAW & PUB. POLICY 148 (2009).

Diana Zacharias, *The UNESCO Regime for the Protection of World Heritage as a Prototype of An Autonomy-Gaining International Institution*, 9 GERMAN L. J. 1833 (2008).

## Additional Readings

Neil Brodie, *The Market in Iraqi antiquities 1980-2008*, found at: http;//www.stanford/edu/group./chr/cgi-bin/drupal/files/Market%20in%20Iraqi%20antiquities%20(2008)%20txt.pdf.

Asif Efrat, *Protecting against Plunder: The United States and the International Efforts against Looting of Antiquities*, found at: http://lsr.nellco.org/cornell/clsops/papers/47.

Asif Efrat, *Governing Guns, Opposing Opium: A Theory of Internationally Regulated Goods*, found at: http://works.bepress.com/asif_efrat/1/.

Kalliopi Fouseki,*Conflict Resolution in the Management of In-Situ Museums*, found at: http://papers.ssrn.com/sol3/papers.cfm?abstract_id=1484888.

Bruno S. Frey and Paolo Pamini, *Making World Heritage Truly Global: The Culture Certificate Scheme*, Institute for Empirical Research in Economics, University of Zurich working Paper No. 419, found at: http://ssrn.com/abstract=1427793.

Kevin Gibson, *Profit from the Priceless: Heritage Sites, Property Rights and the Duty to Preserve*, 114 BUS & SOC. REV. 327 (2009).

David S. Gold, *Is There Any Way Home? A History and Analysis of the Legal Issues Surrounding the Repatriation of Artwork Displaced During the Holocaust*, found at: http://works.bepress.com/david_gold/1/.

Stephanie Goldfarb, *Lessons in Looting*, JOURNAL OF ART CRIME 43 (2009).

David C. Gray, *A No-Excuse Approach to Transitional Justice: Reparations as Tools of Extraordinary Justice*, found at: http://digitalcommons.law.umaryland.edu/fac_pubs/798/.

Tran Huu Tuan and Stale Navrud, *Applying the Dissonance-Minimising Format to Value Cultural Heritage in Developing Countries*, 53 AUSTRALIAN JOURNAL OF AGRICULTURAL AND RESOURCE ECONOMICS 327 (2009).

Reto M. Hilty, *Rationales for the Legal Protection of Intangible Goods and Cultural Heritage, Max Planck Institute for Intellectual Property, Competition & Tax Law*, found at: http://papers.ssrn.com/sol3/papers.cfm?abstract_id=1470602.

Law Library of Congress, Cyprus: *Destruction of Cultural Property in the Northern Part of Cyprus and Violations of International Law,* April 2009, found at: http://ahiworld.org/AHIFpolicyjournal/pdfs/cyprus_destruction.pdf.

Maria Lusiani and Luca Zan, *Institutional Transformation and Managerialism in Cultural Heritage: Heritage Malta,* found at: http://papers.ssrn.com/sol3/papers.cfm?abstract_id=1481165.

Nathan Murphy, *Splitting Images: Shared-Value Settlements in Nazi-Era Art Restitution Claims,* found at: http://works.bepress.com/nathan_murphy/1.

Alexis H. Rossman, *Painting Preemption with the Wrong Brush: The Misapplication of the Preemption Doctrines in Von Saher v. Norton Simon Museum of Art*, found at: http://works.bepress.com/alexis_rossman/1/.

Arthur F. Salomons, *Good Faith Acquisitions of Movables*, found at: http://papers.ssrn.com/sol3/papers.cfm?abstract_id=1515719.

Joseph Saweka, *Reconciling Policy and Equity: The Ability of the Internal Revenue Code to Resolve Disputes Regarding Nazi-Looted Art*, found at: http://works.bepress.com/joseph_sawka/1/.

Ryan M. Seidemann and Rachel L. Moss, *Places Worth Saving: A Legal Guide to the Protection of Historic Cemeteries in Louisiana and Recommendations for Additional Protection*, found at: http://works.bepress.com/ryan_seidemann/4/.

Sid Ahmed Soufiane, *The Strategy of Management of Cultural Heritage in Algeria. Case study Law 98-04*, found at: http://papers.ssrn.com/sol3/papers.cfmd? abstract id=1529086.

Valentina Sara Vardi, *What Role Do Museums Play in the Globalization of Culture?: Museums and Protection of Underwater Cultural Heritage, Solving the Pirate's Dilemma*, found at: http://www.law-archaeology.gr/ClientFiles/Articles/Vadi_Museums_UCH.pdf.

Ana Filipa Vrdoljak, *Cultural Rights: The Possible Impact of Private Military and Security Companies*, found at: http://works.bepress.com/ana_filipa_vrdoljak/13/.

### New Journals

*Journal of Art Crime*, edited by Noah Charney and published by the Association for Research into Crimes Against Art.

## New Web Sites

Cultural Heritage Resource, found at: http://www.stanford.edu/group/chr/drupal/view/chronicle.

## Blogs

Antiquities News and Topical Debate, found at: http://eftis.blogspot.com/.

Antiquities Watch, Cultural Property and the Law, found at: http://antiquitieswatch.wordpress.com/.

Archaeopop, found at: http://archaeopop.blogspot.com/.

Art Crime Blog found at: http://art-crime.blogspot.com/search?q=.

Art Theft Blog, found at: http://arttheftcentral.blogspot.com/search?q=.

Cardozo Art Law Blog found at http://cardozoartlawsociety.blogspot.com/.

The China Art Law Blog found at: http://www.chinaartlaw.com/.

Ethical Antiquities Blog found at: http://piecesofthepastethicalantiquiti.blogspot.com/search?q=.

Hellenic Society for Law and Archaeology, found at http://www.law-archaeology.gr/Index.asp?C=196.

LCCHP Cultural Heritage Law Blog found at: http://culturalheritagelaw.blogspot.com/search?q=.

Pieces of the Past: Ethical Antiquities Collecting, found at: http://piecesofthepastethicalantiquiti.blogspot.com/2009/07/question-for-collectors.html.

Portable Antiquity Collecting and Heritage Issues, found at http://paul-barford.blogspot.com/.

Tiffany Jenkins, found at: http://tiffanyjenkinsinfo.wordpress.com/.

The Cultural Property and Archaeology Law Blog, found at: http://culturalpropertylaw.wordpress.com/.

The Provenance Network, found at: http://groups.google.co.uk/group/the-provenance-network.

## Webinars

Plundering the Past, found at: http://www.sbs.com.au/dateline/story/about/id/600132/n/Plundering-the-Past.

# Recognizing Career Achievements in Cultural Resource Protection

• • •

*Martin McAllister*

### Special Agent David Griffel

**Upon Retiring from Cultural Resources Law Enforcement**

Special Agent David Griffel retired on January 1, 2010, from his position with the Law Enforcement and Investigations unit of the USDA Forest Service. Protection of cultural heritage resources was a significant component of Dave's 34 year career with the Forest Service.

Dave graduated from the University of Idaho in 1975 with a B.S. degree in wildlife biology. He began his long career of federal service by working seasonally in various wildlife positions for the Forest Service, the Bureau of Land Management, and the U.S. Fish and Wildlife Service between 1974 and 1980. In 1980, Dave was hired as a permanent wildlife biologist on the Bridger-Teton National Forest in Jackson, Wyoming. In 1989, Dave became a program manager for law enforcement and wildlife resources on the Uinta National Forest in Provo, Utah. In addition to serving as a law enforcement officer, he directed both the law enforcement and wildlife and fisheries management programs on the forest.

In 1994, Dave attended and graduated from the Criminal Investigator Training Program at the Federal Law Enforcement Training Center. He then became a Special Agent assigned to the Intermountain Regional Office of the Forest Service in Provo. His responsibilities included investigation of complex criminal activities occurring in the Intermountain Region, which is comprised

cultural resource protection laws and NAGPRA on their lands. One of Dave's most interesting cases involved the theft of a time capsule from a schoolhouse at the mining ghost town of Aurora on National Forest lands in Nevada. The contents of the time capsule included three newspapers that dated to 1870. In a pre-trial diversion, the two defendants agreed to forfeit the time capsule and its contents to the Forest Service and they were then donated to the Nevada State Historical Museum. Dave also has investigated two cases involving theft of paleontological resources. Even as Dave's Forest Service career comes to an end, he is working on an ARPA case in Idaho that will be the subject of judicial action after his retirement.

Over the past nine years, Dave also has made a substantial contribution to training law enforcement officers, archaeologists, and others in the area of cultural resource law enforcement. Serving as a guest investigator instructor through the courtesy of the Forest Service, he has participated in 10 classes offered by the firm of Archaeological Resource Investigations (ARI). These classes have been attended by 283 participants from the Forest Service, the Bureau of Land Management, the National Park Service, the U.S. Fish and Wildlife Service, the U.S. Army, and various other federal and state agencies and tribes. During these classes, Dave has made presentations on archaeological crime scene investigation, investigative methods for archaeological crime, and the Polar Mesa Cave Case. He also has served at the lead instructor for the archaeological crime scene practical exercise that is an important component of the classes.

Dave also participated as a Forest Service law enforcement representative at the 2003 Society for American Archaeology conference at which the society's Professional Standards for the Determination of Archaeological Value were developed for use in cases involving unauthorized damage to cultural heritage resources. His perspective as an investigator of these crimes kept the archaeologists who participated in the conference well grounded in terms of the legal standards for expert witness credibility that are necessary to meet the damage assessment needs of investigators and prosecutors.

Dave's career in law enforcement with the Forest Service has been an outstanding one and he has played an important role in the protection of the cultural heritage resources of the United States over the last 15 years. He has always approached his efforts to protect cultural heritage resources with a high degree of professionalism, energy, and commitment. His work in this area undoubtedly will be missed in the Forest Service after his retirement. Fortu-

of the National Forest lands in Utah, Nevada, southern Idaho, and western Wyoming. The crimes Dave investigated included wild land arson, timber theft, fraud, theft and destruction of government property, assault on federal officers and employees, and manufacturing and cultivation of controlled substances. It was during this time that he also became involved in the investigation of violations of the Archaeological Resources Protection Act (ARPA), the Native American Graves Protection and Repatriation Act (NAGPRA), and other federal laws protecting cultural heritage resources.

In late 1994, Dave took over the investigation of looting that was occurring at a prehistoric site located on the Manti La Sal National Forest in southern Utah. The investigation of unauthorized activities at this large cave site, known as Polar Mesa Cave, had begun in 1990 and some suspects had been identified, but no charges had been filed. Dave worked with former Assistant United States Attorney Wayne Dance of the Utah U.S. Attorney's Office to initiate a systematic investigation of the case using strategies that included: gathering and organization of previously collected evidence; extensive suspect interviews; grand jury testimony by 39 witnesses; DNA analysis of dust masks and cigarette butts collected at the cave; use of undercover informants wearing body wires; service of 19 search warrants and seizure of over 1,000 photographs, 28 of which showed looting at the site and looted artifacts; and, finally, grand jury indictments of the suspects on various felony charges. The case resulted in guilty pleas from 10 defendants to 19 felonies, including nine for violations of ARPA and the remainder for perjury, injury to government property, theft of government property, and conspiracy to violate ARPA. Cumulative criminal penalties for the defendants resulting from the case included six years of imprisonment, 24 months of home confinement, 30 years of supervised probation, and $23,550 in restitution to the government. Also, a collection of over 500 artifacts taken from the site was forfeited to the government, as was a Ford pickup truck belonging to one of the defendants. Until recently, the Polar Mesa Cave case was the largest archaeological violation case that had occurred in terms of its prosecutorial outcome. Dave subsequently received the Forest Service Chief's national award for Special Agent of the Year, primarily for his work on this case.

Dave also has investigated a number of other cases involving cultural heritage resources, one of which resulted in felony convictions of three defendants for looting a rock shelter site on National Forest land in Utah. He also has been involved in eight cases that resulted in civil penalties under ARPA and has assisted several states and counties in the investigation of violations of

nately, however, Dave will continue to work with ARI to provide consulting and training on the investigation and prosecution of unauthorized damage to cultural heritage resources. This means that the expertise he has developed in this area will continue to be available for the foreseeable future despite his retirement from the Forest Service.

## In Memoriam

### Curly Bear Wagner

In this last year we experienced the loss of the pipe carrier, Blackfeet historian, and voice of Native American culture and property rights, Clarence "Curly Bear" Wagner.

Curly Bear loved to tell stories, and hundreds, if not thousands, of people loved to hear them. Through these stories he carried understanding of tribal culture and its people all through Montana and the country, to audiences who came to know of painful history in a way that engendered respect for and admiration of Indian people. He helped to establish the "Native American Speaks" program at Glacier National Park, in which he was a frequent presenter, up until just before his death at age 64. One of his favorite topics was the Blackfeet point of view of the meeting of Indians with Meriwether Lewis in 1806. In 1994, he founded the Going-to-the-Sun Institute to share traditional Blackfeet culture through educational programs.

Curly Bear also worked at sites of archaeological excavations, hoping to protect the tribal knowledge gained from these sites in order to support his desire that sites of sacred importance to tribes be preserved. He often worked closely with the Montana State Historic Preservation Office to identify sites of significance to tribes and worked on an archaeological project on Ted Turner's Flying D Ranch, near Bozman.

Curly Bear was a warrior in the battle to achieve repatriation of Native American ancestors and their cultural items from the collections of museums. In 1988, he was a member of a delegation to retrieve and repatriate Blackfeet remains from the Smithsonian Institution. He then went on to work for passage of the Native American Graves Protection and Repatriation Act (NAGPRA). Using NAGPRA, he took part in the Blackfeet repatriation from the Field Museum in the 1990s. His healing presence could be felt at NAGPRA Review Committee meetings, such as the one in Norman, Oklahoma, in 1997, whether he was in front of the room giving voice to Indian people or sitting in the back giving spiritual support.

# Table of Cases

• • •

*Agudas Chasidei Chabad v. Gourary*, 650 F. Supp. 1463 (E.D.N.Y. 1987), *aff'd*, 833 F.2d 431 (2d Cir. 1987). 185, 208
*Agudas Chasidei Chabad v. Russian Federation,* 528 F.3d 934 (D.C. Cir. 2008), *aff'g in part and rev'g in part* 466 F. Supp. 2d 6 (D.D.C. 2006). 167, 173, 181-186, 189-191-194, 197,203
*Altmann v. Republic of Austria*, 317 F.3d 954 (9th Cir. 2002). 175-177, 180-187, 193-204
*Ancient Coin Collectors Guild v. U.S. Dep't of State*, Civ. Case No. 07-2074, 2009 U.S. Dist. LEXIS 109303 (D.D.C. Nov. 20, 2009). 139
*A-S-P Associates v. Raleigh*, 298 N.C. 207, 258 S.E.2d 444 (1979). 71
*Banco Nacional de Cuba v. Sabbatino*, 376 U.S. 398 (1964). 141, 187-189, 208-211
*Bell v. Hood*, 327 U.S. 678 (1946). 184, 207
*Bd. Of Supervisors v. Stickle Town of Painter*, 239 Va. 343, 389 S.E.2d 702 (1990). 72
*Bonnichsen v. United States*, 357 F.3d 962 (9th Cir. 2004), *amended,* 367 F.3d 864 (9th Cir. 2004). 78, 84
*Bowie-McCready v. Morristown Zoning Board of Adjustment*, No. A-6071-06T2, 2008 N.J. Super. Unpub. LEXIS 1377 (App. Div. Sept. 12, 2008). 53, 70
*Brown v. State of Hawai'i*, Civ. No. 07-00556 ACK-LEK, 2009 U.S. Dist. LEXIS 106418 (D. Haw. Nov. 13, 2009). 76, 83
*Brown, as Trustee of Deca Trust v. Mitchell-Innes & Nash*, No. 06 CIV. 7871 (PAC), 2009 WL 1108526 (S.D.N.Y. Apr. 24, 2009). 122, 126
*California-Nevada Annual Conference et al. v. City and County of San Francisco*, 173 Cal. App. 4th 1559 (2009). 52, 70

# *Yearbook* 2010 Contributors and Editorial Board

• • •

**Gillian Bearns** is a land use attorney whose work focuses primarily on cultural resource law and First Amendment law. She previously taught preservation planning and preservation law in the Department of Historic Preservation at the University of Mary Washington in Fredericksburg, Virginia. She went on to work for the land use and zoning practice group of Robinson & Cole, LLP in Hartford, Connecticut, where she represented clients before local historic district commissions and other local land use boards and commissions. Currently, Ms. Bearns is working in the DC metro area as a consultant on federal lawsuits involving First Amendment rights and local land use regulation. Ms. Bearns received her law degree from Western New England College School of Law in Springfield, Massachusetts, and her masters in regional planning from the University of Massachusetts, Amherst.

**L. Eden Burgess** is an associate in the Washington, D.C., office of Andrews Kurth LLP, where she focuses on general litigation matters including art recovery and cultural property cases and has written and spoken on these subjects. She received her J.D. from George Washington University Law School, with honors.

**Eve Errickson**, the *Yearbook* editorial board member for the State and Local Practice Area, is Contracts Manager for the National Trust for Historic Preservation, and works extensively with the Trust's historic sites. In that capacity, she drafts, implements, and enforces contracts relating to treatments of historic, nonhistoric, and contributing structures at the NTHP's historic sites. She is licensed to practice law in the District of Columbia and Virginia, holds a J.D. from the University of Cincinnati, and an M.A. from George Washington University in American Studies/Historic Preservation. Prior to being at the National Trust, Eve worked in the Office of the General Counsel at Howard Hughes Medical Institute.

**Patty Gerstenblith**, Editorial Board, International Practice Area, President of Board LCCHP, is Distinguished Research Professor at DePaul University College of Law, where she is Director of DePaul's Center for Art, Museum and Cultural Heritage Law. She served as Editor-in-Chief of the INTERNATIONAL JOURNAL OF CULTURAL PROPERTY from1995 to 2002, as a public representative on the President's Cultural Property Advisory Committee in the U.S. Department of State from 2000 to 2003, and as Co-Chair of the American Bar Association's International Cultural Property Committee from 2002 to 2006. Her most recent books include the second edition of ART, CULTURAL HERITAGE, AND THE LAW and IRAQ BEYOND THE HEADLINES: HISTORY, ARCHAEOLOGY, AND WAR (co-authored with Benjamin R. Foster and Karen Polinger Foster). She received her J.D. from Northwestern University and a Ph.D. from Harvard University in Fine Art and Anthropology.

**Melanie Greer** is a law student at DePaul University College of Law.

**Lydia Grunstra** is a 2010 degree candidate at American University Washington College of Law. She holds an M.S. in European Archaeology from Oxford University and a B.A. in English from Columbia University. In 2008, she contributed to the State Burial Law Project as a summer law clerk for the National NAGPRA Program.

**Sherry Hutt**, Senior Editor, is the program manager for the National NAGPRA program, in the Department of the Interior, formerly a Superior Court Judge in Arizona, an assistant United States Attorney assigned to ARPA cases, and trustee of the Heard Museum, she is the co-author of CULTURAL PROPERTY LAW (2004), HERITAGE RESOURCES LAW (1999), ARCHEOLOGICAL RESOURCE PROTECTION (1992), and co-editor of PRESENTING ARCHAEOLOGY IN COURT (2006). In addition to the J.D., she holds a Ph.D. in forestry.

**Thomas Kline**, Editorial Board, Art Market Practice Area, Board member LCCHP, is a partner in the Washington, D.C. office of Andrews Kurth LLP, has represented governments, museums, churches, foundations, and families, including Holocaust survivors and heirs, in recovering stolen art appearing in the United States. He has also represented a major American museum in responding to a Holocaust claim. Mr. Kline co-teaches a seminar, "Stolen and Illegally Imported Art and Cultural Property," at the George Washington University Museum Studies Program. Mr. Kline writes and speaks on the subject of restitution of stolen art, and appeared before the Presidential Advisory Commission on Holocaust Assets in the United States. He is a member, Editorial Board, KUNST UND RECHT (Art and Law), www.kur-journal.de.

**Gary Nurkin** was an Assistant District Attorney in Nassau County, where he handled environmental crimes, among others, and was a trial attorney, in the appeals bureau, and then chief of the environmental and frauds bureau. Gary joined the EPA in 1989 as a Regional Enforcement Counsel, became Assistant Regional Counsel, and, for two years, was a Special Assistant United States Attorney handling environmental cases. A graduate of Chicago-Kent College of Law, Gary has also been an adjunct faculty member at Seton Hall University School of Law and Pace University School of Law, where he taught cultural property law. His undergraduate and graduate degrees are in anthropology.

**Nathaniel R. Orpen** is employed at Galena Law Firm, P.A., in White Bear Lake, Minnesota, where he works in the areas of estate planning, medical assistance planning, personal injury, real estate, business, criminal, and property law. He is a graduate of William Mitchell College of Law in St. Paul, Minnesota, and is a member of the Minnesota bar. Nathaniel received his B.A., cum laude, at Gustavus Adolphus College in St. Peter, Minnesota, where he majored in History and Political Science.

**Lucille Roussin**, Editorial Board, Museum Practice Area, Board Member LCCHP, is an advisor to SAFE, Saving Antiquities for Everyone. She is the founder and director of the Holocaust Restitution Claims Practicum at the Benjamin N. Cardozo School of Law in New York City, where she teaches a seminar, Remedies for Wartime Confiscation. She also teaches a course on "Art, the Law and Professional Ethics" at the School of Graduate Studies at the Fashion Institute of Technology. She is an associate with the firm of McCallion & Associates and earned her law degree in 1996 from the Benjamin N. Cardozo School of Law, where she was a Belkin Scholar. She was Deputy Research Director of the Art and Cultural Property Team of the Presidential Commission on Holocaust Assets and was an associate in the Art and International Law Practice Group at Herrick, Feinstein LLP in New York City. In 2001, she negotiated the first restitution of a rare Jewish ritual object to a private family in the United States.

**Amelia Borrego Sargent** graduated from Georgetown University in 2002 with a double major in Russian and Medieval Studies. In addition to studying law at Stanford Law School, she has an M.A. in Medieval Studies from the University of Toronto and is a Ph.D. Candidate in Comparative Literature at the University of California, Berkeley, where she studies medieval English, French, and Latin literature. She is interested in international and comparative law, intellectual property, and art law. She has studied and lived abroad in St. Petersburg, Russia; Rome, Italy; and The Hague, The Netherlands.

**Rob Roy Smith** is of counsel with the Indian Law Group of the law firm Ater Wynne, LLP in Seattle, Washington. He received a J.D., cum laude, with a certificate in natural resources and environmental law from Northwestern School of Law of Lewis and Clark College. He has extensive experience advising Indian tribal clients and those doing business in Indian Country on all aspects of federal Indian law, including economic development, cultural resource protection, taxation, tribal sovereignty, and Indian gaming. He is an adjunct professor of Federal Indian Law at Seattle University School of Law.

**David Tarler**, Assistant Editor, Editor Enforcement Practice Area, Board member LCCHP, is a Near Eastern archaeologist and an attorney. From 1978 to 1990 he was a senior staff member of the City of David excavation project, in Jerusalam, Israel. After completing his legal studies, in 1993, he served as a consultant to the Archeology Program and the Native American Graves Protection and Repatriation Act Program of the National Park Service, in Washington, DC. In 2006, he became the enforcement and training coordinator for the National NAGPRA Program. During 2001–2002, he provided assistance to staff at the United States Sentencing Commission working on Federal Sentencing Guideline 2B1.5, which applies to crimes involving cultural heritage resources. He was a contributing editor for Hutt, Blanco, & Varmer, HERITAGE RESOURCES LAW (1999), and PRESENTING ARCHAEOLOGY IN COURT (2006).

**James Van Ness**, Editorial Board, Board member LCCHP, is the acting Deputy General Counsel (Environment & Installations), Department of Defense. In this capacity, he is responsible for advising senior DoD officials on legal matters related to natural and cultural resources management, environmental planning, and consultation with indigenous peoples. Mr. Van Ness earned an LL.M. from the University of Washington; a J.D. from the University of Iowa; and a B.S. from Iowa State University. He is a member of the adjunct faculty at The George Washington University School of Law.

# Index